? De opdrejvende Breta...
(The Drifting Britannia)

Yacht with King on board.
Launch of the Royal Sovereign
at Chatham

Great Ships

1
Dockyard model of the *St Michael*, a 90-gun ship built in 1669.

NMM

Great Ships

The Battlefleet of King Charles II

by Frank Fox

CONWAY MARITIME PRESS
GREENWICH

Jacket Front
An English fleet at sea in the
1680s, a detail from a large
painting by Willem Van de
Velde the Younger. The
three-decker in the foreground is
the 100-gun *Prince* of 1670. In
the middle distance at centre is a
stern view of the 70-gun *Lenox* of
1678, while the vessel just astern
of the *Prince* is probably one of
the nine 90-gun ships built in
1678-1685.

Property of a private collector. Half of a
large painting by the Younger. It is signed
and dated; but the date is difficult to read
and has been interpreted by some
authorities as 1684 and by others as 1689.
The other half of the picture shows a
Dutch fleet, including the *Gouden Leeuw*
and *Gouda*. It represents an obviously
friendly meeting, with boats crossing
between the flagships.

Jacket back
A close-up of the *Prince* model.
See Plates XXIII-XXV.

Crown Copyright. Science Museum,
London.

Endpapers.
A drawing by Willem Van de
Velde the Elder showing a
concentration of warships lying
in the River Medway. It was
probably made on the occasion
of a royal visit to the fleet in late
1685. The scene is continued on
the back endpaper. The ships
named by Van de Velde on the
front endpaper are (left to right):
the *London, Duchess, Windsor
Castle, Albemarle* and *Britannia*
(with a yacht wearing the Royal
Standard nearby). On the back
endpaper are the *Neptune, Breda,
Prince* (Union at the mizzen),
Royal Sovereign (Union at the
main), *Royal Oak, Suffolk,
Henrietta* yacht, and *Victory*. The
scene is viewed from Chatham
Dockyard, with Rochester in the
left background and Upnor Castle
in the right background. This is
one of a series of drawings which
show the 1st Rate *Britannia* being
moved from Chatham to a
semi-permanent mooring
alongside the *Prince* off
Gillingham. This took place in
late 1685 or possibly early 1686.

British Museum. Elder, ?1685. Only the
faint inscriptions are in the hand of the
artist; the bold inscriptions, in a different
hand, contain a number of errors.

© Frank Fox 1980
First published in Great Britain 1980 by
Conway Maritime Press Ltd,
2 Nelson Road, Greenwich,
London SE10 9JB

ISBN 0 85177 166 1

Designed by David Mills
Typeset by Sunset Phototype, Barnet
Artwork by Letterspace, Barnet
Text printed in Great Britain by
Page Bros (Norwich) Ltd
Colour plates printed in Great Britain by
Exallprint, Tunbridge Wells
Bound by Newdigate Press, Dorking

Contents

	Note on Illustrations	
	Acknowledgements	
	Introduction	7
Chapter 1	The Restoration Fighting Ship	11
Chapter 2	The Fleet at the Restoration *Early Stuart Survivors*	31
Chapter 3	The Fleet at the Restoration *Inheritance from the Interregnum*	51
Chapter 4	The Early Restoration Period *1660-1667*	73
Chapter 5	First Rates *1668-1675*	95
Chapter 6	Continental Navies	115
Chapter 7	The Middle Restoration Period *1668-1676*	135
Chapter 8	The Thirty Ships *1678-1685*	153
Appendix I	List of Ships in Service 1660-1685	173
Appendix II	Abstract of Fleet Strength 1659-1685	183
Appendix III	Ordnance Establishment of 1666	183
Appendix IV	Ordnance Establishment of 1677	186
Appendix V	Ordnance Establishment of 1685	191
Appendix VI	Gunport Configurations	195
Appendix VII	Establishment of Cabin Allowances 1673	197
	Drawings of a First Rate	198
	Glossary	204
	Sources and Bibliography	206
	Index	207

Acknowledgements

No work involving numerous and widely separated sources could ever be possible without the cooperation of a very great many people. This author was particularly fortunate in that respect; so much so that merely to list the contributions of everyone to whom he is indebted would require a full chapter. Appended to the bibliography is a list of nearly forty public and private institutions whose collections were consulted. Without exception their curatorial and administrative staffs cheerfully satisfied every request, often going far beyond what is normally asked of them. Their gracious assistance is deeply appreciated.

Valuable aid was received from a number of kind people who generously made their personal collections available, often accepting great inconvenience in their willingness to help. Thanks are due to Mr and Mrs Paul Mellon, to Mrs R C Anderson, and to Miss Catherine Baer for allowing the reproduction of Van de Velde drawings in their possession; to the Kriegstein family of Roslyn NY for photographs of the *Coronation* model; and equally to the many private contributors who have preferred to remain anonymous. Grateful acknowledgement is offered to the Master and Fellows of Magdalene College, Cambridge, and the Trustees of the British Museum for permission to employ documents from their collections. The author expresses his gratitude to Arnold S Lott and Robert F Sumrall for their critical examination of the work and their extremely helpful suggestions; also to Kathy Hayden, Glenda Philpot, and Becky Wilson for typing a difficult manuscript and the complicated appendix tables; and to Liz, the author's wife, for suggesting many useful stylistic and grammatical improvements.

Very special thanks are due to Michael S Robinson, who freely shared his extensive knowledge of the Van de Veldes and their works. Mr Robinson's assistance extended to every phase of research: steering the author towards little-known collections, helping with ship identifications, interpreting faint inscriptions in seventeenth century Dutch, and locating important documentary sources. He also read portions of the manuscript, correcting several of the author's misconceptions and suggesting valuable improvements. Without his continuous encouragement very little could have been accomplished, and this constitutes a debt which can never be fully repaid.

Note on Illustrations

Each illustration and its caption is preceded by a number – a roman numeral for the colour plates, and arabic numerals for the remainder. The captions are followed by credits, repeating the numbers where necessary, which quote: the location of the work pictured and any reference number; the photo credit if different from the location of the work; the author of the work ('Elder' and 'Younger' refer to the Van de Veldes); the date if known; inscription, if any, with translations; and in some cases information which is useful to a serious student but which is inappropriate for the caption. Abbreviations used in the credits are:

NMM – National Maritime Museum, Greenwich

V&A – Victoria and Albert Museum, London. (Photos: Crown Copyright)

USNA – US Naval Academy, Annapolis, Maryland

Boymans – Boymans van Beuningen Museum, Rotterdam

Goethe Museum – National Forschungs- und Gedenkstätten der klassischen deutschen Literatur, Weimar

Introduction

Accounts of battles and biographies of admirals are only a part of the naval history of any era. The ships that made up the fleets are themselves an important consideration. Without an understanding of their qualities, it is easy to form distorted views of decisions and events.

Historians of twentieth century sea warfare can make use of literally hundreds of books giving detailed descriptions of the warships of the various nations, along with the political and economic conditions under which they were built. For students of the sailing ship era such sources are extremely rare. There are a number of excellent surveys of naval architecture, but by their very nature these can provide no more than a rudimentary treatment of any particular period. Others are outdated volumes giving wildly inaccurate information. There is obviously a need for sources which not only describe shipbuilding trends, but also compare the characteristics of individual vessels. This book is an attempt to satisfy part of that need for one small segment of English naval history, the 25-year reign of King Charles II, 1660–1685.

That era, the Restoration period, was a time of very special importance for the development of the Royal Navy. England was then involved in a complex three-way naval rivalry with the Netherlands and France. The outcome of this contest was not decided until long after the end of the period. However, in Charles II's reign the Navy's responses to the challenge led to the first clear formulation of the administrative and tactical ideas which eventually carried England to world-wide maritime supremacy. A new class of professional administrators evolved the basis for a support establishment of unprecedented reliability and efficiency. At sea a group of talented commanders taught themselves a tactical system that lasted for well over a century. The Navy's leadership, from the King down, was marked by vitality, initiative, and an innovative attitude not yet hampered by the weight of tradition.

The same vitality was also evident in the shipbuilders. It was during the Restoration period that the Royal Navy's warship designs finally crystallized into the basic forms they were to retain even into the nineteenth century. As significant as these developments were, few of the shipwrights looked upon their creations as mere pieces of military hardware. In that age more than any other, ships were also meant to be admired as things of beauty. Restoration men-of-war,

decorated with loving care by the now-forgotten masters of Baroque woodcarving, were in themselves a unique art form. For that reason alone they are worthy of careful study.

The book is limited in coverage–with some deviations–to the English-built warships which were afloat between 1660 and 1685. Brief accounts of the important maritime events of the period are included; but most of the space is devoted to the characteristics, appearance, armament, and histories of the ships themselves, along with the circumstances in which they were built. For comparative purposes, there is also a chapter on the shipbuilding efforts of the most important Continental navies. The emphasis throughout is on the larger vessels, for the simple reason that the big ships had the most impact on the course of events.

The scope is actually slightly greater than it seems. A large proportion of Charles II's warships were built in previous reigns, and with these vessels it is possible to trace the evolution of naval architecture from the beginning of the century. In addition, ships of the Restoration Navy made up the bulk of the English fleet for many years after 1685. Their influence on the designs and events of later periods is mentioned as well.

Information about the design and appearance of seventeenth century English warships is available from a number of sources, but these are less than satisfactory for much of the century. The archaeological examination of wrecks provides useful information about guns and metal fittings, but hulls are seldom preserved. Construction draughts from before 1700 are extremely rare, whilst written records are often incomplete and sometimes contradictory. Vessels dating from after the 1640s are represented by a number of incredibly detailed models, but many remain unidentified. In at least some cases the models were made before the ships, and they do not necessarily reflect the appearance of the completed products. For these reasons naval archaeologists have had to deal with the seventeenth century in generalities, with only a few vessels–usually the same ones–being discussed in detail.

The reign of Charles II is one period for which knowledge of individual ships can be obtained in considerable depth. This is because of two extraordinary research 'windows'. The first of these was provided by the presence on the scene of Samuel Pepys. At the Restoration Charles II re-established the Navy Board, the body which had been the fleet's main administrative arm in early Stuart times. Through patronage the 27-year-old Pepys obtained the Board's junior post, that of Clerk of the Acts. At first he was completely ignorant of the Navy, but he quickly familiarized himself with every aspect of shipbuilding, dockyard operations, and financial management. A tireless, methodical, and (relatively) incorruptible civil servant, he soon made himself an indispensable factor in the administration. He became the Navy's chief lobbyist in Parliament and eventually gained a seat in the Commons. By the end of his career he had become the King's personal adviser in naval affairs, holding the post of Secretary of the Admiralty with almost summary powers.

Mr Pepys had a habit—endearing him forever to historians—of writing down everything he saw and heard. His priceless diary gives behind-the-scenes information of a type which is available for few other ages. He also compiled exhaustive statistics on the ships, providing useful data which would otherwise be extremely difficult to obtain.

2
Samuel Pepys, by Kneller.

NMM. Painting by Sir Godfrey Kneller.

The other window opening on to the Restoration Navy is in many respects even more important than Pepys. This source is found in the works of the superbly talented marine artists of the time. Most of them were Dutchmen trained in the same traditions of draughtsmanship that produced Rembrandt and Hals. Marine art had flourished in the Netherlands for centuries, but few artists achieved the almost photographic standards of accuracy attained by the ship portraitists of Restoration times. Among the better ones were Jan van Beecq, Jieronymus van Diest, and Isaac Sailmaker. The greatest of all were the two Willem Van de Veldes, father and son. The Van de Veldes were not only accurate, but prolific. Between them they produced thousands of drawings and hundreds of paintings of ships and naval events. They were among the first war artists, observing the English and Dutch fleets in battle from their own little galliot. Both could draw very quickly, and events were recorded as they occurred.

Van de Velde the Elder (1611–1693) is considered to have been inferior to his son as a painter. As a pure draughtsman, however, the Elder was without peer. He also perfected an unusual medium—the *grisaille*, or *pen-painting*—in which a scene was scratched on to a canvas or panel which had been pre-coated with white paint. Few artists have mastered this technique. Van de Velde the Younger (1633–1707) was the greatest marine painter of the Dutch Baroque. Few artists have matched the magnificence of his colours, and even fewer have so successfully solved the difficult perspective problems of objects in the sea. These talents were combined with a thorough understanding of all of the parts of the ships and their equipment.

For the naval archaeologist the pure ship portraits are the most useful. Before 1673 most Van de Velde drawings were of Dutch ships, but even then they occasionally found opportunities to portray ships of other nations. The earliest drawings of English vessels were produced during the Civil War (1642–1649), when the Elder witnessed a confrontation of Royalist and Parliamentary fleets off Hellevoetsluis in 1648. Other English ships were portrayed by both father and son between 1660 and 1664, when both made several visits to England. In 1672 the Younger emigrated to England, and the Elder had joined him by early 1673. Once there they were hired by Charles II to be the Royal Navy's official artists, the Elder 'for taking and making draughts of seafights' and the Younger 'for putting the said draughts into colours for our own particular use'. From that point until their deaths they were almost continually employed in drawing and painting English men-of-war.

The drawings and paintings reproduced in this book are only a tiny fragment of the known inventories. They have been selected primarily on the basis of archaeological value rather than artistic merit. The object has been to show at least one likeness of every major vessel of which a portrait has been identified. This calls for a certain amount of caution, since the identification of the ships in the drawings is not always an easy matter. The Van de Veldes frequently did not bother to include inscriptions. Even when they did, later collectors sometimes snipped them off to make the pictures fit frames for which they were not intended. Other inscriptions have faded with age, and in any event both the Elder and the Younger often wrote with barely legible scrawls. The problem is also complicated by the imaginative attempts of the Dutch-speaking artists at phonetic spellings of English ship names. Thus *Charles* becomes *Siarles*, *Woolwich* becomes *Woleg*, and *Happy Return* becomes *Hopritorn*. Others defy interpretation.

Some vessels portrayed in the drawings can be identified from features known from written sources or elsewhere, and in other cases decorative details and gunport arrangements provide clues. Where only a few ships of a certain class were built, a process of elimination can be used to some extent. This is, however, an uncertain method because the Van de Veldes are known to have made drawings of entirely imaginary vessels. Since most of the paintings and drawings reproduced in the book are the work of the Van de Veldes or their studio, only works by other artists are identified as to authorship.

Some of the terminology used in the book requires explanation. The now customary 'HMS' before an English warship's name was not in use in the Restora-

3
Willem Van de Velde the Elder, probably self-portrayed.

NMM. Inscribed 'WVV'.

9

4
Willem Van de Velde the
Younger as portrayed by Kneller
in 1680.

NMM. Mezzotint after Sir Godfrey
Kneller, 1680.

tion period, but–also contrary to modern practice–ship names were invariably preceded by 'the'. In the seventeenth century the standard linear measure, the foot, varied in length from country to country. To make comparisons meaningful all dimensions of Continental warships have been converted to the English foot of 305mm. The modern calendar had not yet been adopted in seventeenth century England, so that English dates were ten days behind those on the Continent. Following the customary compromise, all dates are here expressed in the Old Style, except that the year has been adjusted to begin on 1 January rather than 25 March.

1. The Restoration Fighting Ship

Warships were the most complex industrial products of seventeenth century England. Their construction involved the efforts of skilled artisans in many seemingly unrelated trades and involved the produce of forests as far away as Russia and New England.

New ships were ordered by the King himself, after discussion with the Privy Council and the Admiralty. In the first half of the reign the Admiralty was the responsibility of James, Duke of York, the Lord High Admiral. From 1673 the office of Lord High Admiral was replaced by a commission headed by Prince Rupert as First Lord. Charles, James and Rupert all had a good understanding of naval architecture, and they were often personally involved in matters of ship design. Many more vessels were planned than built. Most of the money had to come from a Parliament which was seldom willing to vote funds for new construction unless the need seemed desperate.

Once a ship was authorized the design and construction were carried out by one of the royal dockyards or, on contract, by a private builder. The responsibility for providing shipbuilding materials lay with the Navy Board. This was composed of four 'Principal Officers': a Comptroller, a Treasurer, a Surveyor, and a Clerk of the Acts. These were assisted by several 'Commissioners for the Navy' who managed supply operations and dockyard activities. The Navy Board also maintained the Navy's accounts and provided most of the needs of the active fleet, although some commodities, such as ordnance and clothing, were supplied by separate organizations.

Dockyards

Five royal dockyards—Chatham, Portsmouth, Woolwich, Deptford, and Harwich—were used for shipbuilding in Charles II's reign. Some of the dockyards served other purposes as well. Chatham on the River Medway, and Portsmouth on the Channel, were accessible from important fleet anchorages and were consequently used as operational bases and supply centres. They also had ample space for accommodating the ships in *ordinary* (the decommissioned reserve fleet). The very old dockyards at Woolwich and Deptford were located in the Thames just below London. They were too far from the sea to make good fleet bases, and both were employed almost exclusively in the building

and repair of ships. A new installation at the North Sea port of Harwich was opened in 1664. It was intended mainly as a forward supply depot and emergency repair station for ships damaged in battles against the Dutch. Though not a permanent royal dockyard, its facilities were often used for shipbuilding. A small dockyard at Sheerness, at the junction of the Thames and Medway, was actually little more than a supply centre which could be reached more easily than Chatham. It was not used for shipbuilding until the reign of William III.

Royal shipwrights snobbishly claimed that contract-built vessels were invariably of poor design and cheap construction. There is little evidence that this was so, but private builders could indeed produce

5
King Charles II.
NMM. Painting by Sir Peter Lely.

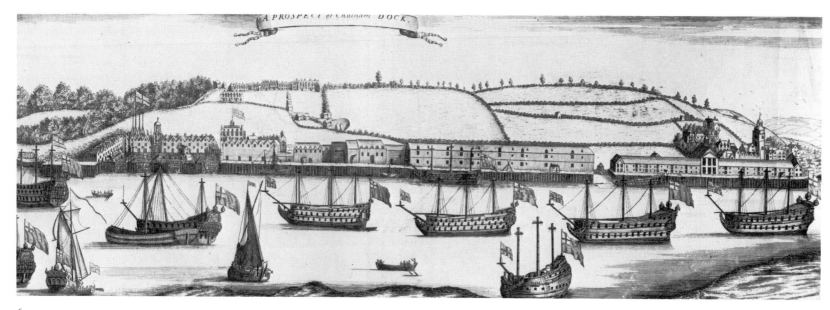

6

Chatham Dockyard around
1690.

NMM. Anonymous engraving after an
unidentified artist, c1690.

less expensive ships than could the government's
yards. This was partly because the royal dockyards were
plagued by habitual corruption at all levels. In addition
labour shortages, strikes, and outright mutinies occurred frequently due to the Navy's inability to pay the
workers' meagre wages. The private yards offered little
more, but at least they paid regularly. The Admiralty
unquestionably shared to some extent the shipwrights'
prejudice against contract building. A hint of this can
be found in the fact that most contracts were placed
with yards in the Thames, where the Navy Board could
constantly monitor the work.

In Restoration times the private facilities doing the
most business with the Navy were the yards of Sir
Henry Johnson at Blackwall and Captain William Castle at Deptford. The only builder outside the Thames
to receive important contracts was Francis Bayley of
Bristol.

Dockyard Organization and Master-Shipwrights

A typical dockyard was a sprawling installation covering several acres. It included building slips, along with
dry and wet docks for repair services. There were bar-
racks, warehouses, ropewalks, and a masthouse for
shaping heavy spars. Large open spaces were used to
store piles of uncut oak and elm logs, sorted according
to size. Sawpits were nearby. Mast timbers were stored
in mud or underwater, in a pond with locks to maintain
the proper water level. Masts were installed in the ships
by a crane usually mounted on a floating platform
called a hulk.*

A dockyard employed numbers of variously trained
'artificers'. There were shipwrights, sawyers, rope
makers, caulkers, painters, carvers, and hundreds of
common labourers. The administrative staff consisted
of a clerk of the cheque, a storekeeper, two masters
attendant, and the clerk of the survey. The latter was
assisted by a team of 'timber tasters', or wood inspec-
tors. This babel was orchestrated by a multi-talented
official known as the master-shipwright.

Apart from organizational ability, a master-
shipwright had to have a high degree of expertise in the
arts of ship carpentry, naval architecture, draughtsmanship, and even forestry. These talents were
acquired through a lengthy apprenticeship. The secrets
were often passed from father to son, and some
families–those of Pett and Shish in particular–produced many generations of famous shipbuilders.

Some master-shipwrights were like Jonas Shish of
Deptford, who was described by diarist John Evelyn as
'a plaine honest Carpenter (master builder of this
Dock) yet one that can give very little account of his
art by discourse, as hardly capable to read, yet of
greate abilitie in his calling: They ben Ship-Carpenters
in this Yard above 100 yeares'. Evelyn also reported
that 'It was the costome of this good man, to rise in the
night, and to pray kneeling in his owne Coffin: which
many yeares he had lying by him'. At another extreme
was Pepys' educated and articulate friend Sir Anthony
Deane. At ease with kings, the brilliant Deane was also
an insufferably arrogant and difficult taskmaster.
Others were brazenly corrupt panjandrums like Commissioner Peter Pett, a 'knave' according to Pepys.

Despite their eccentricities the English shipwrights
were recognized as the best in the world. Their services
were sought at some time or another by nearly every
navy in Europe. Using primitive rule-of-thumb
methods, they consistently produced intelligently
designed, well-built vessels which could often survive
forty years or more of hard service.

Design

The problems involved in designing a sailing warship
were extremely complex. Many qualities were
demanded. The ship was expected to be able to bear a
heavy armament carried as far above the water as
possible. Great strength of construction and ample
stowage capacity were also required. She should have
steady riding characteristics, rolling neither deeply nor
quickly and able to carry sail without heeling excessively. She should be a fast, weatherly, and manoeuvr-

*A hulk was the hull of an
old ship modified for
any auxiliary purpose.

able sailer. All of these qualities had to be combined in the most economical hull possible.

At the centre of the designer's problems were the matters of buoyancy and stability. For the ship to be able to ride at a desirable waterline, the shipwright had to provide sufficient displacement, or underwater volume. Stability–the tendency of a vessel to remain upright and resist capsizing–was obtained only by a low centre of gravity. Weight added high in the ship had a negative effect, and the higher it was added, the worse the effect. By itself, a fully equipped sailing warship was inherently unstable. The centre of gravity had to be lowered artificially by *ballast*, inert deadweight piled in the hold. But if the hull lacked sufficient initial displacement the necessary ballast could not be added because it would make the hull ride too low in the water. The underballasted ship would be *crank*, heeling excessively from the force of the wind on the sails.

The great difficulty was that nearly all the qualities desirable in a warship caused adverse effects on stability, and were furthermore in direct competition with each other. The requirements for strength of construction and weight of ordnance, along with all above water fittings and superstructures, competed for shares of the allowable topweight. The height of the batteries, a matter directly related to stability, also entered

into this competition. A further claim on the topweight was made by the masts and spars. These had to be quite large, since an extensive sail area was one of the principal requirements for speed. The sail area itself had a negative effect on stability, simply because it was the very means by which the wind would try to roll the ship over. All the desirable qualities necessitated an ample displacement. Another quality, stowage capacity, did not require displacement from the stability viewpoint, but it did demand a voluminous hold.

Unfortunately for the designer, there was one very important matter standing in the way of attainment of these goals. This was the fact that an indispensable requirement for good sailing qualities was a hull form of low water resistance. Such a hull was one which became narrow, or *fine*, towards the ends. The narrowing forward was necessary for speed, while at the after end it conferred good handling characteristics by providing a smooth flow of water to the rudder. The trouble was that fine lines meant a reduction in the underwater volume, placing a serious limit on the desperately needed displacement. This created a vicious circle from which the only escape was an increase in dimensions. That, however, violated the requirement for economy. As a result, the design of a sailing

7
A dockyard model of a 50-gun ship of the 1680s.

Photo courtesy USNA.

man-of-war was always a series of compromises, with some qualities sacrificed in favour of others.

In the seventeenth century the dimensions, strength of construction, armament, height of the batteries, and stowage capacity were usually specified by the Admiralty. The master-shipwright's responsibility was to determine the most advantageous layout and hull form, along with a compatible rigging plan, all without sacrificing stability. Unfortunately, no one was entirely sure just what the best hull forms were. The naval architects of the day were severely handicapped by a profound lack of knowledge of the mathematical relationships involved in buoyancy and stability, and they had only a dim comprehension of the mechanics of water resistance. One fairly serious misconception was the widespread belief that a narrow beam was necessary for fast sailing. Nevertheless, by intuition, experience, and his family's secret formulae the designer was usually able to work out a reasonably satisfactory plan. The wise shipwright always fudged upwards a little on the dimensions to work in all the extra stability he could. This was because he could be quite certain that captains and crews would eventually find a hundred ways to overload the ship.

Once the basic arrangements were settled, the master-shipwright and his assistants prepared a series of draughts in 1:48 scale. No actual construction draughts of this period are known to have survived, but they are often mentioned in correspondence and other accounts of the time. Copies of the draughts were sometimes delivered to the dockyard's model shop. There two dozen or more craftsmen built an intricately detailed model of the ship, usually in 1:48 scale also. The model was not used in the ship's construction, but was apparently intended for public relations in the same manner as a modern architect's model. Dockyard models were prepared for most of the larger vessels and some of the smaller ones. Many are now displayed in museums around the world, and they provide a valuable source for the appearance and design of the ships.

The draughts to be used in the actual construction of the vessel were taken to a large building called the mould loft. There, on a perfectly smooth wooden floor, the ship's lines were laid out full size and patterns prepared for shaping the various timbers.

Timber

Warships of the seventeenth century were made almost entirely of wood. Iron bolts were used to join some parts, but most timbers were fastened by wooden treenails, or *trunnels*. All but a few of a ship's structural members were made of sturdy and durable English oak, and the construction of a large man-of-war could consume well over 3000 trees. England was fairly well endowed with oak, but there were never enough of the oddly shaped trees which alone could produce the large curved or bent 'compass timbers'. Timbers of this sort, such as sharply angled *knees*, had to come from single pieces of wood which had grown to the right shape. The largest oak timber in a ship was the sternpost. Because of powerful stresses imposed by the rudder it could not be built up from smaller pieces. A large warship required a perfectly straight sternpost over 30ft long and well over 2ft thick.

In Elizabethan and early Stuart times shipbuilding timber had come mainly from the northern counties, but by 1660 the forests there were practically exhausted. In Charles II's reign much of the Navy's oak came from the Forest of Dean in Gloucestershire and two forests in Hampshire. Other supplies were provided by civilian contractors. Logs were usually shipped to the dockyards in uncut form, but occasionally templates were sent to the forest for on-site cutting. A few ships were actually built on a slipway at the edge of the Forest of Dean.

Less expensive, lower quality oak could be used for the planks covering a ship's sides and the *deals* forming her decks. For these purposes 'east country timber' from Norway and Sweden was purchased pre-cut.

8
Longitudinal section of a 100-gun three-decker, engraved after Edmund Dummer. The internal arrangements are somewhat simplified; there is very little shown beneath the orlop, for example.

Pepysian Library, Magdalene College, Cambridge. Engraved after Edmund Dummer, c1680.

THE
Perspective Appearance
OF A SHIPS BODY
In the Mid-ships
DISSECTED

9
An unusual section by Dummer
of a 90-gun three-decker.

Pepysian Library, Magdalene College,
Cambridge. Engraved after Edmund
Dummer, c1680.

Masts and spars were made of fir, pine or spruce. When possible each mast came from a single tree; for a big ship this meant timbers 100ft long and nearly 4ft thick at the base. Conifers of this size were difficult to find in Europe, but England was fortunate in having the use of the great pines of New England. If such mighty logs were not available it was necessary to use 'made-masts' built up from thinner sticks. Topmasts and large spars were usually fashioned from 'Riga fir'. This was named after the Baltic port from which it was purchased, but it actually originated in the forests of central Russia. Spruce, obtained from Norway, was used for smaller spars and poles.

Construction

The first stage of actual construction was the laying of the *keel*, or backbone. This was one of the few parts that could be made of elm, which was cheaper than oak and could withstand prolonged immersion equally well. The keel consisted of up to five overlapping segments securely scarphed together. Laid across the keel, and attached to it, were as many as eighty pairs of ribs, or *frames*, which formed the shape of the ship's sides. Each frame had several overlapping sections. The segments crossing the keel were called *floors*, and

each floor was extended by several *futtocks* which curved around the bilge. Above the waterline the futtocks were themselves extended by lighter *top timbers*, interrupted at intervals to form gunports. Longitudinal strength was provided by several bands of timbers called *wales* which were laid along the outside of the frames for the entire length of the hull. The lower, or great wale, near the waterline was always the heaviest. In the mid-seventeenth century each wale was normally composed of two strakes.

Before oak timbers went into a vessel it was desirable to 'season' them in the open air for two or three years to dry the sap. If this was not done the hull quickly rotted. To obtain extra seasoning a ship under construction was often allowed to rest on the slip 'in frame' (unplanked) for several months. At the end of this period the hull was covered with external planking to a depth of as much as 8in. Other planking–the *ceiling*–was laid inside the frames. The ceiling was secured by internal ribs called *riders* (amidships), *breasthooks* (forward), and *crutches* (astern).

A transverse section of the hull underwater was nearly semicircular amidships with only a slight flattening near the keel. Towards the ends of the ship the sections gradually became 'V'-shaped, and finally 'Y'-shaped. The tail of the 'Y' was formed by expanses of *deadwood* which aided steering and provided resistance against rolling. The broadest part of the hull was just above the waterline amidships, above which the hull had a considerable inward slope, or *tumblehome*.

From the after end of the keel the sternpost slanted upwards almost vertically. Its upper parts were connected to the frames by curved *transom timbers*, producing the uniquely English 'round tuck'. In Continental warships the sides terminated aft in a right angle, forming a 'square tuck'. In both systems the flat upper parts of the stern projected aft several feet beyond the sternpost.

Forward, an extension of the keel curved upward to form the *stem*. A piece of deadwood, the *cutwater*, extended the keel beneath the stem and slanted upwards into a long beak protruding forward above the waterline. The cutwater and beak were held in place by thick horizontal knees called *cheeks*. Abaft the beak the hull was squared off several feet aft of the stem by the *beakhead bulkhead*. In large seventeenth century vessels the bulkhead could be as much as two decks high. A short platform—the *beakhead*—was fitted in the space between the bulkhead and stem, and on this short deck were the 'seats of easement' which served as the crew's sanitary facilities. From each of the forward corners of the forecastle a heavy timber called a *cathead* protruded over the water. It functioned as a davit to hold a suspended anchor clear of the ship's side. *Head-rails*—usually three in number on each side—curved downward from beneath the catheads to the level of the beakhead and then swept forward and upward to meet above the tip of the beak.

Decks

The main transverse members of the hull were the deck beams, which were supported by knees fixed against the inner sides. To help keep the ship's centre of gravity from being excessively high the decks were placed as low as possible and very close together. There was seldom much more than 5½ft of space between each deck and the overhead beams. This made life uncomfortable for the crew, but habitability had a rather low priority in the King's Navy.

By the middle of the seventeenth century a fairly standard deck arrangement had evolved for English men-of-war. The lowest level of a ship was the inner bottom, or *floor*. A quantity of ballast was placed here to improve stability and trim, and the floor also had storerooms for provisions, spirits and fresh water. The lowest deck proper was the *orlop*. It contained the cable tiers and several cabins and storerooms. The area of the orlop just abaft the mainmast was called the *cockpit*, which in combat served as a surgery ward and battle dressing station. Beneath the after end of the orlop, well below the waterline, was the powder magazine. No flame could ever be allowed in this space, and the only light had to come from a lantern in an adjacent compartment.

Above the orlop were one, two or three *battery decks* along which was ranged most of the armament. It was

these decks only that were referred to when a vessel was described as a two-decker or three-decker. The tiller entered the hull just below the overhead of the *gun-room*, the compartment at the after end of the lower deck. The use of a wheel for steering did not become common until after 1700, and in the seventeenth century the tiller was swung by a lever called a *whipstaff* which was operated from the deck above. In a three-decker the hull was pierced amidships at middle deck level by an *entry port* for ease of access, this opening being found usually on the port side. The after end of the upper deck contained the *great cabin*, providing comfortable accommodation for the senior officer. Three-deckers had another great cabin on the middle deck. The great cabins had access ports leading to the *quarter-galleries*, serving as officers' privies, that projected from the ship's sides at the stern.

A series of superstructures was built above the battery decks. The forward end of the upper deck was sheltered by a *forecastle* in most ships, though this was sometimes omitted to save topweight. The cook's hearth was located beneath the forecastle, on the middle deck in three-deckers and on the upper deck in smaller ships. The uncovered area of the upper deck abaft the forecastle was called the *waist*. The after part of the upper deck was covered by the *quarterdeck*, extending to the stern from a point abaft the main-mast. The cabin under the forward part of the quarter-deck served as a wardroom for the officers. This area was called the *coach* in large ships, but in two-deckers it was usually called the *steerage* since it was also the space in which the helmsmen operated the whipstaff. In three-deckers the steerage was on the middle deck.

On the after end of the quarterdeck itself there was a comfortable cabin called the *roundhouse*, forward of which was an anteroom, or *cuddy*. In a rather confusing piece of terminology, an unusually spacious cuddy was called the *coach* in large two-deckers. These spaces were sheltered by the deck known as the *poop*. On the after end of the poop there was usually a boxlike structure only 2 or 3ft high in which the ship's trumpeters were expected to sleep. In very large vessels this was sometimes replaced by an upper roundhouse covered by a short deck called the *topgallant poop* or *poop royal*.

The lowly seamen who made up most of a ship's crew slept on the lower deck in 'hammacoes' slung from the overhead beams. The space allotted for each man was usually no more than 18in wide. The petty officers and mates did have tiny individual cabins, though they were nothing more than portable canvas screens erected between the guns. In fact, all internal bulkheads were removable. To reduce the danger of splinter casualties they were always taken down and stowed in the hold before battle.

Decoration

Once planking and decks were in place, an army of wood-carvers swarmed over the hull to provide decoration appropriate for a ship 'fit to defend a kingdom'. The figurehead—a lion except in the largest vessels—was placed on the beak. Vertical *headpieces* shaped into human or animal forms crossed the headrails, and other figures adorned the bulkhead. On the ship's side wreaths were fitted around the gunports of the upper deck and quarterdeck–a particularly English characteristic, seldom seen on Continental vessels. Quartergalleries were an art form in themselves, coming in an endless variety of fanciful shapes and surmounted by turrets, domes, and spires. The flat projecting sternpiece was well suited to receive decoration. Its lower parts were taken up by the windows of the important cabins, while the upper areas were usually dominated by the Stuart royal arms. The stern was flanked by larger-than-lifesize human forms called *quarterpieces*. In Charles II's reign genuine gilt was allowed only for the arms on the stern, the glitter of the other carvings usually being simulated by a mixture of tar and yellow paint.

The mid-seventeenth century marked the height of the Baroque age, and this was naturally reflected in naval decorative styles throughout Europe. English ships displayed in addition a somewhat Gothic quality. This was especially noticeable in the bows, sterns and bulkheads, which were characterized by rows of strongly expressed verticals and horizontals.

The treatment of the ship's sides followed a standard pattern throughout the Restoration period. The lower wale and adjacent strakes were painted black, while the areas above the upper wale were either black or blue. The remaining expanses of the sides were 'paid' with a clear varnish, leaving a natural wood colour. Internally, all surfaces except the decks were painted red to lessen the bloody horrors of battle. Variations

were allowed for officers' spaces such as the roundhouse and coach, where more comfortable blues, greens and dark wood shades predominated. Regulation ceased entirely in the great cabin, which had panels 'very curiously wrought and gilded with divers histories, and very much other work in oil colours'.

Launching

When a new vessel was ready for launching, the King himself selected her name. Before then she would have been identified only as 'the great ship building at Chatham', or something to that effect. Charles II regularly attended launchings at Thames yards. Drummers and trumpeters were hired 'for sounding on the occasion', while the Navy's official artists–the Van de Veldes–were often nearby with pencil in hand.

On the Continent, ships entered the water in an incomplete state and were finished alongside a quay. In England it was customary to delay the launching until the ship was entirely complete except for masts and rigging. In place of the masts, thin poles were installed to display the Royal Standard, along with the ensign and the flags of the Union and the Admiralty.

English warships were always launched stern first. Since a building slip had a considerable slope, gravity provided much of the force necessary to move the ship, but gangs of workers with jacks and heavy tackles were usually needed as well. Some particularly balky vessels required several days of sustained effort by hundreds of labourers. Things were much easier if, as was sometimes the case, the ship had been built in a drydock. It was then only necessary to open the locks and await the tide.

10
Launching of a 3rd Rate around 1675, perhaps the *Defiance*.

NMM No 1109. Younger, c1675.

Refits, Repairs, and Rebuildings

The dockyards, in addition to building new ships, were constantly occupied in repairing and modernizing existing vessels. These repairs came under four basic headings:

Repairs of operational damage. In wartime, such repairs consisted only of replacing burned or broken planks and timbers. The only object was to get the vessel back into action as soon as possible.

Correction of design defects. Repairs in this category were administered mainly to new ships, sometimes before they had even been to sea. The most common defect was poor stability. This was caused by a ship having been given either excessively fine lines or a disproportionately narrow beam. Such a vessel usually lacked the displacement necessary for carrying the weight of her ordnance, and would be topheavy and crank, heeling alarmingly under even light breezes. The dockyard's usual cure was a process known as *girdling*, in which an extra thickness of planking was added externally near the lower wale. The additional weight in this area resulted in a lower centre of gravity at the cost of a certain amount of speed.

Replacement of decayed timbers. The worst enemy of a wooden man-of-war was not cannon balls, but an insidious fungus known as dry rot. This is actually a misnomer, since it was most damaging in damp, poorly ventilated spaces. Its most vulnerable targets were the floors, futtocks, riders and beams surrounding a ship's hold. The onset of dry rot was often greatly delayed in vessels built of well-seasoned timbers. It was also a negligible problem in ships on active service, since in that circumstance the hold was frequently aired and inspected, and the ship's carpenter and his mates could correct many problems before they became serious. The real trouble came with the ordinary fleet (ships laid up out of service). The rot often raged unchecked in these neglected, unventilated vessels. Most of the Navy was in ordinary in peacetime, and even in wartime it was customary to lay up all but a small 'winter guard' during the cold months. Dockyard repairs for dry rot sometimes meant nothing more than the replacement of a few infected timbers. On other occasions the

11, 12, 13

These drawings show the extent to which the appearance of a ship could be changed by even a relatively minor repair. This vessel is the 54-gun *Happy Return*, originally built as the *Winsby* in 1654. She is shown before (11) and after (12) a repair administered in 1678. She received new quarter-galleries, hancing pieces, and figurehead, along with circular wreaths in place of the original square ones around the gunports of the upper tier. The third view (13) shows the stern entirely redecorated above the level of the upper deck.

11. Boymans No 374. Elder, c1675. Inscribed 'happy retorn'.

12. NMM No 1207. Younger, 1678. Inscribed 'd hapritorn vertumert' and 'vertumert 1678' (the *Happy Return*, rebuilt in 1678).

13. NMM No 1206. Younger, 1678. Inscribed 'd haperitorn neu vertumbert 1678' (the *Happy Return* newly rebuilt in 1678).

11

12

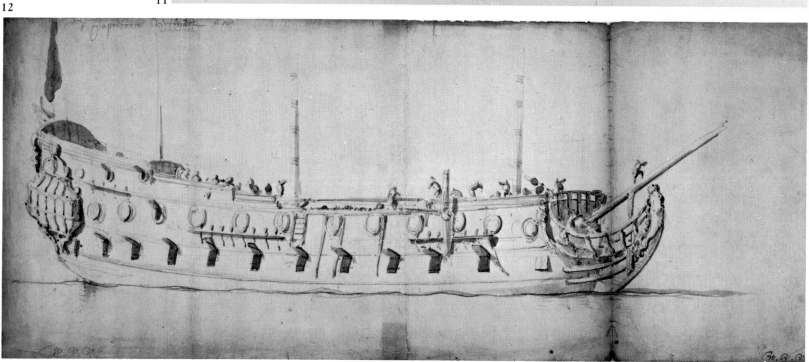

victims' ravaged skeletons had to be almost entirely rebuilt.

Modernizations. From time to time an elderly man-of-war was modernized to bring its characteristics into line with more recent vessels. A typical improvement was reducing topweight by shortening, lowering, or removing superstructure decks. Stability could be further enhanced by increasing the beam. This was accomplished either by girdling or by 'furring', which meant packing extra strips of timber against the outer surfaces of the frames. By Restoration standards many of the older warships had clumsy underwater lines, with an excessive amount of *rake* (the overhang of the stem and sternpost). Such vessels usually emerged from major refits with reshaped bows, wider sterns, and longer keels. In many cases they also received entirely new decorations in the latest styles.

Even though modernized vessels were sometimes much altered in both dimensions and appearance, it is a mistake—with a few exceptions—to consider them new ships. 'Before and after' portraits by the Van de Veldes usually show the positions of the original gunports unchanged, at least on the battery decks. This is an indication that the locations of the frames remained undisturbed. In addition it should be noted that the gundeck length often remained the same even when all other dimensions were altered.

There is much confusion about the meaning of rebuilding. In the eighteenth century a 'rebuilt' ship was actually an entirely new vessel incorporating 'serviceable timbers' from an old ship which had been broken up. A true refit was termed a 'great repair' or 'small repair' depending on the extent of the modifications. What was called a 'rebuilding' in the seventeenth century was usually the same as an eighteenth century great repair, while the sham 'rebuilding' of the later periods was rarely practised in Restoration times.

Rigging

The standard three-masted rig for English men-of-war of the mid-seventeenth century is illustrated elsewhere in this book. The system had been almost fully developed by the early years of the century, and there were only a few significant advances until after 1700. A distinguishing characteristic of seventeenth-century rigging was the *spritsail topmast*—with its tiny square sail—rising vertically from the tip of the bowsprit. Another was the location of the *chain wales*, or *channels*, to which the lower ends of the shrouds were anchored. In seventeenth century English ships the main and fore channels were sited above the gunports of the lower tier, while the mizzen channels were usually placed beneath the quarterdeck ports. In the next century the channels gradually moved upwards.

One improvement during the seventeenth century was the use of triangular fore and aft sails rigged forward of the masts. These *staysails* had been used in small craft since the fifteenth century, and they finally appeared in ship-rigged vessels around 1660. Prior to the introduction of staysails the only fore and aft sail had been the *mizzensail*.

During the Restoration period topgallant masts and sails were often omitted to improve stability. Speed was seldom critical in battle, since a fleet was limited to the pace of its slowest units. In any event, the fastest warships of the day could make little more than 8 or 9kts under the best conditions.

Ordnance

Naval guns of the seventeenth century were smooth-bore muzzle-loaders made of either brass or cast iron. Except for small swivel pieces, they were mounted on low, slab-sided, four-wheeled wooden carriages. The guns could fire either solid iron balls or, for anti-personnel effects, clusters of small balls called *grapeshot*. There were also several types of chain and bar shot for attacking sails and rigging. The responsibility for providing guns and ammunition for both the Army and Navy lay with an interservice organization called the Ordnance Board.

The different sizes of ordnance had long been known by a system of ancient names. Although these terms were still in use, a more convenient system—based on the weight of the roundshot—was gradually gaining acceptance in Restoration times, as shown in the accompanying table.

able, since extra ports could be added on the forecastle, quarterdeck and poop if space permitted. Next, the size of the largest individual pieces was limited by the strength of the ship's timbers. The relatively light frames of the smaller two-deckers could not safely withstand the immense recoil shock of the larger guns, and the huge cannon-of-seven were reserved exclusively for the most heavily built three-deckers. Finally, the total permissible weight of armament was a function of the ship's size and stability. In Restoration times a typical English man-of-war carried one ton of ordnance for every eight or nine tons of burden (the standard size measure for ships of the sailing era). This ratio remained fairly constant throughout Charles II's reign, although for most vessels the sizes and numbers of guns carried varied greatly from time to time.

English ships were, ton for ton, far more heavily armed than Continental warships. One disadvantage of this was that the lower tier had to be carried only 3 or 4ft from the water. This meant that even in moderate seas and weather the heaviest guns in the ship were unworkable on the lee side.

The Rates

The Navy's warships were classified according to importance into six *rates*, the 1st being the most powerful and the 6th the weakest. These had originally been established in the late 1640s to differentiate the pay scales of the officers and petty officers. Those serving in larger vessels were deemed to have more important positions and were accordingly paid on higher scales. By 1660 the rates had become convenient terms for describing the different types of warships in much the same manner as 'cruisers' and 'destroyers' in the twentieth century. There was a certain amount of overlap in size and armament between the various rates. This was because old units were seldom reclassified, while over the years the size of new ships of each rate became considerably larger. The overlap in the numerical strength of the armament was sometimes remarkable (see table). This was not, however, a good measure of the relative firepower of the ships, since the larger rates usually carried heavier guns.

Naval Ordnance In Use 1660-1685

Type	Weight of shot (lb)	Diameter of shot (in)	Bore (in)	Length (ft)	Weight (lb)
Cannon-of-seven	42	6.7	7.0	9½-10	5500-6500
Demi-Cannon	32	6.1	6.4	9 - 9½	4100-5400
24pdr	24	5.5	5.8	9 - 9½	3600-4500
Culverin	18	5.0	5.3	9 - 9½	3200-4200
12pdr	12	4.4	4.6	8½- 9½	2700-3500
Demi-Culverin	9	4.0	4.2	8 - 9	2100-3100
Saker (large)	7¾	3.8	4.0	7 - 8½	1800-2600
Saker (ordinary)	6	3.5	3.7	6 - 8½	1300-2200
Saker (light)	5	3.3	3.5	5 - 7	750-1600
Minion	4	3.0	3.2	4½- 5	625- 750
3pdr	3	2.8	2.9	4½- 5	400- 500
Falcon	2½	2.6	2.7	4 - 4½	275- 350
Falconet	1¼	2.0	2.1	3½- 4	200- 250

Variations in weight were due partly to differences in length and partly to the fact that iron guns were usually heavier than those made of brass. In addition to the normal lengths and weights listed above, some calibres came in special sizes.

Each ship was assigned a mixture of calibres, generally with a different size for each deck. A big three-decker might actually mount armament on five levels, so there would be five calibres. For reasons of weight distribution the heaviest guns were always mounted on the lower deck, while the lightest were placed in the upperworks.

The armament establishment for a given vessel depended on several factors. First of all the maximum quantity of guns was determined simply by the number of available gunports. This was to some extent vari-

Numerical Range of Armament of Each Rate

	1666	1675	1685
1st	80-102	90-100	90-100
2nd	56- 92	56- 84	64- 90
3rd	56- 70	58- 74	60- 74
4th	38- 62	40- 60	30- 56
5th	20- 38	24- 40	28- 38
6th	4- 20	4- 20	4- 18

The smallest warships, the 6th Rates, had only a single complete deck and seldom carried guns larger than sakers. Charles II also possessed a number of speedy and magnificently decorated royal yachts. These were comparable in size and firepower to the smaller 6th Rates, and were used for combatant duties

14
Seventeenth century guns were usually loaded from inboard, with the guns run in. As these Van de Velde sketches show, they could also be loaded from outboard by a dare-devil seaman straddling the barrel or perched on a channel. This method, employed when crews were undermanned, was practised most commonly in merchantmen.

NMM No 106. Younger, ?1664.

in wartime. The 5th Rates were small two-deckers, usually mounting their guns in a complete lower tier but only a partial upper tier. The 3rd and 4th Rates were two-deckers with full tiers of guns on both levels. These two classes were identical in design, the only differences being in size and armament.

All the ships of the two highest rates were three-deckers, and it was to these vessels that the term 'great ships' really referred. The larger 2nd Rates had three complete tiers of guns and were scarcely distinguishable from 1st Rates. The smaller—and older—2nd Rates were usually lacking a forecastle. They had only a partial upper tier, with the waist left empty of guns. Some of this group were ancient relics from the early Stuart and Elizabethan periods. They were smaller than many 3rd Rates, and were retained in the 2nd Rate only because of their three decks.

Only the most powerful three-deckers were classed as 1st Rates. They were given lavish decoration, and unquestionably existed in part because of their propaganda value. The very size and cost of such ships limited the scope of their employment. They were so expensive to maintain and so difficult to man (with 700-800 crewmen required for each) that they were seldom commissioned except in national emergencies, and even then the Admiralty was rarely willing to risk them outside home waters. In addition they were clumsy to manoeuvre and had an embarrassingly deep draught. However, when a 1st Rate could be brought alongside an enemy, the broadside was absolutely devastating. Charles II's 1st Rates were in action more frequently than those of any other period; and in his time, at least, they certainly justified their cost many times over.

Officers and Crew

The gorgeous ornamentation of seventeenth century men-of-war could not hide the fact that the ships were actually cramped, uncomfortable, and filthy places for human beings to live. Sanitary facilities were entirely inadequate. With hundreds of men living in close proximity, the ships were breeding places for all sorts of infectious diseases. Dietary deficiencies made other contributions to ill-health, and mortality rates of 15 per cent per year were not looked upon as especially bad. Shipboard boredom was relieved mainly by alcohol, and in its allotment of beer and spirits the Navy was truly munificent. There is plenty of evidence that in some of His Majesty's ships everyone from the captain down stayed in an almost perpetual state of drunkenness.

The pay and the amount and quality of food appeared adequate on paper, but the Navy's weak financial condition often made it impossible to fulfil the established allowances. When crews were paid at the end of a commission, wages often came in the form of 'tickets'. These were vouchers which could be converted to cash only at the Navy Office in London. To avoid making this journey the seamen could cash in their tickets with private brokers in the seaport towns, but only at a substantial discount. Shipboard discipline was not as tight as it became in the following century, but punishments could nevertheless be brutal. With all of this it is remarkable that the King's ships could be manned at all.

All the nation's seamen, with the exception of those in certain essential occupations, were legally liable for service. While it is true that large-scale impressment was always required in wartime, surprising numbers of men volunteered. This was partly due to genuine patriotism and the fact that the term of service was normally short, since most ships were paid off and decommissioned at the end of each summer. A number of volunteers were also attracted by the cash bounties which were offered as an inducement. Since no bounties had to be given to pressed men, each campaign began with the strange spectacle of the press gangs desperately trying to intercept the volunteers before they could reach the enlistment centres.

The officer corps was very small; in Charles II's reign only large ships had more than one lieutenant, and even the greatest three-deckers normally had only two. Consequently the various non-commissioned officers had greater responsibility than in later periods. Next in command after a ship's lieutenants was the *master*, a warrant officer appointed by the Navy Board. Although not commissioned, he was entitled to the same shipboard social privileges as the lieutenants. The master was responsible for navigation and the safe operation of sails and rigging. He was assisted by several mates, in addition to locally recruited pilots who were supposed to be familiar with the waters in which the ship was operating; good navigation charts were all but non-existent.

Next in line after the master was the *gunner*, whose responsibility was the maintenance and operation of the ordnance. His assistants were called *quarter-gunners*. The *carpenter* and his crew maintained all of the woodwork in the ship, and the *boatswain* was responsible for deck fittings, ground tackle, and the physical condition of sails and rigging. The *coxswain* took care of the ship's boats, while the *quartermasters* and their mates kept the helm and ensured the proper stowage of the hold and cable tier. Three somewhat more prestigious positions were filled by civilians.

15, 16
Two royal yachts, the *Kitchen* (15) and the *Charles*. These speedy little vessels, originally intended as pleasure craft, proved to be excellent wartime scouts and advice boats.

15. NMM No 665. Younger, ?1686.

16. NMM No 1108. Younger, c1675.

These were the medical officer, or 'chirurgeon'; the *purser*, functioning as paymaster and supply officer; and the chaplain, usually called the 'minister'.

Other specialized skills and duties were carried out by the armourer, gunsmith, cooper, cook, steward, trumpeter, swabber, and barber, along with the 'yeomen of the sheets' and the 'yeomen of the powder'. The bulk of the crew was made up of able seamen and relatively unskilled ordinary seamen. There were also several midshipmen, or officers in training, plus a number of boys and 'gromets'. The latter were young sailors intermediate in rank between boys and ordinary seamen. In addition to the normal ship's complement, the officers were allowed to have servants, some of whom could be maintained at the expense of the Navy. The captain's servants usually included musicians and secretaries.

The commissioned officers came from two types of backgrounds. One type were professionals who had learned their trade in the wars of the Commonwealth. They were called 'tarpaulins', and at least some had risen from the ranks. Among the tarpaulins were most of the more famous commanders, including George Monck (Duke of Albemarle), Edward Montagu (Earl of Sandwich), Sir William Penn, Sir John Lawson, Sir John Harman and Sir Christopher Myngs. The other type were the 'cavalier' or 'gentlemen' officers. They included a certain number of men who had gained their positions purely by patronage. Others were experienced commanders who had learned their business with Prince Rupert's Royalist squadron in the final years of the Civil War. Many cavalier officers, such as Sir Thomas Allin, Sir Robert Holmes, Sir Edward Spragge and Sir William Berkeley, were every bit as worthy of command as the tarpaulins.

Various political and tactical disputes cut across the lines established by the class differences, so that the officer corps was always split into a number of bickering factions and cliques. All were intensely jealous of each other's glory; almost every battle, however successful, was followed by a round of arguments and backbiting. They were to a man bloodthirsty and violent, with personalities as baroque as the decorations on their ships. They tended to err on the side of rashness rather than caution, a trait Nelson would have admired. Most of them loved a *mêlée* type of battle above all else, and

17
The Anglo-French fleet struggling to form line ahead as the Dutch (background) approach at the First Battle of Schooneveld in 1673. On this occasion the fleet never did get itself sorted out, and the result was a very confusing battle. This is one of series of eyewitness views by Van de Velde the Elder; his vantage point was the English ketch in the left foreground. Another drawing from the same series is reproduced as 165.

NMM No 396. Elder, 1675.

18
A pair of royal yachts sailing very close to the wind. The attitude of the flags and vanes gives an idea of the weatherliness of these nimble craft.

Rupert Preston, Ltd, London. Painting by the Younger.

the efforts of the fleet commanders to control the individualism of their subordinates was often a hopeless task. Charles II was generally well served by his sea officers. That they failed to win their wars was not due to incompetence, but to the poverty of the government and the skill and determination of the opponents.

Plate I
A storm-damaged English two-decker digs her nose into a heavy sea. While the hull form of Restoration warships provided some resistance against rolling, their relatively fine ends allowed them to pitch violently.

Rijksmuseum, Amsterdam. Painting by the Younger.

Plate II
A privately owned dockyard at Deptford, portrayed in Restoration times by an anonymous painter. A large East Indiaman lies in the drydock in the centre. In the river at the left is one of the King's yachts, while in the right foreground are several well-armed merchantmen.

NMM. Anonymous painting, probably dating from the 1660s or 1670s.

Plate III
A large 1st Rate, the 100-gun *Prince* of 1670, portrayed by Jan van Beecq in 1679. Although a beautiful painting, it is unfortunately inaccurate in many respects: it shows one too many gunports in the upper tier and disagrees with other portraits of the ship in the details of the stern, quarter-gallery, and hull decoration. However, the small projecting stern gallery is shown correctly.

NMM. Painting by Jan van Beecq, 1679.

Plate IV
Royal yachts departing for the Netherlands in 1677 with the newly wedded William of Orange and Princess Mary. The yachts are shown passing Erith, below Gravesend. The ship on the right should be the 3rd Rate *Mary*, which escorted the yachts on the journey.

NMM. Painting by the Younger, 1677.

Plate V
A fine painting by Isaac Sailmaker of the 6th Rate *Saudadoes*. She had been built as a yacht in 1670, but was rebuilt as a 6th Rate in 1673. This is one of the finest Sailmaker pictures known, and it and several others which the artist produced in the 1670s and 1680s show a degree of accuracy rivalling the works of the Van de Veldes. One of the ships in the background – the nearest two-decker – can be identified from decoration as the 4th Rate *Woolwich* of 1675.

From a private collection. Painting by Isaac Sailmaker, c1675.

I

II

III

IV

V

Battle Tactics

Fleets of the Restoration period normally attempted to sail into battle with the ships arrayed in a single-file 'line-ahead' formation. This arrangement gave every unit a clear field of fire and allowed excellent mutual support. It presented only the well-armed broadsides, giving the enemy no opportunity of inflicting murderous raking fire through the vulnerable bows and sterns. It also permitted the commander to retain some degree of control over the course of events.

The line of battle dominated naval tactics even into the twentieth century, but in Charles II's time it was a relatively recent development. Even then it was realized that its use demanded considerable organization. Fleets of the period often comprised 75 ships or more, and such a line might stretch 7 to 10 miles. English fleets were normally divided into three squadrons, designated Red, White and Blue. The Red squadron usually formed the centre of the line and was directed by the commander-in-chief. The White squadron, under the second in command, or admiral of the White, formed the van. The rear position was taken by the Blue squadron, commanded by the admiral of the Blue. The squadrons were themselves organized into three divisions. Each van division was commanded by a vice-admiral (of the Red, White or Blue), each

centre division by the squadron commander, and each rear division by a rear admiral (also of the Red, White, or Blue). Within each rank the flag officers of the Red were the most senior and those of the Blue the most junior. The order of divisions was customarily reversed in the Blue squadron, with the vice-admiral of the Blue commanding the rear division. This was done so that if the fleet came about together (placing the Blue squadron in the van) the leading elements would not be commanded by the most junior flag officer.

Early experience with the line of battle (in the 1650s) made it evident that any weak ship was a liability. It could easily be overwhelmed or driven out of place, leaving a gap which might compromise the whole fleet. In Charles II's reign vessels smaller than 4th Rates disappeared from the line and were relegated to subsidiary duties. The 5th Rates stood by to tow or otherwise assist damaged vessels, while the 6th Rates and yachts were used to relay signals and deliver messages. Both classes were also expected to intercept and dispose of the enemy's fireships.

In theory a system of flag signals made it possible to carry out a fairly wide range of co-ordinated manoeuvres. Actually the vagaries of the winds and the differing sailing qualities of the ships sometimes made nightmarish snarls of the simplest evolutions. Once battle was joined the line often dissolved entirely.

19
A typical seventeenth century fireship, the converted merchantman *Thomas and Elizabeth*. Most fireships, but evidently not this one, had downward opening port lids to prevent the flames from being confined within the hull. Note the sally port in the lower tier aft.

NMM No 681. Younger, c1690. Inscribed 'd Tomas d lisbet fer.' The *Thomas and Elizabeth* was purchased in 1688 and expended in 1692.

With signalling useless in the dense clouds of smoke, ships blundered about blindly, each fighting its own private battles.

Naval guns of the seventeenth century had extreme ranges of well over a mile. Such distances were described as 'random shot', which gives an idea of the accuracy to be expected. Fire was usually withheld until the range was under 500yds. At least in the early stages of an engagement each ship discharged its guns in nearly simultaneous salvoes called broadsides, but disciplined firing could not usually be maintained for long. The combatants sometimes closed until their sides were actually grinding together. This called for musketry and hand-to-hand fighting as each crew sought to board and capture its opponent. For this purpose every English ship above the 5th Rate carried a contingent of 'The Duke of York and Albany's Maritime Regiment of Foot'. These were the ancestors of the modern Marines.

While many vessels were forced to surrender or were taken by boarding, surprisingly few men-of-war were actually sunk by gunfire. A ship's carpentry crew was usually able to plug any underwater shot holes before extensive flooding could take place. Horrifying powder explosions occurred occasionally, but these were almost invariably caused by accident or negligence.

A more common cause of destruction was fire. In wooden ships caulked with pitch and tar nearly everything would burn. To take advantage of this obvious weakness Restoration battle fleets were normally accompanied by a number of *fireships*. These were incendiary vessels filled with inflammable substances and fitted with grappling hooks suspended from the rigging. They were usually converted from merchantmen or obsolete small warships. Manned by daredevil volunteers, fireships were set aflame and steered against the sides of opposing men-of-war. At the last moment the crew would attempt to escape to a boat towed astern. The best defence against a fireship was to cut the tow cable before the attack began, but once ignited, these deadly vessels could be dealt with only by gunfire and evasion. They were in many respects the seventeenth century equivalents of modern torpedoes, especially in their psychological effects. The approach of a blazing fireship was often enough to unnerve the steadiest crew. They could be sent to spread disorder and confusion in the enemy's line or be launched in mass attacks against his flagships. They were most effective against immobilized targets, such as grounded or dismasted vessels. While the Dutch were the undisputed masters of these tactics, the English had successes as well. The most notable came at the Battle of Lowestoft in 1665, when fireships delived the *coup de grace* to a defeated, disordered Dutch fleet.

2. The Fleet at the Restoration
Early Stuart Survivors

At the Restoration Charles II inherited fifteen warships of the two largest rates. Of these, two 1st Rates and nine 2nd Rates were holdovers from early Stuart reigns. Despite their advanced years they were by no means obsolete. They were of sound construction and heavy armament, and most still had many years of valuable service remaining.

The 'Prince Royal'

The older of the two 1st Rates was the *Prince Royal* (or *Royal Prince*) of 1610. She may not have been the world's first three-decker–some Spanish 'galleons' of the early 1600s may have been triple-tiered–but she was certainly the first in England. The *Prince Royal* was

20

The *Royal Prince* as she appeared shortly after the Restoration.

V&A No 4694. Elder, c1661, but masts and flags probably added later. Several inscriptions, including 'd . . . prinse roijall' and 'tot tiattum' (at Chatham). The *Royal Prince* was docked for a large repair in 1661 and was not refloated until 1663.

21
The *Royal Prince* in her final form.

conceived in 1607 when a shipwright named Phineas Pett prepared, on his own initiative, a model of a great ship of unprecedented size. King James I saw the model and, recognizing the prestige value of such a vessel, ordered her construction. Many of the shipwrights and naval authorities were openly critical of the apparently top-heavy design and its then-astronomical £20,000 price tag. It was also charged that her builder was an embezzler and that he was using green, unseasoned timbers. The Pett family, however, was long established in the dockyard hierarchy, and they rushed to his defence. Additional support came from Nottingham, the Lord Admiral, and Henry, Prince of Wales. With their powerful assistance Phineas survived three courts of enquiry.

The ship was ready for launching at Woolwich on 24 September 1610. A great crowd, including the King and court, gathered to watch. Phineas Pett then suffered his worst embarrassment when it was discovered that the ship's beam was too great to permit her to pass through the mouth of the dock. Red-faced dockyard workers hurriedly widened the opening, but few notables were present when the mighty *Prince Royal* was floated out on the next tide at 2 o'clock in the morning.

As built, the *Prince Royal* was 115ft on the keel and 43 or 44ft in beam. The rake of early Stuart warships was very long by later standards, so Pett's vessel may

have been as much as 155ft on the gundeck. Although originally intended as a 64-gun ship, she carried only 55 as completed. Early portraits show heavy gratings over the waist, forecastle and quarterdeck, so that she could almost be described as a four-decker. With her towering sides the *Prince Royal* was probably very unstable, and by 1623 the grating over the forecastle had been removed. By the time of the Restoration the others had disappeared as well.

The *Prince Royal* was greatly modified during her career, and by 1660 Pett would not likely have recognized her. The first refit came in 1621, when it was found that Phineas had indeed used bad timbers in building the ship. The repairs cost £6000–nearly a third of the original cost. The *Prince Royal* was more extensively modernized in 1641, and it was probably at that time that she exchanged her old-fashioned flat stern for the more up-to-date 'round tuck'. She also received ornate quarter-galleries and a large equestrian figurehead. She was then rated at 64 guns, but during Commonwealth times, when she was known as the *Resolution*, she packed in as many as 88.

In 1663 the again renamed *Prince Royal* emerged from the drydock at Woolwich after yet another major refit. Exactly what was done to the vessel is not known, but the 1663 version does not seem to have been considered a new ship. 'Before and after' views by the Van de Veldes show only slight differences in appearance, but the dimensions apparently changed drastically. The keel length after 1663 was 132ft and the beam 45ft 2in. The increase in beam could have been obtained by furring the frames, but the 17ft increase in keel length must have resulted from major structural modifications. Part of this may be accounted for by reductions in the rake both fore and aft, which would have allowed greater displacement and consequently an improvement in stability. It could be that the entire hull was lengthened as well. Unfortunately neither the original nor the final gundeck length is known, but for the 1660s a keel of 132ft corresponds to a gundeck of over 160ft. In her final form she mounted up to 92 guns.

England fought no wars involving major naval engagements in the early Stuart period, and the *Prince Royal* had no chance to prove herself in battle until the First Anglo-Dutch War (1652–53). Despite her great age at the time–over 40 years–she was still one of the most formidable warships afloat. As the *Resolution*, she was engaged–victoriously–at the battles of the Kentish Knock, North Foreland, and Scheveningen. She served on each occasion as the fleet flagship.

In Charles II's reign the *Prince Royal* survived the Battle of Lowestoft (1665), but in the Four Days' Battle (1666) she ran aground and was captured and burned by the Dutch. Her loss caused shock and dismay throughout England; she had been held in much the same regard as the ill-fated *Hood* in the twentieth century. Said Sir Thomas Clifford, who witnessed the disaster, 'She was like a castle in the sea, and I believe the best ship that ever was built in the world to endure battering, but she is gone, and this is an ill subject to be long upon'. In all, the *Prince Royal*'s career spanned 56 years.

The 'Royal Sovereign'

As great a man-of-war as the *Prince Royal* was, she was dwarfed by the other early Stuart 1st Rate, the 100-gun *Royal Sovereign*. This awesome vessel was, like the *Prince Royal*, built mainly to demonstrate the prestige of the reigning monarch, in this case Charles I. Her genesis occurred in June 1634, when the King paid a visit to Phineas Pett at Woolwich dockyard. The two met in the hold of an uncompleted vessel–the *Leopard*–and there discussed the construction of a super-ship. Word of these plans soon reached Trinity House, whose authorities were considered experts in naval architecture. They were appalled. In their eyes the building of the *Prince Royal* had been a serious mistake; an even greater project was an outrage. Despite their protest that 'neither can the art or wit of man build a ship well conditioned and fit for service with three tier of ordnance', preparations for the vessel's construction were begun in the winter of 1635.

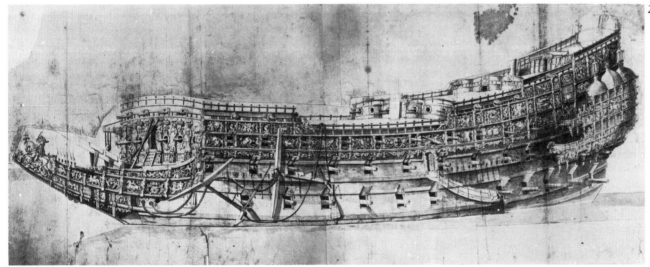

22

22, 23, 24
Van de Velde produced a detailed portrait of the original *Sovereign of the Seas* (22), perhaps taken from the Payne engraving. The other two drawings show the *Royal Sovereign* as she appeared through nearly all of Charles II's reign.

22. Photo: NMM. Original last noted in the collection of the late J S Morgan. ?Elder, date unknown.

23. NMM No 488. Younger, ?1673. Inscribed 'soeverijn' and 'd Roijal soeverijn.' Note that for a wartime Commission the enormous and much treasured central stern lantern has been replaced by a smaller and presumably more expendable one.

24. Royal Canterbury Museum. Elder, 1673. Inscribed 'roijal soeverijn 1673'.

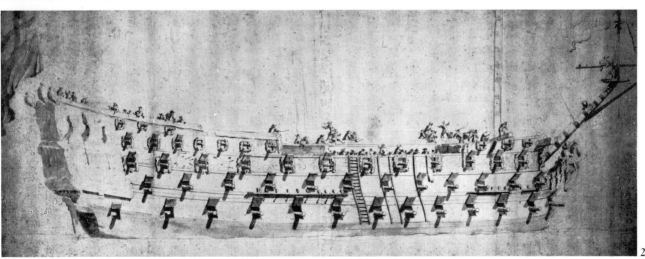

23

24

No expense was spared. To avoid repeating his earlier mistake with the *Prince Royal's* timbers, Pett personally combed Chopwell Forest, near Durham, and selected the oaks to be felled. Many of the frames were shaped at sawmills in the forest and shipped to Woolwich ready for assembly. The transportation of the timbers was a major operation in itself. They had to be dragged overland as much as 20 miles to the nearest seaport. 'One great piece of timber, which made the kelson, was so great and weighty that twenty-eight oxen and four horses with much difficulty drew it from the place where it grew, and from whence it was cut, down unto the water side'.

The amount of timber that went into the ship was so great that two small vessels—the *Greyhound* (120 tons) and the *Roebuck* (90 tons)—were built entirely from the 'chips' or waste. With all the advance staging of materials, the actual construction of the great ship went rapidly. Her keel was laid in December 1635 and the launching took place in October 1637.

In every statistic the *Sovereign of the Seas*, as she was christened, was many years ahead of her time. Her gundeck was 167ft 9in long and she was 127ft on the keel. Her beam was 46ft 6in inside the planking and 47ft 11in outside. Both the beam and the draught (23ft 6in) were greater than that of any other seventeenth

26

26

Warships lying in ordinary off Gillingham in 1685. The three-decker seen head-on at right is the *Royal Sovereign*, showing the lion figurehead she received in her 1684 great repair. Nested together at left are the 1st Rates *Prince* and *Britannia*, while the three-decker in the middle distance at centre is the 2nd Rate *Neptune*.

Boymans No 202. Elder, 1685. Inscribed on the left 'roijal prins' and 'britanje', and on the right 'd Neptunis' and 'dit nieu opgemaecht souvaereijn' (this the newly rebuilt *Sovereign*). Probably part of the same series as the endpapers.

34

century English warship. She was consequently much more stable than many later three-deckers. Unfortunately, this was partly negated in her earlier years by heavy gratings which were placed over the waist, forecastle and quarterdeck.

The 'Sovereign of the Sea's' armament (as originally fitted)

Lower deck

broadside	20 cannon drakes
stern chasers	4 demi-cannon drakes
bow chasers	2 demi-cannon drakes
luffs	2 demi-cannon drakes

Middle deck

broadside	24 culverin drakes
stern chasers	4 culverins
bow chasers	2 culverins

Upper deck

broadside	24 demi-culverin drakes
stern chasers	2 demi-culverins
bow chasers	2 demi-culverins

Quarterdeck	6 demi-culverin drakes
Forecastle	8 demi-culverin drakes
	2 culverin drakes
Poop	2 demi-culverin drakes

In later years the composition of the *Sovereign*'s ordnance varied considerably. The term 'drake' referred to a gun with a taper-bored chamber intended for light charges. It was commonly shorter than normal and made of rather thin metal. The standard long gun, described as 'fortified', was made of thicker metal and had a true-bored chamber intended for heavy charges.

Her builder had planned for only 90 guns, but Charles I insisted that she carry at least 100. Although a number of English 1st Rates built later in the century had 100 guns, the *Sovereign* was at all times allotted more powerful ordnance than the others. As originally outfitted she actually carried 104 guns, all of brass (see table).

25
The *Sovereign* was the flagship of Vice-Admiral Sir Joseph Jordan at the Battle of Solebay in 1672.

NMM: Greenwich Hospital Collection. Painting by Sir Peter Lely.

One dismaying feature of the *Soveriegn of the Seas* was her extremely high cost. Modern naval administrators may derive some solace from the fact that cost overruns have not been peculiar to the twentieth century. The original estimate was only £13,680. By the time she was ready for sea over £40,000 had been obligated, not counting the cost of the guns (another £25,000). No English warship exceeded this until the 1750s; by then inflation had doubled all prices. To pay for the *Sovereign* and several other new warships, Charles I resorted to the unpopular Ship Money Tax which was an important cause of his eventual downfall.

A large portion of the *Sovereign*'s cost was absorbed by the most spectacular ornamentation ever provided for a ship. Her decorations are said to have been designed by Thomas Heywood and Sir Anthony van Dyck and executed under the direction of master-carver Gerard Christmas.

The figurehead was an equestrian effigy of Edgar the Peaceful trampling seven kings. Her headrails were decorated with greyhounds, dragons and the various insignia of the royal arms. All the hull above the upper wale was covered with friezes depicting Roman Emperors and the signs of the zodiac, along with helmets, weapons, drums, and other paraphernalia of warfare. The stern displayed a bewildering array of statuary. The upper part was dominated by a Winged Victory, flanked by Neptune, Jupiter, Hercules, and Jason. A wide vertical panel beneath contained the royal arms and the plumes of the Prince of Wales. The

bulkheads at the breaks of the forecastle, quarterdeck, poop and topgallant poop were also encrusted with elaborate forms. Later experience showed that a profusion of inboard carvings was unwise because of the risk of splinter casualties in battle; even so such decoration was not abolished in the Royal Navy until the end of the century. It was not unusual for crews to chop away much of this useless froth before going into action. The carvings of the *Sovereign* were coated, not with the yellow paint which was the rule in later ships, but with real gilt. To the Dutch, who later fought her many times, she became known as the 'Golden Devil'.

The design of the *Sovereign* was as revolutionary as her decoration. The original version of the *Prince Royal* had been little more than an outsized Elizabethan galleon. The *Sovereign*'s design, with flush decks and rounded stern, was so advanced that with only superficial modifications she would not have looked out of place in the battle lines of 1800.

Because of the expense of operating such a vessel she was rarely commissioned in peacetime. She spent most of her time as a tourist attraction. John Evelyn first saw her in July of 1641:

'The 19th we rod to Rochester, and having seene the Cathedrall, we went to Chatham to see the Sovraigne, a mo[n]strous Vessel so call'd, being for burthen, defense and ornament the richest that ever spread cloth before the Wind; and especially for this remarkable, that her building cost his Majestie the affection of his subjects, who quarreld with him for a

27
The launching of the 'rebuilt' *Royal Sovereign* in 1701. One of the largest ships in the world at the time, she was pierced for 112 guns.

NMM No 733. Younger, 1701. Inscribed 'Roijal Soverijn 1701.'

trifle (as it was manag'd by some of his seacret Enemys, who made this an occasion) refusing to contribute to their owne safety, or his glory'.

The *Sovereign*'s enormous stern lantern delighted many observers. One was Samuel Pepys:

'. . . down we went to see the Sovereign, which we did, taking great pleasure therein, singing all the way, and, among other pleasures, I put my Lady, Mrs Turner, Mrs Hempson, and the two Mrs Allens into the lanthorn and I went in and kissed them, demanding it as a fee due to a principall officer, with all which we were exceeding merry, and drunk some bottles of wine and neat's tongue, &c'.

Like the *Prince Royal*, the *Sovereign* was brought up to date by occasional refits. The first occurred in 1651, when as much topweight as possible was removed to improve the ship's stability. The heavy gratings over the waist (which by that time had been at least partly planked over) were removed, the forecastle was reduced in height, and the quarterdeck was shortened. The topgallant poop was dismantled, and the forward extensions of the quarter-galleries were taken off. In addition, the long head was replaced by a shorter and more seaworthy structure.

In this form the *Sovereign* fought her first major battle, that of the Kentish Knock in 1652. Although it was said that she sank a Dutch ship with a single broadside, the *Sovereign*'s role was otherwise rather ignominious. Because of her ultra-deep draught she ran aground at a critical time and was lucky to escape destruction. After that the Commonwealth's admirals dared not risk her further. She spent the rest of the First Anglo-Dutch War safely in port.

Another major repair–sometimes described as a rebuilding – was administered to the *Sovereign* in 1659–60, by Captain John Taylor at Chatham Dockyard. The extent of Taylor's modifications is not certain. A drawing by Van de Velde the Elder dating from about 1673 shows the *Sovereign* with only superficial changes from her original appearance. An obvious difference is the increase in the number of gunports in the upperworks. It should be recalled that Phineas Pett had planned for only 90 guns. In order to carry 100 it had been necessary to point the extra ones in fore and aft directions, including across the waist from the forecastle and quarterdeck. The improved arrangement permitted full 50-gun broadsides for the first time. The 1673 drawing also shows one port worked into the upper tier aft in the space made available by the removal of the upper quarter-gallery's forward extension. Whether these changes were made in 1651 or 1660 is not known, but the 1673 drawing shows no changes in the siting of the *original* gunports. This proves, at least, that Captain Taylor did not disturb the positions of the original frames.

In Charles II's reign the *Sovereign* (properly *Royal Sovereign* from 1660) was engaged against the Dutch at the St James Day Fight of 1666 and also in the four main fleet actions of 1672–73. Surprisingly, she was less popular as a flagship than many of the other three-deckers. She fought two battles as a private ship (ie with no flag officer aboard). When she was finally used as the fleet flagship in the last two engagements of 1673, it was only because the admiral's first choice had proven unsatisfactory. There was certainly nothing wrong with the *Sovereign*'s fighting qualities. With her generous beam she was an unusually stable gun platform, so much so that she was outfitted in the 1670s with 24pdrs on the middle deck instead of the normal culverins. No other three-decker was so equipped. Prince Rupert wrote to the King in 1673; 'The *Sovereign* is the best ship you have for riding as well as sailing'.

One reason the *Royal Sovereign* was unsuitable as a flagship may have been that, despite her size, she lacked adequate cabin space to accommodate the small army of adventurers who made up the staff of a Restoration fleet commander. Her uppermost cabin had been removed in 1651, and a survey report dating from 1675 proposed, among other things, 'to make her stern 6ft broader at the transom'. This indicates that her after parts were narrower than had become customary by the 1670s, so she may well have been somewhat uncomfortable for senior officers.

The 1675 survey had come about because the *Royal Sovereign*'s ancient timbers were showing signs of deterioration. Unfortunately, the £16,000 needed for her rehabilitation could not be obtained. The repairs were put off from year to year, until Robert Lee, Master Shipwright at Chatham Dockyard, finally took the ship in hand in the early 1680s. He found her in a very shoddy condition. By the time he had finished with her in 1684 she was 'almost new'. Lee increased the keel to 131ft and the beam to 48ft 8in, but made no change in the gunport arrangement. He also gave her a lion figurehead, along with new and more stylish quarter-galleries and stern decoration.

She saw further combat in the 1690s, this time against the French at the Battles of Beachy Head and Barfleur. In 1696 the Admiralty was planning to rebuild her once again, but on the night of 27 January, at Chatham, a lighted candle was negligently left unattended in one of the ship's cabins. A fire broke out which the caretaker crew was unable to control. The watch on the nearby vessels was so slipshod that no one noticed the *Royal Sovereign*'s distress, and the trouble was first observed from the shore. By the time help arrived it was too late to do more than pick up the survivors.

Her name was not officially removed from the lists. Work on a new and even larger *Royal Sovereign* began almost immediately. The Admiralty made a point of using a few timbers from the burned out wreck so that the new vessel could be officially described as having been 'rebuilt'. She was launched in 1701 and survived until 1768.

Early Stuart Second Rates

The nine early Stuart 2nd Rates which survived into Restoration times were among the most interesting vessels in the fleet. By 1660 they already had long and glorious histories. The *Vanguard* of 1615 and the *Rainbow* of 1617 were actually rebuilt versions of Elizabethan warships. Both were important participants in the battles against the Spanish Armada. In those engagements the *Rainbow* was the flagship of Admiral Lord Henry Seymour, while the *Vanguard* was captained by Seymour's second-in-command, Sir William Wynter. The *Vanguard* had another unusual exploit. In 1625 she was briefly loaned to the King of France, who used her in an assault on the Huguenot stronghold of La Rochelle. The attack failed dismally but 'as for the *Vanguard*, she mowed them down like grass'.

28, 29, 30, 31
Early Stuart men-of-war had rather angular sterns. These vessels are shown as they appeared in the late 1640s and early 1650s, when all four were armed with 40-56 guns. On this page are the *Convertine* (28) and *Lion* (29); opposite are the *St George* (30) and *Garland* (31). The *Garland* is shown with Commonwealth arms in 1652, while the others date from 1648.

28. V&A No 4695. Elder, 1648. Drawn off Hellevoetsluis during the confrontation of the Parliamentary and Royalist fleets. The identification of this ship is not certain, and it could be the *Antelope* instead.

29. Boymans No 400. Elder, 1648. Drawn off Hellevoetsluis during the confrontation of the Parliamentary and Royalist fleets. The beast above the counter is unmistakably a lion, but lions were too common a decorative theme to make the identification of the ship a certainty. The *Unicorn*, also present in the Parliamentary squadron, was probably similar.

30. Atlas van Stolk. Elder, 1648. Inscribed twice 'd s Joris.' Drawn off Hellevoetsluis during the confrontation of the Parliamentary and Royalist fleets.

31. V&A No D241-1890. Elder, 1652. Drawn in Dutch waters after being captured at the Battle of Dungeness in 1652. Inscribed 'de roosekrans' (the *Rozenkrans*, as the *Garland* was renamed in the Dutch service).

Five other ships originated in James I's reign between 1620 and 1623; the *Victory*, *Swiftsure*, *St George*, *St Andrew*, and *Triumph*. The *Unicorn* and *James* (called *Old James* after 1660) dated from Charles I's time. All had been modified by dockyard refits. The *Vanguard* is known to have been modernized in 1631, the *Victory* in 1646, and the *Swiftsure* in 1653. Some were updated following severe battle damage in the First Anglo-Dutch War. Later portraits testify to other undocumented repairs and modifications.

All these vessels were three-deckers. The upper deck was originally nothing more than a grating over the waist, but by the mid-1640s it had been planked over. In their earlier years most pre-Commonwealth ships had a complex deck arrangement. There was often a fall in the lower deck aft, and sometimes a fall was present in every deck. In the 1640s some of these vessels had raised forecastles, but there was usually no proper quarterdeck. Abaft the waist was an isolated deck cabin–an early form of coach–which was separated from the great cabin by a short uncovered space. Passage around the coach was by narrow gangways which were raised several feet to give guns within the coach access to broadside ports.

By 1660 the early Stuart ships had been given a simpler configuration, with three complete flush decks and a short quarterdeck and poop, but no forecastle. One unit, the *Old James* of 1634, apparently had this arrangement from the start. In their final form the early Stuart 2nd Rates mounted complete tiers of guns only on the lower and middle decks. The upper tier was interrupted by an unarmed waist. Ships with this arrangement have been described as 'semi-three-deckers' or 'three-deckers spoilt'.

The details of their armament varied considerably, both from time to time and from ship to ship. All had originally carried fewer than 50 guns, but in Charles II's reign they were rated at 60–70 guns. The lower tier included at least a partial battery of demi-cannon, while the middle deck was armed with culverins or 12pdrs. Lighter pieces were carried on the upper deck and quarterdeck.

Because of their approaching obsolescence the old 2nd Rates had low priorities for rebuilding after 1660. The only one to be extensively modified was the *Victory*, which was enlarged in 1665 to carry 80–84 guns. In the mid-1670s the Admiralty considered a plan to uncover the waist of the *Old James* and lengthen her hull to make her conform to the larger 3rd Rates. The upper deck may have been removed–she was classed as a 3rd Rate after 1677–but nothing else was ever done. The others were almost entirely neglected. Van de Velde portraits from the 1670s and 1680s show the *St George* without a figurehead and another unit with no quarter-galleries. Even so the Navy was happy to have them in the battle line. All nine saw hard fighting in

the Second Anglo-Dutch War, during which three were lost. The *Swiftsure* was taken by the Dutch in the Four Days Battle of 1666; the *Vanguard* was sunk to avoid capture in 1667; and the *St Andrew* was wrecked accidentally. The *Swiftsure* served under Dutch colours as the *Oudshoorn* and fought against her prior owners on several occasions. Despite Dutch attempts to disguise her, English sailors easily recognized her even from a distance. The remaining six units fought in all of the main fleet engagements of the Third Anglo-Dutch War.

Their last years were spent peacefully in reserve. The *Rainbow* ended up as a sunken foundation at Sheerness in 1680. The *Old James* was sold in 1682, and the *Triumph* and *Unicorn* were sold in 1688. The *Victory* was broken up in 1691. The final survivor, the *St George*, was still afloat as late as 1697, although she had been a nameless hulk for the previous ten years.

32, 33
These small three-deckers illustrate typical configurations of Early Stuart warships in Civil War and early Commonwealth times. The first vessel (32) is the *Constant Reformation*, flagship of Prince Rupert's forlorn Royalist squadron at the end of the Civil War. She foundered in the Atlantic in 1651. The damaged vessel (33) may be the *Leopard* of 1635, shown on her arrival in the Netherlands after being captured at the Battle of Leghorn Roads in 1653. Apparently most other Early Stuart ships were rebuilt or at least 'modernized' between 1653 and 1660.

32. NMM No 753. Elder, 1648. Drawn off Hellevoetsluis during the confrontation of the Parliamentary and Royalist fleets.

33. NMM. Elder, ?1653.

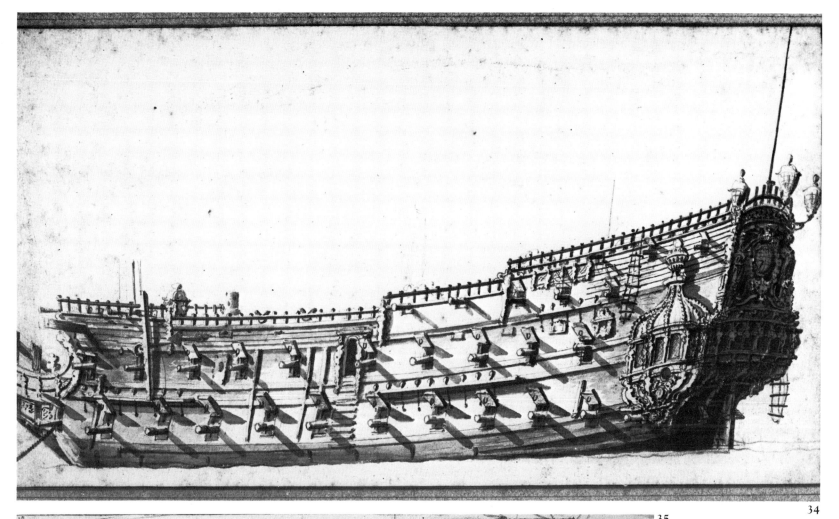

34, 35
An early Stuart 2nd Rate (34) –
probably the *Rainbow* – just after
the Restoration. The stern
decoration is typical of the
1650s, except that a royal
emblem has been hastily
installed in place of the
Commonwealth arms. The other
drawing (35) shows the *Rainbow*
only a year or two later
redecorated with new
quarter-galleries and a few other
minor changes. Though pierced
for at least 64 guns, the *Rainbow*
seldom carried more than 56.

34. Nederlandsch Historisch Scheepvaart
Museum, Amsterdam. Elder, ?1660.

35. Boymans No 390. Elder, c1661.
Inscribed 'no 10' and 'de rijnbouw oft
ramboul' (the *Rainbow* or . . .). Another
inscription at lower left reads 'schout bij
nacht van de witte van het voorschip tot
aent waeter verbrandt daer . . .' (The
Rear-Admiral of the white burned from
end to end . . .). This inscription is
probably erroneous, since it seems to refer
to the partial burning of Rear-Admiral of
the White Thomas Graves' *St Andrew* at
the Battle of Scheveningen in 1653.

36

An unidentified Early Stuart 2nd
Rate, possibly the *Victory*.
Shown with Commonwealth
emblems on the stern, but with
the plumes of the Prince of
Wales over the quarter-gallery.
Note that she still has a
forecastle.

NMM No 30. ?Younger, c1655. The
decoration is appropriate for the *Victory* or
Triumph. However, the feathers over the
quarter-gallery make the *Victory* more
likely, since she was originally built for the
Prince of Wales.

37, 38

The *Triumph* (37). Although the
other 2nd Rate (38) cannot be
identified with certainty, the
Unicorn is known to have had
this gunport arrangement. The
St George was similar in
configuration, but was without a
figurehead from at least 1672. In
its place was a triangular slab
with a painting.

37. Boymans. Elder, c1675. Inscribed 'de
trijphun triphunse', probably two separate
attempts at spelling the ship's name.

38. Rijksmuseum, Amsterdam. Elder,
?1661.

39

The damaged *Swiftsure*,
portrayed after her capture in the
Four Days' Battle of 1666.

NMM No 280. Elder, 1666. Inscribed 'de
swifsieure bij . . . vewallen' (the damaged
Swiftsure).

38

39

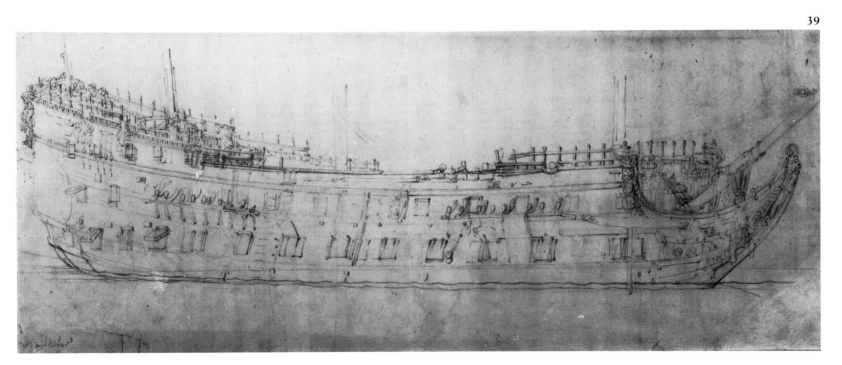

43

40, 41

Two 'mystery ships' showing some characteristics of Early Stuart men-of-war in the 1670s. The *St George* had a cut-off beak like the first 2nd Rate (40), but differed in other respects. The 2nd Rate missing with the quarter-gallery (41) shows decoration of around 1670, but is certainly a much older ship.

40. NMM No 492. Younger, *c*1675. The old *St Andrew* and *Vanguard* must have looked something like this ship, but both were lost long before the probable date of the drawing. It has been suggested that it might be an Algerine corsair.

41. Mr and Mrs Paul Mellon Collection. Younger, *c*1675. This appears to be a redecorated version of an old 2nd Rate, but it could also be the *French Ruby*, a prize which was taken in 1666 and extensively rebuilt in 1672.

41

Plate VI

The English fleet returning from Spain with Charles, Prince of Wales, in 1623. The *Prince Royal* leads the line, followed by the *St Andrew*. Despite the tubby appearance of the ships, this painting by Cornelis Vroom is probably quite accurate.
NMM. Painting attributed to Cornelis Vroom.

Plate VII.

The capture of the *Royal Prince* at the Four Days' Battle. The loss of this famous old ship came as a great shock to the English public. The Dutch flagship off the *Prince*'s starboard bow is the 72-gun *Gouda*. She wears the flag of Admiral Cornelis Tromp at the main and that of Rear-Admiral Isaac Sweers at the mizzen. Tromp, who received the surrender, had shifted to Sweers' ship when his own *Hollandia* had been disabled. De Ruyter's *Zeven Provincien* is in the middle distance at right. Van de Velde should have shown the ships of Tromp's squadron with ensigns of nine rather than six stripes, an anomaly probably explained by the much later date of the painting.
Gallerie J Kraus, Paris. Painting by the Younger, mid 1670s.

Plate VIII

The *Sovereign of the Seas* as she appeared shortly after her completion. An engraving by John Payne.
NMM. Engraving by John Payne, *c*1640.

Plate IX

An anonymous view of the original stern of the *Sovereign of the Seas*. She is portrayed with shipwright Peter Pett, who assisted his father Phineas in the ship's construction. The isometric perspective in the view of the ship indicates that the painting was probably made from the shipwright's draught. It unaccountably shows a square tuck, though the *Sovereign* is believed to have been built with curved transoms. This feature – along with the row of impossible gunports below the lower deck – may be the work of an ill-advised restorer.

NMM. Anonymous painting, *c*1640.

Plate X

This portrait of the *Royal Sovereign*, attributed to Jacob Knyffe, shows the events of 12 June 1673, when the King and the Duke of York held a council of war with Prince Rupert aboard the *Sovereign* off the Buoy of the Nore. The yacht is the King's favorite, the *Cleveland*. The *Sovereign* here seems much closer to her original appearance than is shown by Van de Velde portraits of similar date. It may that Knyffe used an earlier picture as his guide, perhaps one dating from the 1650s.

Parker Gallery, London. Attributed to Jacob Knyffe, 1673.

VI

VII

PRÆGRANDIS ILLIVS ATQ. CELEBERR. NAVIS SVB AVSPICIS CAROLI MAGN: BRIT: FRA: ET HIB: R

VIII

Tritons auspicious Sound ush'er Thy raigne
O're the curl'd billowes, Royal SOVERAINE,
Monarchal Ship, whose Fabryck doth outprize
The Pharos, Colosse, Memphique Pyramide;
And seemes a mouing Towre, when sprightly gales
Quicken the motion, and embreath the sailes.
Wee y⁴ haue heard of SEAVEN, now see y⁴ EIGHT
Wonder at home: of Naual art the height.
This Britain ARGO putts down that of Greece
Be Deck't with more then one rich Golden Fleece
Wrought into Sculptures, which Emblematize
Pregnant Conceipt to the more Curious eyes.
Neptune is proud e'th burden, and doth wonder
To heare a Fourefold Tire out-rore Ioue's Thunder.
Onn then Triumhal Arke, with EDGAR's fame,
To CHARLES his Scepter y⁴ y⁴ Trident claime.
Tho: Cary.

Cum priuilegio
ad imprimendum solum

IX

X

42, 43, 44
Three views of the *Old James,*
showing the ship as she appeared
about 1675. Except for the
Stuart arms and cipher, the stern
decoration is in a typical
Commonwealth style.

42. Boymans No 442. Elder, *c*1675.
Inscribed 'de gems' and 'de ould jems.'

43. NMM. Younger, *c*1675.

44. NMM No 495. Younger, *c*1675.
Though this ship seems very similar to
other drawings of the *Old James,* the
identification is not entirely certain.

44

3. The Fleet at the Restoration
Inheritance from the Interregnum

The years of the Civil War and the following Interregnum were sad times for the Stuart dynasty. The same periods were, however, extremely important for the development of the Navy. During the Civil War great advances were made in ship design, and the advances were put into effect on a large scale under the Commonwealth and Protectorate. It was during those times that England became a truly global power, and by the time of the Restoration the fleet was unquestionably the most powerful in Europe.

Warships of the Civil War, 1642-1649

Although the execution of Charles I did not occur until 1649, the Navy was under the control of the Puritan-dominated Parliament from 1642. The Parliamentary Navy was able to carry out only a very limited shipbuilding programme because of the dislocations of the Civil War. Even so, it was a significant period in the history of English naval architecture, brought about by the introduction of the *frigate*, a remarkable new type of warship.

It should be noted that the word *frigate*, as used in the 1640s, had little in common with its many later meanings. In Commonwealth times it was often used to describe warships of any size, while in Restoration times it came to mean combatant vessels smaller than 4th Rates. In its earlier usage the meaning was somewhat more specific.

The frigates of the 1640s incorporated no really new features; rather did they represent a new emphasis in design philosophy. An early Stuart warship–even a

45
An unidentified Parliamentary 4th Rate of 42 guns, probably portrayed around 1675. The *Constant Warwick* was very similar.

NMM No 460. Elder, c1675.

small one—was essentially a floating fortress stressing defensive characteristics: massive timbering to withstand roundshot, and high sides to deter boarding. With so much topweight already expended on the ship's own timbers, the designer could work in a heavy armament only by sacrificing the fine hull lines necessary for speedy sailing. The frigate represented the opposite ideal. Light timbers were employed, unnecessary superstructures were avoided, and decks were flush with low overheads. The considerable savings in topweight made it possible to bear a respectable armament while still retaining fast lines. Such a vessel was not

expected to withstand heavy shot, but was well suited for scouting, commerce raiding, and various 'hit and run' operations. This was hardly a new idea. It was simply a return to the concept of the lean, 'race-built' Elizabethan galleons which had so perfectly expressed the 'singe the king's beard' philosophy of Drake and Hawkins. This had somehow been lost in the intervening decades.

Like many other advances in English ship design, the frigate was a foreign invention. The word itself was first used to describe a type of small sailing ship with auxiliary oars which was employed in Spanish treasure

46

47

46, 47
The *Adventure* (46) and *Tiger*, armed with guns in the waist, around 1675. Note that the lower strake of the *Tiger's* channel wale terminates abaft the main channels, a feature typical of these lightly built ships.

46. NMM No 442. Younger, c1675. Inscribed 'd adventer'.

47. Mr and Mrs Paul Mellon collection. Younger, c1675.

fleets of the sixteenth century. The name was then adopted by the corsairs of Dunkirk and Flanders, whose shipwrights developed the type into full-sized men-of-war. In the 1640s the Flemish pirates became particularly bold in the Channel and North Sea, and it

was then that the qualities of their ships began to be taken seriously in England.

The first English example was copied from a pair of captured Dunkirkers, the *Swan of Flushing* and the *Nicodemus*. The designer was Peter Pett, a nephew of

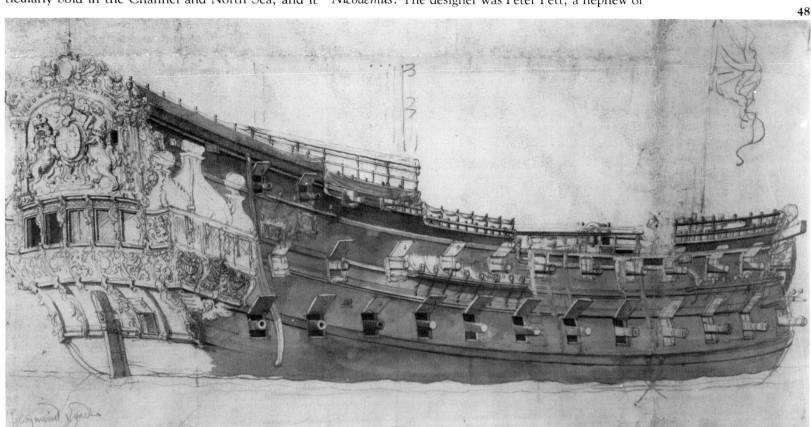

48

49

48, 49
The 3rd Rates *Plymouth* (48), about 1675, and the *Gloucester* (49).

48. NMM No 535. Elder, c1675. Inscribed 'pleijmoud vergadt' (*Plymouth* frigate).

49. Boymans. Elder, c1680. Partially cut-off inscription reads '. . . stor'. Inscribed in another hand, 'de Star'.

50, 51, 52, 53
These detail drawings show the port quarters of the Commonwealth 3rd Rates *York* (50), *Monck* (51), *Montague* (52), and *Dunkirk* (53) as they appeared in 1673-1675.

50. NMM No 449. Detail of a drawing by the Elder, 1674. Inscribed 'de Jorck'.

51. NMM No 536. Detail of a drawing by the Elder, *c*1675. Inscribed 'de Monck'.

52. NMM No 69. Detail of a drawing by the Elder, *c*1673. Inscribed 'de vergadt montegu' (the frigate *Montague*).

53. Boymans No 335. Detail of a drawing by the Elder, *c*1675. Inscribed 'de duinkerk'.

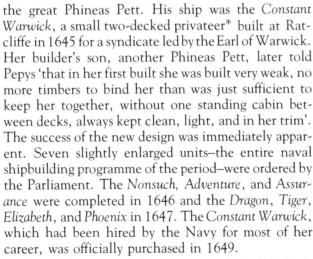

the great Phineas Pett. His ship was the *Constant Warwick*, a small two-decked privateer* built at Ratcliffe in 1645 for a syndicate led by the Earl of Warwick. Her builder's son, another Phineas Pett, later told Pepys 'that in her first built she was built very weak, no more timbers to bind her than was just sufficient to keep her together, without one standing cabin between decks, always kept clean, light, and in her trim'. The success of the new design was immediately apparent. Seven slightly enlarged units–the entire naval shipbuilding programme of the period–were ordered by the Parliament. The *Nonsuch*, *Adventure*, and *Assurance* were completed in 1646 and the *Dragon*, *Tiger*, *Elizabeth*, and *Phoenix* in 1647. The *Constant Warwick*, which had been hired by the Navy for most of her career, was officially purchased in 1649.

The Parliamentary frigates were flushed-decked, with a short quarterdeck and poop, but to save topweight no forecastle was provided. This turned out to be a mistake. With their fine lines the ships could pitch deeply, and the low freeboard forward made them very wet in a seaway. Pepys wrote of the *Constant Warwick*:

'She is said to have cut through the water so that the waves have gone over her head in such a manner as that her commander has told Sir P [Phineas] Pett that he has sometimes been afraid that she would never have appeared above water again'.

Another problem with the absence of a forecastle was that in a two-decker it left no covered space available for the cook's fire-hearth other than the hold. This was an inconvenient location for a number of reasons, not the least of which was the problem of smoke dispersal. In addition, war experience in the early 1650s showed that some shelter forward was desirable in battle. Short forecastles were consequently added in 1653 and 1654.

At least some of these ships–possibly all–were initially equipped with sweeps, or long oars, for use when

*A privateer was a privately-owned man-of-war licensed to attack the shipping of selected nations. In the seventeenth century the distinction between privateering and outright piracy was often rather blurred.

the wind failed. The sweeps, another characteristic borrowed from the Dunkirkers, were operated through small ports sited between the guns of the lower tier. This seemingly useful feature remained in vogue for only a few years, though it was reintroduced in the 1670s.

All eight ships survived into Restoration times, and some were still in service in the 1690s. They had originally been equipped with 32–34 guns, probably arranged in a complete lower tier but with the upper tier unarmed in the waist. In Charles II's reign they were classed as 4th Rates of 40–46 guns, usually but not always with two complete tiers. While nearly all English warships afloat in 1660 showed large numerical increases in armament in later years, the actual weight of armament seldom changed appreciably. All that usually happened was that heavy pieces were exchanged for more numerous light ones. In the mid-1670s the smaller 4th Rates, including those of Parliamentary age, were armed with culverins or demi-culverins on the lower deck and sakers on the upper deck. In addition a few light sakers could be mounted on the quarterdeck. At least one ship, the previously speedy *Constant Warwick*, was rearmed with an excessive weight of ordnance. She was thereafter described as a 'slug'.

In the Restoration period the Parliamentary 4th Rates were often used as convoy escorts or independent cruisers. Several distinguished themselves. In 1666 the *Adventure*, sailing alone under Captain John Torpley, successfully defended herself against four French warships in a five-hour battle. Only eleven days later she

defeated three men-of-war from Flushing, sinking one and driving off the others. In 1681 the same ship outfought a 46-gun Algerine corsair called the *Golden Horse*. This was a gory duel lasting thirteen hours. Another celebrated one-to-one action–such affairs were suprisingly rare in the seventeenth century–was fought by the *Tiger*. In 1674 she captured the Dutch ship *Schakerloo* off the harbour of Cadiz following a dramatic challenge by the Dutch captain.

Commonwealth Two-Deckers

Except for the eight 4th Rates of 1645–47, all the large English-built two-deckers at the beginning of Charles II's reign dated from the Commonwealth period. In all the Navy built an impressive total of seventeen 3rd Rates and twenty-eight 4th Rates between 1650 and 1659. Fifteen of the larger rate and twenty-five of the smaller were still afloat in 1660. Most of these vessels were produced between 1650 and 1654. The magnitude of this programme outstripped the capacity of the Navy's dockyards. Many of the ships were built under contract at Wapping, Ratcliffe, Blackwall, Limehouse and other yards. Two 3rd Rates–one of which was a rebuilt version of an older ship–and one 4th Rate were built in 1658–59.

It has often been assumed that the sober Puritans omitted frivolous and expensive decoration from their warships. This was true only to the extent that the use of gilt was discontinued in favour of yellow paint. Van de Velde drawings show some Commonwealth vessels festooned with carvings even more elabroate than had

54

Dockyard model showing the
clean, graceful hull of a
Commonwealth 3rd Rate. Note
the curve of the cutwater, typical
of ships built before the
mid-1660s; and the absence of
quarterdeck gunports. One of
the earliest Admiralty models
still in existence, it is shown as it
appeared in the early 1900s, with
eighteenth century rigging.

Photo: Statens Sjöhistoriska Museum,
Stockholm. Model: USNA. This
photograph was made just before the
model received a gross 'restoration' which
rendered it almost unrecognizable. The
dimensions do not perfectly match any
ship, but are very close to those of many
3rd Rates of the early 1650s.

been customary earlier. Commonwealth warships had a much less angular appearance than their early Stuart predecessors. The straight head of the older vessels gave way to a more seaworthy structure which swept upward in a graceful curve. A snarling, leonine 'beaste' almost invariably formed the figurehead, while the use of decorative wreaths around at least some of the upper deck gunports became common after 1650. These were usually squarish or irregular in shape, but small circular wreaths were also popular. The stern usually–but not always–bore the double-shielded Commonwealth arms. The Puritans were apparently not too concerned about this. Van de Velde drawings of the Battle of Scheveningen (1653) show one of the older English ships still bearing the royal arms.

As soon as Charles II was invited to return to England the entire fleet had to be hurriedly redecorated with Stuart emblems and ciphers. Pepys reported in the Diary (11 May 1660) that 'this morning we began to pull down all the State's arms in the fleet, having first sent to Dover for painters and others to set up the King's'. Van de Velde drawings show evidence of more extensive redecorations later.

The names of many of the vessels commemorated Civil War victories of the Parliamentary armies. These were natually repugnant to Charles II, and one of his first official acts was to change the offending names.

Third Rates

The Commonwealth 3rd Rates were essentially scaled-up versions of the Parliamentary frigates. However, since such important ships were meant to have better staying power in a fight, they had to be built of more sturdy timbers. The result was a well-balanced compromise between offensive and defensive capabilities. The 'great frigates', as they were at first called, became the prototypes for all the Royal Navy's two-decked ships-of-the-line for the following century and a half.

Ships Renamed in 1660

Rate	Commonwealth Name	Name from 1660
1st	Naseby	Royal Charles
	Richard	Royal James
	Resolution	Royal Prince
2nd	Dunbar	Henry
3rd	Speaker	Mary
	Worcester	Dunkirk
	Bridgewater	Anne
	Langport	Henrietta
	Lyme	Montagu
	Marston Moor	York
	Newbury	Revenge
	Torrington	Dreadnought
	Tredagh	Resolution
4th	President	Bonaventure
	Gainsborough	Swallow
	Preston	Antelope
	Maidstone	Mary Rose
	Nantwich	Breda
	Taunton	Crown
	Winsby	Happy Return
5th	Basing	Guernsey
	Fagons	Milford
	Selby	Eagle
	Grantham	Garland
	Cheriton	Speedwell
	Wakefield	Richmond
	Bradford	Success

55, 56
Commonwealth warships were occasionally modernized in Restoration times. The 3rd Rate or large 4th Rate (55) is decorated in a purely Commonwealth style except for the royal arms on the stern. The other vessel (56) is similar in many details and may be a redecorated version of the same ship. The quarter-galleries and the upper parts of the stern were changed, and the quarterdeck gunports sited farther aft.

55. NMM No 1197. Younger, probably around 1660, but possibly as late as 1673.

56. NMM No 1093. ?Elder, c1675. Possibly the *Dreadnought* or *Henrietta* (both 3rd Rates) or the *Leopard,* a large 4th Rate of 1659.

57, 58
The 3rd Rate *Revenge* (57)
shown in 1673, compared with a
dockyard model of a very similar
ship. The gunport arrangement
of the model is similar to that of
the *Revenge* and *Montagu*, but
the dimensions are closest to
those of the *Antelope* of 1651
(wrecked 1652).

57. NMM No 443. Younger, 1673.
Inscribed 'd reevense 1673'.

58. NMM.

57

58

With few exceptions, most of the 1650–54 units were 116–118ft on the keel and approximately 35ft in beam. The later *Monck* (1659) and the rebuilt *Lion* (1658) retained the 35ft beam, but were reduced in keel length to only 108ft.

The ordnance originally carried by most of the Commonwealth 3rd Rates comprised 50 guns: 20 demi-cannon, 6 culverins and 24 demi-culverins. At first few guns were mounted above upper deck level. In the Restoration period the armament was gradually increased numerically, with corresponding reductions in calibre. During the Second and Third Anglo-Dutch Wars most carried 58 guns. From the mid-1670s the usual establishment was 60–62 guns, with 24pdrs and 12pdrs on the battery decks and light sakers on the forecastle and quarterdeck. A pair of 3pdrs were sited on the poop.

The oldest of the 3rd Rates, the *Mary* (ex-*Speaker* of 1650) deserves special mention. She was built at Woolwich by yet another Pett, this one named Christopher. As the first of the 'great frigates', her design was to some extent experimental. She was 116ft on the keel, 143ft 3in on the gundeck, and 34ft 4in in beam. She was at first not entirely successful, but after a girdling widened her to 35ft 6in she became a much-admired vessel. Another modification of uncertain date (but prior to 1689) increased the beam to 36ft 8in.

As late as 1664 the Admiralty specified that the *Mary*'s dimensions be copied in a class of projected 3rd Rates.

Battle Honours of the 'Speaker'/'Mary'

Major Fleet Engagements

19 May 1652	Dover
28 Sept 1652	Kentish Knock
30 Nov 1652	Dungeness
18-20 Feb 1653	Portland
2-3 June 1653	North Foreland
31 July 1665	Scheveningen
3 June 1665	Lowestoft
25 July 1666	St James Day
28 May 1672	Solebay
28 May 1673	1st Schooneveld
4 June 1673	2nd Schooneveld
11 Aug 1673	Texel
1 May 1689	Bantry Bay
12 Oct 1702	Vigo Bay

Notable Minor Actions

8 Sept 1656	Cadiz
20 April 1657	Tenerife
8 May 1671	Bugia Bay
22 Feb 1692	Désirade

59
The *Mary* (ex-*Speaker*).

NMM No 62. Elder, ?1660. Inscribed 'spijcker genaemt . . . den 4 kante gesnede poorten' (named *Speaker* . . . the square carved ports) and, apparently written at another time, 'de Pr Marije' (the *Princess Mary*).

60
Sir William Penn, who flew his flag from the *Speaker* in the First Anglo-Dutch War.

NMM: Greenwich Hospital Collection. Painting by Sir Peter Lely.

Fourth Rates

The many 4th Rates of the 1650s were built in a variety of sizes. The smaller ones had a keel length of about 100ft and a beam near 30ft. The largest were as much as 109ft on the keel and over 33ft in beam, scarcely smaller than some of the 3rd Rates. Like the related Parliamentary frigates, most of the earlier units were built without forecastles. However, combat experience in the First Anglo-Dutch War showed this to have been an unwise omission. Forecastles were added as quickly as possible, and most 4th Rates completed after about 1652 incorporated them from the start.

Most of these vessels were originally designed to carry 38–44 guns, including a partial tier of demi-cannon. The Admiralty experimented with a number of armament configurations for large and medium-sized 4th Rates in the 1660s and early 1670s. By the mid-1670s two basic arrangements had been found satisfactory. The larger vessels–the *Newcastle*, *Yarmouth*, *Happy Return* and *Leopard*–were rated at 54 guns; 24pdrs were mounted on the lower deck and sakers above. The other group was allowed 46–50 guns, usually 48. They had culverins on the lower deck and sakers on the upper. Both classes carried a few light sakers on the quarterdeck, though no guns had originally been mounted there.

The Commonwealth 4th Rates proved to be versatile and useful vessels. The battle record of the *Mary* was rivalled by the 4th Rate *Ruby* of 1651, with thirteen major fleet actions and many minor ones to her credit. Most of the 4th Rates were overshadowed in great battles by the larger ships, but many achieved fame in independent actions. Some of their most extraordinary exploits occurred in the Mediterranean in operations against the corsair navies of North Africa.

In 1669 the *Mary Rose*, commanded by Captain John (later Admiral Sir John) Kempthorne, had to

Pepys visited the *Speaker* in April of 1660 (she had not yet been renamed) and as an aside in the Diary noted, 'a very brave ship'. Indeed she was. During her career the *Speaker/Mary* was engaged in the amazing total of fourteen major fleet actions, more than any other vessel in the history of the British Navy. She also took part in a number of noteworthy minor engagements. In the First Anglo-Dutch War she was often used as a flagship, on one occasion by the great William Penn. In all, her history spanned more than half a century. In 1703 the *Mary* was wrecked, with only three survivors, during a gale so violent that it is remembered to this day in southern England as simply The Great Storm.

61, 62
The 4th Rate *Bristol* (61). Though usually rated for 48 guns, she carried 54 in 1673. The very similar *Portland* (62) is shown about 1660 with Commonwealth decoration still in evidence.

61. Boymans No 386. Elder, probably 1673. Inscribed 'de bristoll'.

62. NMM No 854. Elder, ?1660. Inscribed 'd vergadt poortlant' (the frigate *Portland*).

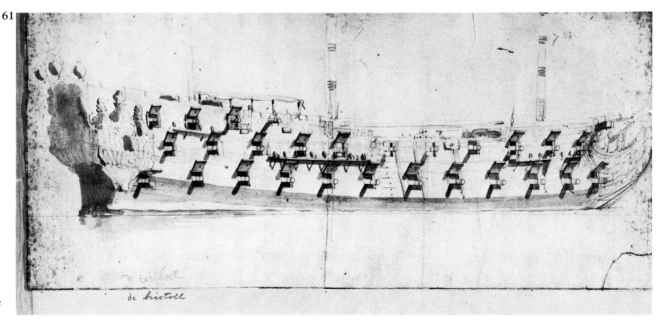

defend a small convoy against an attack by seven Algerine men-of-war. After four hours of desperate fighting the Algerines were forced to retire without harming the convoy. This action–one of the most famous of the age–inspired an overstated rhyme:

Two we burnt, and two we sank,
and two did run away
And one we carried to Leghorn Roads
to show we'd won the day.

62

63

63
A large 4th Rate, the *Newcastle*, armed with 54-56 guns in 1676. Note the castle atop the quarter-gallery.

NMM No 1190. Younger, 1676. Inscribed '. . . kastel 1676'.

64
Fighting against long odds, the *Mary Rose* defends her convoy against seven Algerine corsairs in 1669. A typical Commonwealth 'frigate', the *Mary Rose* was a 4th Rate of 1654. The *Mary Rose* is the large ship on the right. Off her port bow is a merchantman of Hamburg, while the vessels in the right foreground are a Scottish merchantman and the *Roe* ketch. At left centre, seen from the stern, is an English pink (whose panic-stricken passengers mutinied during the fight and unsuccessfully tried to go over to the Algerines). The ship in the left foreground is a French merchantman. In line across the top are the Algerine corsairs *Half Moon, Orange Tree, Seven Stars, White Horse, Hart* and *Golden Lion*. The seventh Algerine, the *Rose Leaf*, is in the right background chasing a prize which the *Mary Rose* had taken earlier but abandoned with sails set before the fight.

Leger Gallery, London. Painting probably by Van de Velde the Younger.

A less publicised but equally remarkable action was fought the following year by the *Advice* of 1650, commanded by Captain Benjamin Young. While escorting a convoy in company with the 5th Rate *Guernsey* (Captain Argentine Allington), she too encountered seven Algerines. All carried between 40 and 56 guns. After two *days* of fighting, the corsairs were put to flight; but both English captains were killed.

The 'Royal Charles'

The 'reign' of Oliver Cromwell began in 1653. The Lord Protector was a king in all but name. As could only be expected, his vanity caused the Navy to concentrate on the construction of heavy 'prestige ships'. This ultimately presented Charles II with four of his most powerful three-deckers.

65

65, 66, 67, 68
Four views of the *Royal Charles* dating from after her capture in 1667. All are Van de Velde drawings except for one (67) attributed to Abraham Storck. Each varies in some details from the others. Note, however, that the mizzen channels are consistently shown beneath the upper deck ports, a very unusual position. The last view (68) obviously differs in several ways, and may be a later rendering done from memory.

65. NMM No 1187. ?Elder, c1667.

66. V&A No 4691. ?Elder, c1667.

67. Rijksmuseum, Amsterdam. Attributed to Abraham Storck, 1672. Shows some confusion over the spacing of the ports of the middle and upper decks. Note the absence of wreaths around the two aftermost upper deck ports, a feature shown in several other portraits of the ship.

68. NMM No 490. Younger, possibly 1672 but probably later. The large port at the break of the forecastle may have had something to do with the ground tackle; the drawing also shows no cathead.

67

68

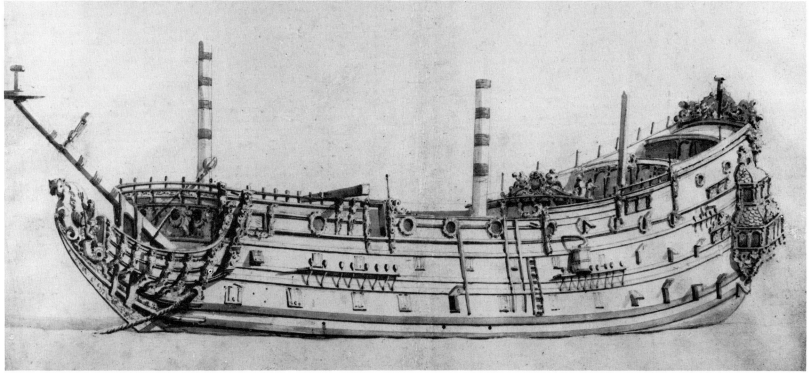

69
Stuart arms from the stern of the
Royal Charles, preserved in the
Rijksmuseum, Amsterdam.

Rijksmuseum, Amsterdam.

Plate XI
One of the best views of an Early Stuart 2nd Rate in Restoration
times is this portrayal of the *Swiftsure* (foreground). She is shown
in Dutch waters with other captured English ships following the
Four Days' Battle of 1666. Except for the royal arms, the
Swiftsure's decoration dated from 1653 when she had received a
major repair. Note the debased English ensign. Just off the
Swiftsure's port broadside is the ship that captured her, the 72-gun
Reigersbergen, or *Blauwe Reiger* (blue heron). Ahead of the
Swiftsure is the Dutch ship *Delft,* flagship of Rear-Admiral Jan van
Nes. At the extreme left is the dismasted flagship of Cornelis
Tromp, the 80-gun *Hollandia.* A captured English hired
merchantman, probably the *Loyal George,* is visible in the left
background.

Rijksmuseum, Amsterdam. Painting by the Younger, *c*1667.

Plate XII
An unidentified English two-decker, probably of Commonwealth
vintage, in action with the Algerine corsairs. Often assumed to be
the *Kingfisher* or *Mary Rose,* but it probably shows neither.

NMM. Painting by or after the Younger, ?1670s.

Plate XIII.
The *Royal Charles* being sailed to the Netherlands following her
capture in 1667.

Rijksmuseum, Amsterdam. Painting by Jieronymus van Diest, *c*1667.

Plate XIV
The damaged *Royal James* is towed out of action on the final day of
the Four Days' Battle. She wears Prince Rupert's flag at the main.

Nederlandsch Historisch Scheepvaart Museum, Amsterdam. Painting by the
Younger, *c*1667.

XI

XII

XXIV

The first and largest of the new 'great ships' was completed by Commissioner Peter Pett (this one the son of old Phineas) at Woolwich in 1655. She was christened *Naseby* in honour of Cromwell's great victory over the Royalists in 1645. With a keel of 131ft and a beam of 42ft 6in (1258 tons) she was considerably smaller than the *Sovereign*. Even so, only one foreign power–Denmark-Norway–had anything to compare with her at the time. The *Naseby* was the flagship of the fleet that sailed to the Netherlands in 1660 to return Charles II to England. The King was delighted with the ship, changing her name to *Royal Charles* on his first night aboard.

The ship's figurehead had outraged Royalist sympathizers. John Evelyn had examined it shortly after the launching in 1655:

'. . . We went to see the greate Ship newly built, by the Usurper Oliver, carrying 96 brasse Guns, & of 1000 tunn: In the Prow was Oliver on horseback trampling 6 nations under foote, a Scott, Irishman, Dutch, French, Spaniard & English as was easily made out by their several habits: A Fame held a laurell over his insulting head, & the word God with us'.

In December of 1663 someone remembered its significance. Pepys reported (14 December):

'But among other things, Lord! what an account did Sir J Minnes and Sir W Batten make of the pulling down and burning of the head of the Charles, where Cromwell was placed with people under his horse, and Peter*, as the Duke called him, is praying to him; and Sir J Minnes would needs infer the temper of the people from their joy at the doing of this and their building a gibbet for the hanging of his head up, when God knows, it is even the flinging away of £100 out of the King's purse, to the building of another, which it seems must be a Neptune'.

He was still grumbling about the waste of money the next day:

'. . . but it troubles me the King should suffer £100 losse in his purse, to make a new one, after it was forgot whose it was, or any words spoke of it'.

The £100 Neptune was an effigy of the trident-bearing deity drawn on a great sea shell by a pair of bizarre aquatic horses. It was unusual in the seventeenth century for English ships to be fitted with anything other than the standard equestrian or lion figureheads.

The *Royal Charles* was one of the Navy's most important units at the outbreak of the Second Anglo-Dutch War (1665–67). She was the fleet flagship in all three of the great engagements of the war. She proved to be a formidable opponent, and the Dutch were unable to defeat her at sea. Then, in 1667, a combination of English negligence and Dutch daring resulted in a shocking coup in which the undefended *Royal Charles* was captured and taken to the Netherlands. She was displayed as a trophy at Rotterdam for several years. Her presence there was considered a personal insult by Charles II, and this made no small contribution to the

ill-feeling that led to the Third Anglo-Dutch War (1672–74). Eventually she became expensive to maintain. The Rotterdam authorities decided in 1672 to have her broken up, but the ruling body of the Netherlands, the States-General, intervened and ordered that she be kept afloat a little longer. In the summer of 1672 she was refitted for possible use in the battle line. The defensive nature of the Dutch strategy, however, precluded the use of a vessel of such deep draught. In April of 1673 she was accordingly sold at auction for 5000 guilders and broken up.

Despite Evelyn's claim that she had '96 brasse Guns', there is no evidence that she ever carried more than 86. A more usual figure was 80. However, had she survived in the Royal Navy much longer than she did, it is probable that she eventually would have been outfitted with over 90.

The 'London' and the 'Henry'

The *Naseby* was followed in 1656 by a pair of 1100-ton 2nd Rates, the *Dunbar* and the *London*, the former being renamed *Henry* at the Restoration. She was built at Deptford by a shipwright named Manley Callis, whilst the *London* was built by Captain John Taylor at Chatham.

Callis and Taylor provided these vessels with three flush decks, but did not add a forecastle. This omission had been considered a fault in small ships, but in a three-decker it was not as serious since the upper deck was already at a considerable height above the water. The location of the cook's fire-hearth was not affected, since in a 2nd Rate it was usually on the middle deck anyway.

Original ordnance establishment of the 'London' and the 'Henry'

Lower deck	12 demi-cannon
	12 culverins
Middle deck	12 culverins
	12 demi-culverins
Upper deck	
forward	6 demi-culverins
waist	4 demi-culverins
aft	6 demi-culverins

The original ordnance establishment was 64 guns (see table), but within a very few years this arrangement had been greatly modified. When Van de Velde the Elder drew the two ships in the early 1660s, there were ten ports a side on the upper deck, three forward and seven aft, but none in the waist. The broadside had been further increased by the provision of four or five ports on each side of the quarterdeck, and they could then accommodate 80 guns. From about 1675, 24 guns were officially allowed for the upper deck of the *Henry*. If this establishment was followed, it must have been necessary again to mount some of the guns in the waist. The 1677 Establishment called for 24 demi-cannon, 26 culverins, 24 sakers, and 8 light sakers for a total of 82

*Presumably Peter Pett, the ship's builder.

69

guns. The *Henry* was one of the few pre-1660 warships that showed a large increase in weight of armament in later years, and that she was able to do so speaks well for her designer's skills.

The *Henry* was in action in all of the battles of Charles II's wars with the Dutch. Her most notable adventure came when she was cut off and surrounded during the Four Days' Battle of 1666. At the time she was flying the flag of Rear-Admiral of the White Sir John Harman. The *Henry* was successively grappled by two fireships, one on each side. Before they could be forced away one of the ship's quarter-galleries was set afire. Some of the crew jumped overboard in panic, and Harman had to use his sword to restore order. While the fires were being put out, the lower deck guns sank a third fireship. Shortly afterwards the flagship of Dutch Admiral Cornelis Evertsen came alongside, and Evertsen demanded the *Henry*'s surrender. Harman, whose ankle had been broken by a falling spar, shouted back 'It's not come to that yet!' His next broadside killed Evertsen. The *Henry* survived this and many later encounters, but an accidental fire destroyed her in 1682.

70
The 2nd Rate *Henry* in the early 1660s. Note the guns on the upper deck and quarterdeck abaft the quarter-gallery.

NMM No 66. Elder, 1660. The upper inscription reads, 'No 6 de dumbbar (lined through) maer nu genaemt heijnrich da duck de glohester henrij Doijael henrich' (the *Dunbar*, but now named *Henry* after Henry, Duke of Gloucester). At lower left: 'de heer . . . skun visad van de Graeff van zandwits montagug blaau vlaggs' (the Lord Ayscue – Sir George Ayscue – Vice-Admiral under Montague, Earl of Sandwich, blue flags). At lower right: 'tot tiattum' (at Chatham). The hull was probably drawn in 1660, but the masts, flags, and the inscription concerning Ayscue date from as late as 1664.

The *London*'s career came to a sudden and unexpected end on 8 March 1665. War had been declared on the Dutch, and the *London* had been selected as the flagship of Sir John Lawson, Vice-Admiral of the Red Squadron. The ship was sailing up the Thames between the Nore and the Hope, where she was to meet Sir John. Some of her 80 brass guns were probably being made ready to fire the noisy salutes which would accompany the admiral's embarkation. At some point an unknown sailor made a mistake in the magazine, and a powerful explosion blew out the ship's bottom.

She sank instantly, and over 300 people were killed. Twenty-five badly shaken survivors–including a woman–were rescued from the poop, which remained above water.

71
Sir John Harman.

NMM: Greenwich Hospital Collection. Painting by Sir Peter Lely.

72, 73
Two views of the ill-fated *London*, shown with Commonwealth decoration in 1660. The Union at the fore is the flag of Sir John Lawson, Vice-Admiral of the fleet which returned Charles II to England.

72. Atlas van Stolk, Rotterdam. Elder, 1660. Masts and flags probably added later. The arms of London are above the rudderhead.

73. NMM No 852. Elder, 1660. Inscribed 'London vis admerael lauson' (*London*, Vice-Admiral Lawson).

The 'Royal James'

The last of the pre-Restoration 'great ships' was launched at Woolwich in 1658. She was another of the fine products of Christopher Pett. The ship was named *Richard*, after Oliver Cromwell's son and successor, but Charles II changed it to *Royal James* in 1660.

The *Royal James* was only 15 tons larger than the *London*, and was classed as a 2nd Rate until 1660. At that point she was called a 1st Rate. She had three full tiers of guns and, unlike the *London* and *Henry*, she was provided with a forecastle. Although the original plans had called for only 70 guns, she was armed with at least 82 during the Second Anglo-Dutch War. One of the few Van de Velde portraits of the ship shows her pierced for 88 guns, including two a side on the forecas-

tle. The *Royal James* had the least elaborate decoration of any of the English 1st Rates: gunport wreaths were limited to the waist and quarterdeck, and the quarterdeck ports were probably not present in her original configuration.

The *Royal James* had a short history. She took a prominent part in the major battles of 1665–66, but in 1667 the disastrous neglect that led to the Dutch capture of the *Royal Charles* also resulted in the burning of the *Royal James*.

A treasured model of this ship was displayed by Samuel Pepys in his house in Seething Lane–he had borrowed it from his friend and patron, the Earl of Sandwich. Unfortunately, this model is believed to be no longer in existence.

74
The *Royal James* (ex-*Richard*) as she appeared in the 1660s. Shown pierced for 88 guns, but the *Royal James* is not known to have carried more than 82.

Boymans No 351. Elder, date uncertain. Possibly drawn from a draught or model in the 1670s.

4. The Early Restoration Period
1660-1667

The fine-looking fleet that Charles II inherited in 1660 was found to be in somewhat less than perfect condition. The warlike Protectorate had commissioned large squadrons almost every year, and many of the ships needed repairs. Of greater importance, the Navy had begun to experience financial difficulty in the years immediately preceding the Restoration. By the time Charles took over, the debt had reached serious proportions. In November of 1660 it was officially reckoned at £1,300,819 8s 0d, an enormous amount in those days. Everything had to be purchased on credit, and the merchant suppliers of timber and stores were able to charge inflated prices to offset the inevitable delays in payment.

The Navy was forced into a period of retrenchment. Most of the money that was made available was consumed by the debt and by the pressing repair requirements. Another large portion was used to maintain active fleets in the Mediterranean, English Channel, and North Sea. Little was left over for shipbuilding, and because of shortages of all commodities—especially labour—the few projects that were undertaken took a long time to complete. This applied to maintenance as well as new construction. Pepys was aboard when the *Royal Prince* was floated out of the drydock at Chatham on 11 July 1663, and he reported in the Diary that she 'hath lain in the Dock repairing these three years'.

The 'Royal Katherine' and the 'Royal Oak'

At the Restoration a 4th Rate, the 54-gun *Princess*, was under construction on the slipway at the Forest of Dean. Except for this vessel, the only new ships larger than yachts to be completed before 1666 were the 2nd Rates *Royal Katherine* and *Royal Oak*. They were laid down in 1661 but not completed until 1664. The *Royal Katherine* was built at Woolwich by Christopher Pett and the *Royal Oak* at Portsmouth by Sir John Tippetts.

The lines of the *Royal Katherine* were designed by the recently established Royal Society to test a new theory

75

75, 76
Two views of the 54-gun *Princess* of 1660. She had an eventful cruise to Gothenburg in the spring of 1667. On the way there she had to fight her way through a Dutch squadron of 17 men-of-war, many of them larger than herself. On the return trip she duelled for four hours with two 40-gun Danish ships. The captain, lieutenant, and master were killed in succession, but with the gunner in command the *Princess* drove off her opponents. The last words of the captain, Henry Dawes, were 'For God's sake do not yield the ship to those fellows!'

75. NMM No 441. Younger, 1673. Inscribed 'd prinsis 1673'.

76. Collection of Katherine Baer, Atlanta, Ga. ?Younger, c1675.

77, 78
The *Royal Katherine*, minus figurehead, in 1673, with John Sheffield, 3rd Earl of Mulgrave, the ship's captain at the time of the Van de Velde drawing.

77. Author's collection. Younger, 1673. Inscribed 'roijal katrijn 1673'.

78. NMM. Engraving after Sir Godfrey Kneller.

of water resistance, but the experiment was unsuccessful. The ship was very unstable and had to be sent back to the dockyard for girdling before she could be sent to sea. This failure was unfortunate since it discouraged the Society from making further suggestions, some of which might have been helpful. The *Royal Oak*, designed by Tippetts' tried methods, was apparently satisfactory from the start.

Not much is recorded about the appearance of the *Royal Oak*. She was lost after only three years–burned by the Dutch–and no reliable portraits have been identified. However, she must have been generally similar to her sister, a ship which is now known in some detail. In size and configuration they formed an almost homogeneous class with the *London* and *Henry*. There was no forecastle and the upper tier had no ports in the waist, though some ordnance may have been sited there pointing over the low gunwale. In such cases canvas 'fights' were usually rigged above the rail for the safety of the gun crews.

royal katrijn 1673

stood this famous man-of-war in good stead throughout her long history. She survived nine major battles, often with harrowing escapes: at the Four Days' Battle of 1666 she ran aground and barely escaped destruction; and in 1667 she had to be sunk in shallow water to avoid being lost in the Dutch raid on the Medway. At the Battle of Solebay in 1672 she was actually captured in an assault by a Dutch boarding party. Her captain, Sir John Chicheley, and all of her other officers were taken off and sent to the Netherlands as prisoners of war. At the last moment the *Katherine* was saved when her lowly 'people' rose against the prize crew and brought the ship home safely. The *Royal Katherine* was finally broken up and rebuilt as a new 90-gun ship of the same name, launched in 1702.

The 'Loyal London'

The second of the three wars between England and the Netherlands broke out in 1665. Tensions had been building for some time, and hostilities had been occurring on the seas and in colonial areas since 1662. Many grievances were involved, but the real cause of the war was commercial rivalry. George Monck, Duke of Albemarle, made the English motive quite clear with the blunt statement that 'What we want is more of the trade the Dutch now have'.

78

When the ships were first planned, it was decreed that 'His Majesty intends them very plain, without any other carving or gilding than the arms on the stern'. This was obeyed to a large extent, at least with the *Royal Katherine*. She had undecorated sides and unwreathed upper deck ports, though exceptions to the order were apparently allowed with the head and quarter-gallery. A 1673 Van de Velde drawing does show circular wreaths for the quarterdeck ports, but these ports may not have been present when the ship was completed. The overall impression was that of a purposeful vessel which must have stood out sharply from her gorgeously ornamented contemporaries. In the Van de Velde drawing this effect is intensified by a missing figurehead, testimony to the hard fighting that the ship had experienced. It would be interesting to know what the figurehead had looked like. After her launching on 26 October 1664, Pepys had reported that 'the King did very much like the ship, saying, she had the best bow that he ever saw'.

The *Royal Katherine* and *Royal Oak* were originally armed with 70–76 guns, including an at least partial tier of cannon-of-seven on the lower deck. The *Katherine*'s armament was later changed on more than one occasion. In the 1670s and 1680s she was usually allowed 26 demi-cannon, 26 culverins, 24 sakers, and 6–10 light sakers, for a total of 82–86 guns. In William III's reign the number of light pieces was again increased, bringing the establishment to over 90 guns. This was a tremendous firepower for a vessel of her size.

At the *Royal Katherine*'s launching a rainbow had appeared just as she took to the water, an omen which

79
Admiral Sir Jeremy Smith, who commanded the hard-pressed Blue Squadron at the St James Day Fight. His flagship, the *Loyal London*, suffered the heaviest casualties in the fleet.

NMM: Greenwich Hospital Collection. Painting by Sir Peter Lely.

The war started on a sour note with the accidental destruction of the 2nd Rate *London* in March of 1665. Despite his grief, Charles II was understandably delighted when the City of London offered–in a moment of generosity later regretted–to donate a new 'great ship' to replace the *London*. The King demonstrated his appreciation by directing that the new ship's

name 'shall be the *Loyal London*'. After bids had been submitted by several shipwrights, the building contract was granted to Captain John Taylor, who had built the original *London*. The authorities apparently had difficulty in getting Taylor to follow the specifications. Charles II was worried that Taylor would 'alter his moulds . . of his New London, that he makes it differ, in hopes of mending the Old London, built by him'.

The *Loyal London* was launched at Deptford 'after three days trials in vain' on 10 June 1666. The ship was originally intended to receive 80 guns; unfortunately all of her 22 cannon-of-seven burst during their proof tests, and she had to join the fleet without them. Replacements were hurriedly supplied from land fortifications, but only ten cannon-of-seven could be found. The shortage was apparently made up by an increased number of light pieces, raising her establishment to a total of 92 guns.

When the *Loyal London* was finally ready for battle, all the misgivings about Taylor's design disappeared. Pepys was told that she was 'the best ship in the world,

large and small'. Another observer reported that the *Loyal London* 'sails better beyond compare than most of the frigates; draws little water for her bulk; and carries her guns eighteen inches higher than the *Royal Charles*; the whole fleet consider her as good a man-of-war as any in the world'.

No portraits of the *Loyal London* are known. The only possible source for her appearance is a model which was made for Sir Jeremy Smith about 1672. The ship served as his flagship at the St James Day Fight of 1666. The model was identified as the *Loyal London* mainly because of Sir Jeremy's association with the ship; there is no way to guarantee its accuracy.

War Construction: The 'Victory'

The Royal Navy's wartime construction efforts were much less ambitious than the programme carried out in the Netherlands. Between 1665 and 1667 the Dutch strengthened their fleet by some forty vessels of 50 guns

80, 81
Dockyard model possibly of the
Loyal London. This model, long
displayed at Trinity House, was
destroyed by a bomb in 1941. A
small panel beneath the upper
row of stern windows contained
the arms of Sir Jeremy Smith and
those of his second wife. It is
presumably the model that
Smith is known to have asked
Jonas Shish, master-shipwright
at Deptford, to make for him in
1672. It is identified as the *Loyal
London* on the basis of Sir
Jeremy's association with the
ship. It could well be the *Loyal
London*. The old photographs
reproduced here show a circular
escutcheon beneath the taffrail
containing a low relief of what
may be the dagger of the arms of
London. On the other hand the
ship looks suspiciously similar to
the *Charles*, a 1st Rate
completed by Shish in 1668.
This problem is complicated by
the possibility that the *Charles*
and *Loyal London*, both Deptford
products, may have been
near-sisters. The model can be
forced to fit the dimensions of
either, but only by assuming an
unusual scale; on the 'even' 1:36
scale it fits no Restoration
warship.

Photos: *Country Life* magazine. Model
formerly displayed at Trinity House, now
replaced by a modern reproduction.

81

or more. During the war the English dockyards produced–besides the *Loyal London*–only five 3rd Rates,
three 4th Rates, and two 5th Rates.

Most of the new ships were authorized just before the
war began. The Navy Board's economies in the early
years of the reign had been so successful that by the end
of 1663 Pepys could write that the Navy 'is quite out of
debt; . . . to hear how our creditt goes as good as any
merchant's upon the 'change is a joyfull thing to consider, which God continue!' Unfortunately it did not
continue for long, but the Navy's finances were still
sound enough in October 1664 for the Lord High

82

83

82, 83

The *Victory* in 1672.
Vice-Admiral Sir Christopher
Myngs (83) was killed in the
Victory on the final day of the
Four Days' Battle. Pepys was
touched when some of the
Victory's crewmen requested a
fireship with which to avenge
their beloved chief.

82. NMM No 394. Younger, 1672.
Inscribed 'd fictori 1672'.

83. NMM: Greenwich Hospital
Collection. Painting by Sir Peter Lely.

Admiral to order the construction of two 2nd Rates, four 3rd Rates and two 4th Rates.

As it turned out the plans proved to be over-optimistic. The two 2nd Rates never material-ized—apparently neither was laid down. They were to have been built at Portsmouth and Woolwich, and were intended to have been about the same size as the *Royal Katherine* and *Royal Oak*. Instead, the Navy had to be content with rebuilding the ancient *Victory* (64 guns), one of the early Stuart 2nd Rates.

The *Victory* received a very extensive repair. By the time she emerged from the dock at Chatham in 1666 she had been enlarged beyond the size of the two cancelled 2nd Rates. She was then allotted 80 guns. It has been customary to list the 1666 version of the *Victory* as a new ship. This seems reasonable in view of the drastically altered dimensions, but in actuality she must have retained a large proportion of the old tim-bers. The ship survived only until 1691, when she had to be broken up. By seventeenth century standards that would have been premature for a ship 'built new' 25 years earlier. The *Victory*'s enlargement may have been obtained simply by extending the keel, fitting a new bow and stern, and furring the original frames. A somewhat similar process is known to have been pro-posed in the 1670s for improving the *Old James* of 1633. In any event, the *Victory*'s alterations made her equal in importance to the *Henry*, *Royal Katherine* and *Royal Oak*. She had been in action half a dozen times in the 1650s, and after her repair she acquitted herself well in both the battles of 1666 and all four engage-ments of the Third Anglo-Dutch War.

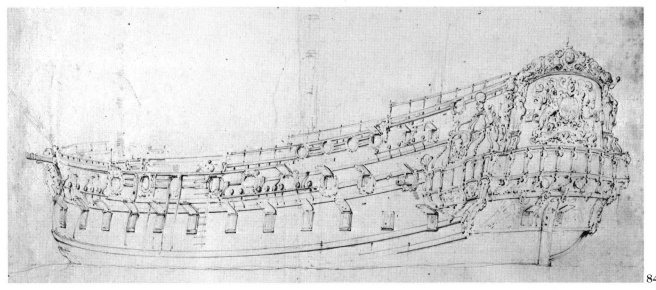

84

85

86

84, 85, 86
Two views of the *Resolution* (84, 86) built by Sir Anthony Deane. The very similar vessel (85) may be Deane's *Rupert*.

84. NMM No 540. Younger, 1676. Contains three inscriptions: in pencil 'reesolue' and 'resoluse', and in ink '1676'.

85. V&A No 4654. Younger, c1675. Not the *Resolution*, but so similar that the ship was very likely designed by the same shipwright.

86. NMM No 1195. Younger, 1676. Inscribed 'reesolusi 1676'.

War Construction: Third and Fourth Rates

Although the 2nd Rates of the 1664 programme were not built, all the 3rd and 4th Rates were laid down in 1665 and launched in 1666. The Admiralty decided from the start to build half the ships by contract, presumably because of the expected wartime demands on the royal dockyards. Of the government-built 3rd Rates, the *Cambridge* was produced by Jonas Shish at Deptford and the *Rupert* by Sir Anthony Deane at Harwich. The 4th Rate *Greenwich* was built at Woolwich by Christopher Pett. The original plans called for one 3rd Rate and one 4th Rate to be built on contract by Francis Bayley at Bristol, while the remaining 3rd Rate was to be ordered on the Thames. In the end Bayley built only the 4th Rate *St Patrick*, and Thames shipwrights obtained contracts for both 3rd Rates. The *Warspite* was built by Sir Henry Johnson at Blackwall, and the *Defiance* by Captain William Castle at Deptford.

Once the war was under way one 3rd Rate and one 4th Rate were added to the building programme, presumably in place of the cancelled 2nd Rates. The 3rd Rate was the *Monmouth*, built by Sir Phineas Pett* at Chatham, and the 4th Rate was Daniel Furzer's *St*

David, built at Conpill. Both ships were completed in early 1667.

In the 1660s the design process for warships began with the Admiralty issuing specifications to the master-shipwrights, citing dimensions, numbers of gunports, and so forth. Each shipwright prepared his design independently of the others, and submitted his draughts to the Lord High Admiral (James, Duke of York). The latter normally referred the plans to the experts of Trinity House for comment. The rivalries among the shipwrights–and their friends–often became particularly intense at these times.

Some of the designs for the new 3rd and 4th Rates reached the Admiralty in March of 1665. Samuel Pepys, as the Navy Board's Clerk of the Acts, was ordered to take the draughts to Trinity House and eventually report their findings to the Duke. Pepys took advantage of his office to pull of a piece of skul-duggery that was typical of the age. He was a supporter of Sir Anthony Deane, the master-shipwright at Harwich–in fact Deane had obtained his position through his friend's recommendation. Instead of going to Trinity House, Pepys rushed home and invited Captain Castle to come and examine the plans, though without

*The son of the Peter Pett who had built the *Constant Warwick*. Yet another Phineas Pett was a grandson of 'old' Phineas who had built the *Prince Royal*.

87
Draught of a 3rd Rate by Sir Anthony Deane, probably dating from the mid-1660s. No ship was built with this gunport arrangement, but the dimensions and the quarter-galleries were similar to those of the *Resolution* of 1667. The *Resolution*'s stern was also similar, except for the substitution of the royal arms for the picture shown in the draught. Its dimensions correspond to a ship with a keel of 120ft, gundeck 148ft, and external beam of about 37ft. The dimensions of the *Resolution* were: keel 120ft 6in, gundeck 148ft 2in, and beam 37ft 2in.

Pepysian Library, Magdalene College, Cambridge.

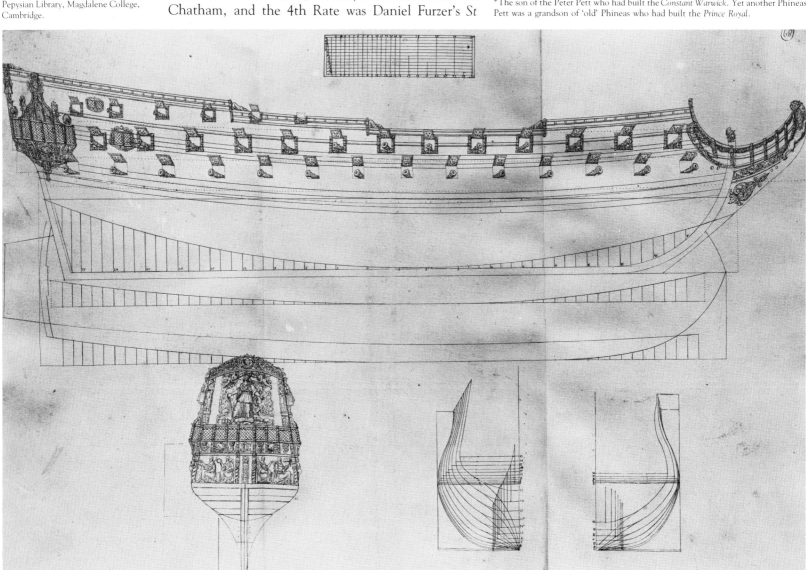

telling him whose they were. Castle first examined a draught by Daniel Furzer, presumably the plans for the *St David*. The Captain thought it an outstanding design. When shown Deane's draught, however, he sarcastically asked 'whether he that laid it down had ever built a ship or no', and said he thought it must be a fake. When Castle had gone, the horrified Pepys rushed off a confidential letter to his friend, explaining what had happened. He also enclosed the draughts of

Furzer and Jonas Shish for Deane to use as guides for modifying his plan. Whether or not Deane changed his draught is unknown, but a year later Pepys 'heard the Duke commend Deane's ship "The Rupert" before "The Defiance", built lately by Castle . . which pleased me mightily'. The *Defiance* was an unlucky ship. She survived the battles of 1666 only to be lost in an accidental fire in December 1668.

88

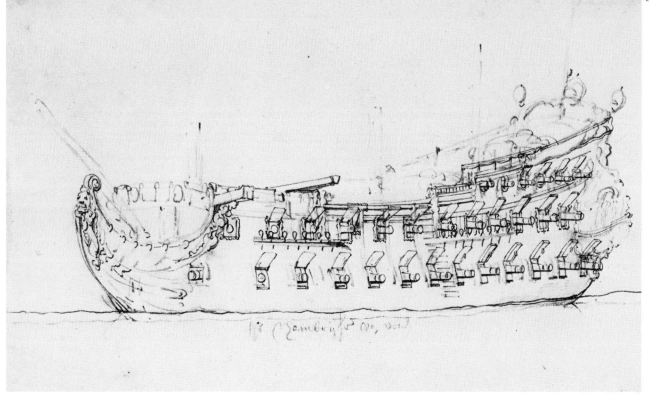

89

88, 89

The 3rd Rate *Cambridge* (88). The uncompleted drawing (89) remains unidentified, but it could be another portrait of the *Cambridge*. Whatever the ship, it shows a fine example of the stern decoration of the mid-1660s. It is probably a 3rd Rate, despite the presence of only three quarterdeck ports. The awning shows that the quarterdeck is long enough for at least three more ports between the hances. The quarter-gallery, with a central arch, seems similar to that of the *Cambridge*.

88. *Boymans No 391. Elder, c1675, but probably worked up later by a different artist. Inscribed 'the Chambrijse van voren' (the* Cambridge *from forward).*

89. *NMM No 503. Younger, c1675.*

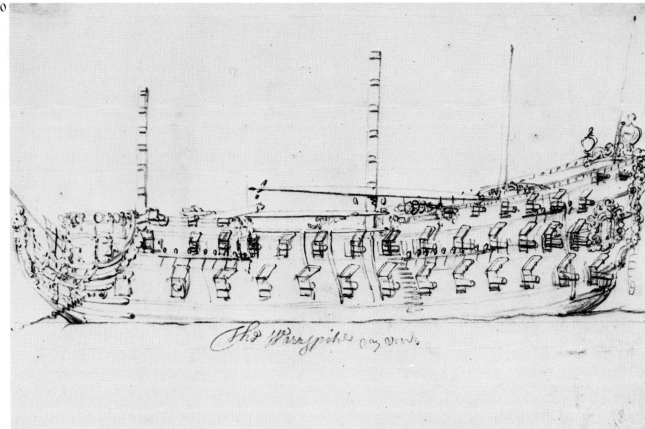

90

The Blackwall-built *Warspite*.
This Van de Velde drawing may
have been 'touched up' by a later
artist. The gunport arrangement
seems muddled and may be
inaccurate.

Boymans No 392. Elder, c1675, but
probably worked up later by a different
artist. Inscribed in an unknown hand 'The
Warrspite' and by the Elder 'van voren'
(from forward). In Van de Velde's original
sketch there may have been only 12 ports
in the upper tier.

The dimensions planned for the new 3rd Rates were copied directly from those of the successful *Mary* of 1650: keel 116ft and beam 34ft 6in. Actually all of the shipwrights exceeded the specifications by substantial amounts. The smallest of the government-built 3rd Rates, the *Rupert*, was 3ft longer than required and nearly 2ft wider. Apparently only the contractors, Johnson and Castle, intended to build close to the specifications. Their vessels as completed were in fact about the same length as the *Mary*. However, while the ships were under construction Charles II saw the plans and personally directed that enough beam be worked in to allow the lower tier to be carried 4ft 6in from the water. The *Defiance* was accordingly widened to 37ft 3in and the *Warspite* to 38ft. In later years Pepys claimed that Deane had suggested this move to the King. If so, it may have been his way of getting back at Castle. The relative failure of the *Defiance* may have been caused by the increase in beam being insufficient to offset the elevation of the batteries.

The *Warspite*, like the 2nd Rates of 1664, was built without gunport wreaths. In this case the omission was not because of an order from the King, but because the ship's builder, Sir Henry Johnson, had a contract dispute with the Admiralty and simply refused to provide them. A Van de Velde drawing also shows the *Warspite* without quarter-galleries, but it is not known whether this was Johnson's doing as well.

The 3rd Rates were originally assigned 64 guns: 22 demi-cannon, 28 culverins and 14 demi-culverins. However, the ships differed so greatly in dimensions and tonnage that in the mid-1670s they were split into two classes. The *Cambridge* and *Warspite* became

70-gun ships with demi-cannon on the lower deck, 12pdrs on the upper, and light sakers and 3pdrs above. The slightly smaller *Rupert* and *Monmouth* were allowed 66 guns with the lower deck armament reduced to 24pdrs. The armament of the three 4th Rates (and also the *Princess* of 1660) was similar to that of the larger Commonwealth 4th Rates. The units that survived the Anglo-Dutch Wars were eventually assigned 54 guns, with 24pdrs on the lower deck, sakers on the upper deck, and light sakers on the quarterdeck.

With the exception of the *St Patrick*, which was captured in 1667, and the *Defiance*, all the 3rd and 4th Rates of the 1664 programme had long and active careers. The *St David* was finally made a hulk in 1691, and the *Cambridge* was wrecked in 1694. The remaining vessels were rebuilt as virtually new ships between 1698 and 1702.

The reason that the Royal Navy was unable to match the output of the Dutch dockyards in the 1660s was that there was simply not enough money. The merchants–for whom the war was being fought–soon tired of the dislocation of their overseas trade. With the nation wracked by plague and economic depression, the tax collectors became increasingly unable to provide the government with the funds it needed. By the summer of 1666 the Navy was again deeply in debt. In early July Charles II unveiled a grandiose shipbuilding plan, but Pepys' Diary entry for 4 July makes it clear that this was little more than propaganda:

'To St James's, and there did our usual business with the Duke, all of us, among other things, discoursing about the places where to build ten great ships; the King and Council have resolved on none to be under

82

third-rates; but it is impossible to do it, unless we have more money towards the doing it than yet we have in any view. But, however, the shew must be made to the world'.

As Pepys feared, little progress was made. One 3rd Rate possibly originating in this programme, Sir Anthony Deane's *Resolution*, was launched in December 1667, but by then the war was over. The *Resolution*, well-known because of an often reproduced Van de Velde painting, was a slightly enlarged edition of Deane's earlier *Rupert* and eventually carried 70 guns. Of the remaider of the 'ten great ships' programme most of the vessels were never built, though a few units completed between 1668 and 1670 may have been long-delayed parts of it.

91

91
The 4th Rate *St David*, built in 1667 but here showing decoration probably dating from the mid-1670s.

Boymans No 332. ?Elder, c1676.
Inscribed 'de sen david'.

92
The 4th Rate *Greenwich*.

From a private collection. Younger, 1679.
Inscribed 'd grinwits 1679'.

92

93

The decisive moment at the Battle of Lowestoft: the Dutch flagship *Eendracht* is torn apart by a terrible explosion. She is visible at centre engulfed by a sheet of flame, with masts crashing down. At left centre are the flagships of the English Red Squadron, with Vice-Admiral Sir John Lawson leading in the *Royal Oak*. Astern of Lawson is Rear-Admiral Sir William Berkeley's *Swiftsure*, followed by the Duke of York's *Royal Charles*. In the left foreground is the large Dutch East Indiaman *Oranje*, which was captured and burned by the English later in the battle. This drawing was probably made as a design for a tapestry sometime after the artist emigrated to England in 1673.

NMM No 445. Elder, c1674.

The Second Anglo-Dutch War

The Second Anglo-Dutch War was a closely contested affair. The advantage repeatedly swung back and forth, as each side gained smashing victories and suffered humiliating defeats in some of the greatest sea fights of all time.

Both nations sent out fleets of over a hundred ships of all sizes in the spring of 1665. The English were commanded by the Duke of York, while the Dutch were under Jacob van Wassenaer, Earl of Obdam. The opponents were closely matched in numbers; the Dutch actually had a slight superiority in the total number of guns, but this was more than offset by the much heavier ordnance mounted in the English ships.

The first clash occurred about 40 miles south-east of Lowestoft on 3 June. It was a long and hard-fought battle, but the result was an overwhelming victory for the English. Obdam's flagship, the 76-gun *Eendracht*, blew up under the guns of the Duke of York's *Royal Charles*, and the leaderless Dutch fleet disintegrated. In their haste to escape several Dutch ships collided with one another. Hopelessly entangled, they fell easy prey to the English fireships. In all the Dutch lost 19 men-of-war and 5000 men against an English loss of a single 4th Rate and about 700 men. The Dutch would have suffered even more severely, but the English pursuit was called off prematurely by an unauthorized order from one of the Duke's retainers.

Plate XV

The *Resolution*, a 3rd Rate built by Sir Anthony Deane in 1667. The Union at the main is probably that of Sir Thomas Allin, who took the *Resolution* to the Mediterranean in 1668.

NMM. Painting by the Younger, 1676.

Plate XVI

The Four Days' Battle, a famous picture by Abraham Storck. The artist was familiar with the Dutch ships, but it was not an eye-witness view and he had no way of knowing the exact appearance of the English vessels. De Ruyter's *Zeven Provincien* is portrayed with scrupulous accuracy, but the views of the *Royal Prince* (right) and *Royal Charles* (right centre) are not reliable. In the left background Sir William Berkeley's *Swiftsure* is being overwhelmed and captured by the *Reigersbergen*. The picture, like many others of this engagement, compresses events both spatially and temporally.

NMM. Painting by Abraham Storck.

Plate XVII

A portrait of the *Royal Katherine*, showing both broadside and stern views, by H Vale. The painting, dating from 1695 or after, seems only tenuously related to the 1673 Van de Velde drawing, and its accuracy is therefore suspect. The date is provided by the presence of a bobstay, which was only introduced into English ships in the mid-1690s. The Earl of Mulgrave commanded the ship in the Third, not the Second, Anglo-Dutch War.

NMM. Painting by H Vale, c1695.

Plate XVIII

The Medway raid, viewed from a point above the Thames with Sheerness in the foreground. This picture compresses the time scale, showing events as if they had occurred simultaneously. The position of the chain is marked by the sunken ships at the centre. In the middle distance the captured *Royal Charles* can be seen with English colours debased. In the right background are the burning *Loyal London*, *Royal James*, and *Royal Oak*, with Dutch warships in action against shore batteries and the guns of Upnor Castle. Attributed to Willem Schellincks; the ships are portrayed more accurately than one would expect from a landscape painter, and Schellincks may have obtained the assistance of a marine artist.

Rijksmuseum, Amsterdam. Painting attributed to Willem Schellincks.

XVI

The Royall Katherine Command.d by John Earl of Mulgrave in the Second Dutch Warr.

XVII

XVIII

Lowestoft was one of the greatest victories in the history of the Royal Navy, and against a different opponent it might have decided the war. But the Dutch only tried harder. Captains who had not done their duty were ruthlessly purged—some were actually shot—and the dockyards worked at full capacity to reinforce the fleet. A supremely talented commander, Michiel Adriaanszoon De Ruyter, was appointed to lead it. The fleets did not meet again in 1665, but in the next year there occurred one of the greatest naval engagements ever fought. This was the Four Days' Battle, lasting from 1–4 June.

Charles II had decided against risking his brother's life again, and the English were under the combined control of Prince Rupert and George Monck, Duke of Albemarle. The Dutch had many new ships, and the fleets would have been evenly matched but for an error by the English command. France, in response to treaty obligations, had declared war on England during the winter. Although Louis XIV actually had no intention of active participation, the English received faulty intelligence that a French squadron was attempting to join the Dutch. Rupert was detached with nearly a third of the fleet to deal with this threat. The mistake was soon discovered, but too late.

On 1 June the rest of the English fleet found De Ruyter's entire array lying at anchor about thirty miles north of Ostend. Despite being outnumbered three to two Monck took the offensive. He maintained the initiative throughout the whole of the first day and part of the next, but the English losses were severe. Vice-Admiral Sir William Berkeley's *Swiftsure* was captured

94
George Monck, Duke of Albemarle.

NMM: Greenwich Hospital Collection. Painting by Sir Peter Lely.

on the first day, and Berkeley was killed. Many vessels, including Rear-Admiral Sir John Harman's powerful *Henry*, were badly mauled and had to limp for home. By the third day the English had so few ships available that a retreat was ordered. The withdrawal was carried out in good order, but late in the day, with Rupert's squadron in sight, a disaster occurred. Monck's rear-

95
This fine grisaille by Van de Velde the Elder shows the Dutch commanders gathering for a council of war shortly before the Four Days' Battle. De Ruyter's flagship, the 80-gun *Zeven Provincien*, is at right, while the vessel on the left is probably the *Delft*, flagship of Rear-Admiral Jan van Nes. At centre and right centre are stern views of the *Stad Utrecht* and the new *Eendracht*, the latter wearing the flag of Lieutenant-Admiral Aert van Nes.

Rijksmuseum, Amsterdam No 2467A2. Grisaille by the Elder, c1666.

guard, including most of the larger vessels, blundered on to a hidden shoal called the Galloper Sand. The deep-draught three-deckers hit the bottom and stuck fast. The *Royal Charles* and *Royal Katherine* got off just in time, but Admiral Sir George Ayscue's *Royal Prince*–the famous giant of 1610–was captured and burned.   On the fourth day Rupert and Monck, with fresh ships available, made one last effort. After a bloody eight-hour *mêlée* in which neither side gained any real advantage, the exhausted fleets parted and made for their own ports. In the confusion a damaged English 3rd Rate, the *Essex*, was left behind and captured.

The Dutch were the undoubted victors. In addition to the *Royal Prince*, *Swiftsure*, and *Essex*, the English lost five 4th Rates–all but one were prizes from the previous year–and two hired merchantmen of 4th Rate size. There were angry recriminations in London, but tactically the fleet had performed very well. The Dutch themselves lost four ships and had many others damaged. Their failure to destroy a smaller English fleet left them with little reason for confidence.

Both fleets were again at sea by mid-July. Neither side had a numerical advantage in either ships or guns, but as usual the English had the heavier metal. For the only time in the war the *Royal Sovereign* was in the line, along with the brand new *Loyal London*.

Battle was joined about 35 miles south-east of Orfordness on 25 July, St James Day. It was a grand set-piece affair, with van against van, centre against centre and rear against rear. After a lengthy struggle the Dutch were driven from the field but the English were themselves too battered to take advantage. With a masterful retreat De Ruyter brought his centre and van squadrons home safely. On the following day the isolated Dutch rear squadron was almost trapped by the whole English fleet, but the opportunity was missed.

Casualties were heavy, but losses in ships were not. The English lost the 58-gun *Resolution* (built 1654) to a fireship attack, and De Ruyter had to abandon two damaged vessels during his retreat. Both were captured and burned by the English. The St James Day Fight was a solid English victory. It was followed up two weeks later when Rear-Admiral Sir Robert Holmes led a light squadron into the undefended Vlie and burned 150 Dutch merchantmen.

In all three of the major open-sea battles of the war the Royal Navy had proved to be superior in both tactics and *matériel*. The remarkable order and discipline of the English fleet was noted by many observers, especially in the Four Days' Battle. Though the line was repeatedly broken, it always re-formed when the smoke cleared.

Both sides bolstered their fleets with merchantmen which were not really suitable as warships. But there was a significant difference. The English merchantmen – manned by naval personnel – were no bigger than 4th Rates, and little was expected of them in the first place.

96
The English bear down on the Dutch to begin the Four Days' Battle. At left is Vice-Admiral of the White Sir William Berkeley's *Swiftsure,* while the 1st Rate at centre is Sir George Ayscue's *Royal Prince.* Hidden off the port side of the *Royal Prince* is Vice-Admiral of the Red Sir Joseph Jordan's *Royal Oak,* with Monck's *Royal Charles* just beyond. The Dutch ship in the left foreground is the 48-gun *Zon.* At right is the Dutch squadron of Lieutenant-Admiral Cornelis Tromp, commanding from the *Hollandia.*

Rijksmuseum, Amsterdam No 2464. Grisaille by the Elder, c1666.

In 1665 the Dutch employed a number of very large Indiamen which made up a substantial proportion of the total firepower. The ships were manned by the Dutch East India Company, and the misbehaviour of some officers and crews was disastrous at Lowestoft.

The most important factor was that the Dutch ships—nearly all of them two-deckers—were more lightly built and less powerfully armed than those of their opponents. There were very few guns in the Dutch fleet larger than 24pdrs. They had few ships which could stand up to the larger English 2nd Rates, not to mention the 1st Rates. The three-deckers formed strong points in the English line like the towers in a medieval fortification. As long as they retained their mobility, they were almost impregnable.

97
Vice-Admiral of the White Sir William Berkeley, who was killed aboard the *Swiftsure* at the Four Days' Battle. At the time of his death this promising Cavalier officer was only 27 years old.

NMM: Greenwich Hospital Collection. Painting by Sir Peter Lely.

98
Sir George Ayscue, Admiral of the White, who surrendered the hopelessly trapped *Royal Prince* at the Four Days' Battle. Ayscue wanted to blow up the ship, but the crew understandably would not allow it.

NMM. Painting by Sir Peter Lely.

99
The 3rd Rate *Essex* of 1653 was captured by the Dutch at the end of the Four Days' Battle. She had been damaged in a collision and was left behind when the rest of the fleet returned to port.

NMM No 63. Elder, c1660. Inscribed 'exsecx van vooren' (*Essex* from forward)

97

98

99

Unfortunately for England, the most glorious victories counted for little in this conflict. The Second Anglo-Dutch War was decided not at sea, but in the banking halls of London and The Hague. The States-General could pay its bills and Charles II could not; it was as simple as that. By marshalling all the financial power of their country the Dutch were able to spend at least twice as much money on the war as the English did. In the absence of adequate sources of revenue the Royal Navy was in arrears from the outset. The victuallers became unwilling supply stores to the Navy without hard cash. This meant that though the Dutch might be driven from the seas by roundshot and grape, the English were driven from it just as surely by want of beef, biscuit, and beer. Because payrolls could not be met, acute manpower shortages developed. Again and again the fleet lay paralysed in port while Dutch convoys sailed home unmolested with the wealth of Africa and the Indies.

After the St James Day Fight the opposing fleets were in sight of each other on only two more occasions, and both times the state of the weather caused Prince Rupert to decline battle. With these decisions, correct though they may have been, Charles II's last chances for victory disappeared.

The Raid on the Medway

In the autumn of 1666 the fleet was laid up for the winter as usual. Most of the 'great ships' were moored off Chatham in the River Medway. It was desperately hoped in England that the fighting would not be renewed. In the deepening depression, the populace lost all enthusiasm for the war. Starving, unpaid seamen rioted daily in the streets. The Dutch themselves had gained nothing by the war, and peace talks were initiated in the winter. The negotiators, however, made little progress. By March it was obvious that the Admiralty would not have enough money to commission the fleet, but Charles was not willing to make peace on Dutch terms. The fateful decision was made to continue the war without using the 'great ships'. They were to be kept in ordinary behind fortifications in the Medway, while the Dutch were to be harried by squadrons of light commerce-raiders.

Such trifling with the great De Ruyter was a grave mistake. If the English ships would not come out he meant to go in and get them. On 7 June his fleet appeared in the mouth of the Thames and boldly pushed into the Medway. On the 12th, a black day for the Royal Navy, Dutch warships smashed through a heavy chain which had been stretched across the river. The English defence could only be described as disgraceful. Soldiers fled in panic, and the officials of Chatham Dockyard thought only of saving their own

100
Engraving of the St James Day Fight, giving the English order of battle. The sinuous shape of the opposing lines is consistently shown in contemporary diagrams of this engagement. Neither Van de Velde was present.

NMM.

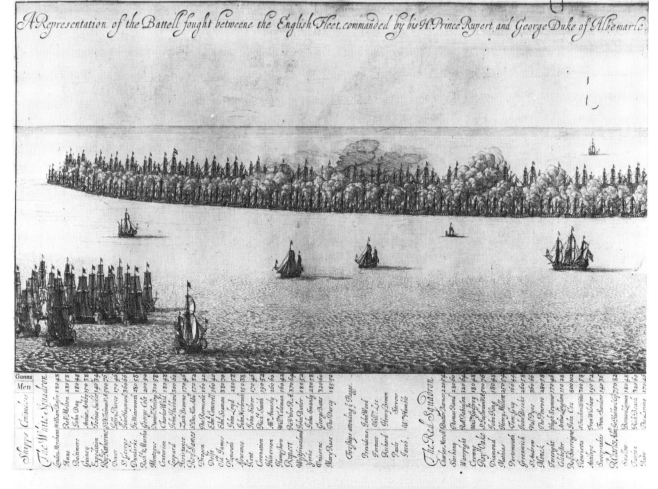

01

possessions. Through incredible negligence the magnificent *Royal Charles* was left exposed and undefended. She was yielded up without a shot. Dockyard workers scuttled as many of the other ships as they could, but this did not prevent an even greater disaster.

On the 13th, with De Ruyter present in person, the Dutch took their fireships up the river. In the culmination of a near-perfect operation, they set fire to three 'great ships' which they found lying sunk in shallow water near the river bank. These were the *Royal James*, *Loyal London*, and *Royal Oak*, all among the finest ships in the fleet. Their hulls had been left exposed to the level of the lower tier, and they burned to the water's edge.

English Losses Related to the Dutch Medway Raid

Rate	Ship	Guns	Fate
1st	Royal Charles	86	Captured
1st	Royal James	82	Burned
2nd	Loyal London	92	Burned
2nd	Royal Oak	76	Burned
2nd	Vanguard	60	Sunk to prevent capture; not recoverable
3rd	House of Sweeds	70	Blockship at Woolwich; not recoverable
3rd	Golden Phoenix	70	Blockship at Woolwich; not recoverable
3rd	Helverston	60	Blockship at Chatham; not recoverable
4th	Matthias	56	Burned
4th	Charles V	52	Burned
4th	Maria Sancta	50	Burned
4th	Unity	42	Captured
4th	Marmaduke	42	Blockship at the chain; not recoverable
5th	Leicester	24	Blockship at Blackwall; not recoverable

In addition the *Royal Katherine, Victory* and *St George* (all 2nd Rates) were sunk to prevent capture. These could not be restored to service for many months. Another blockship at Woolwich, the 4th Rate *Welcome*, was raised but was found to be useful only as a fireship.

101

Admiral Sir Thomas Allin commanded the victorious White Squadron at the St James' Day Fight. His flagship was the *Royal James*.

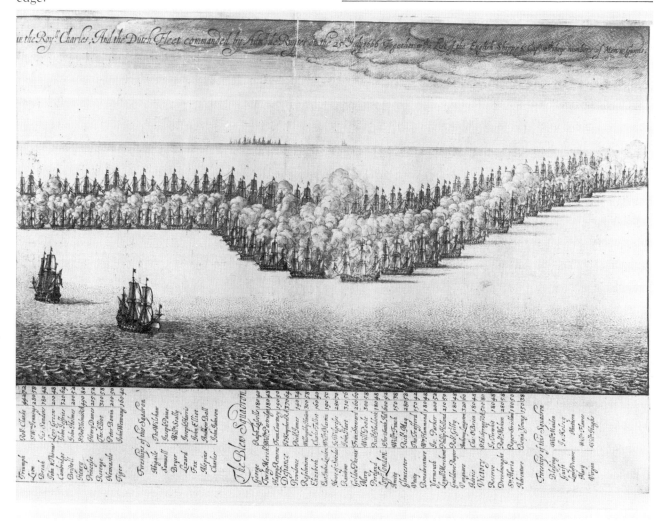

This deed accomplished, the Dutch retired to the Thames and imposed a crippling blockade. With her fleet decimated and her trade strangled, England was out of the war. The Treaty of Breda was signed on 31 July. Louis XIV was alarmed at the extent of the Dutch success, and only the perception that their ally was turning on them prevented the Dutch from imposing onerous terms.

In modern times there is a common view that the raid on the Medway was a mainly psychological blow, and that the loss of 'a few ships' was not especially significant. While the psychological shock was indeed severe, the actual loss in ships was anything but insignificant. It is often forgotten that in addition to the vessels burned or captured, a number of others had to be sacrificed to block the channels leading to Chatham and Woolwich.

It is also frequently forgotten that the Dutch dock-yards had produced so many new ships by 1667 that the English were outnumbered even before the raid. The loss of four great three-deckers–all flagships in the St James Day Fight–was in itself a catastrophe. These were the ships upon which the Royal Navy depended to maintain the balance. Even if by some miracle Charles II had managed to send his entire navy to sea after the Medway raid, it would have been overwhelmingly outnumbered and outgunned by De Ruyter's enlarged and confident fleet. For the first time within memory, England was not the leading naval power.

102

This dismasted vessel is probably the hired merchantman *Loyal George,* shown after her capture at the Four Days' Battle. The English ensign is debased beneath the Dutch colours. Note also the canvas 'fights' draped around the quarterdeck.

Photo: Courtesy Malcolm Henderson Gallery. Original from a private collection. Younger, 1666. The ship is portrayed in the same attitude in the left background of the Younger's painting of the Dutch prizes of the Four Days' Battle.

103

A large English merchantman, portrayed in the 1670s. The long interval in the upper deck ports amidships was probably made necessary by the width of the cargo hatch.

NMM No 497. Younger, c1675.

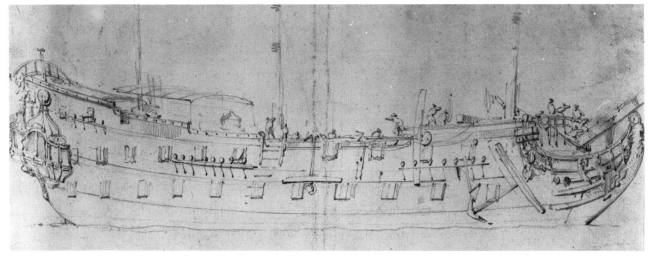

5. First Rates
1668-1675

At the end of the Second Anglo-Dutch War Charles II–bent on revenge–grimly made plans to rebuild his fleet. One fact which seemed proven by the open-sea battles of the Second Anglo-Dutch War was that, tactics and leadership aside, victories had been won and disasters averted mainly by the awesome broadsides of the biggest three-deckers. The Dutch simply could not match them. Because of the Admiralty's negligence in laying up the 'great ships' within reach of De Ruyter, only one 1st Rate–the *Royal Sovereign*–remained at the end of the war. To make matters worse, the French had initiated a vast naval expansion that could not be ignored. It was clear that a major programme of big-ship construction was necessary to restore the fleet to a level of even bare parity.

Through the seventeenth century prior to 1668, the English Navy had been able to acquire only five ships of 1st Rate size: one each in the reigns of James I and Charles I, two under the Protectorate, and in Charles II's time only the donated *Loyal London*. Then, between 1668 and 1675, the perpetually impoverished Restoration government somehow found the means to construct no fewer than eight of these expensive vessels. This was accomplished only by neglecting the lesser rates, but it was still a remarkable achievement.

There had not yet been any moves towards a standardization of the Navy's warship designs. Since the shipwrights tended to view their products primarily as works of art, the new 'great ships' showed a high degree of individuality in both design and decoration. One thing they did have in common was a very heavy armament. This usually comprised complete tiers of cannon-of-seven, culverins and demi-culverins, plus batteries of light sakers and 3pdrs spotted around the upperworks.

By continental standards they had rather fine lines which resulted in a good turn of speed. Combined with their massive armament, this feature demanded some penalty in the matter of stability, and in several the problem was severe enough to require girdling. Fortunately, this proved successful in every case.

In appearance they presented a majestic aspect which thoroughly satisfied the propaganda role demanded by national vanity. The 1st Rates were also well built, and except for one that was lost in battle they had long, if not always active, careers. They still formed the core of the battle fleet at the end of the century. Naturally they attracted the marine artists of the day, and detailed paintings and drawings of all of them exist.

The 'Charles'

The first of the new 'great ships' to appear after the war was the 96-gun *Charles*, built in the royal dockyard at Deptford by Jonas Shish. After the disaster of 1667 the *Charles* must have been a welcome sight. The launch-

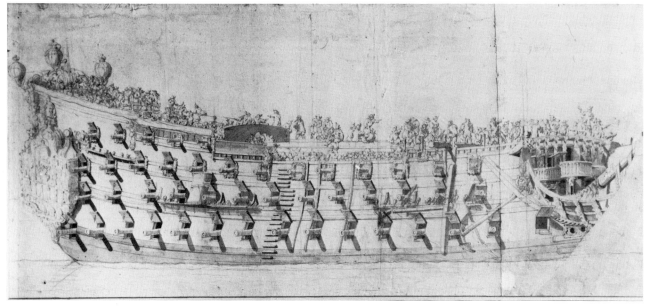

104
The 96-gun *Charles*. Note the unique gallery projecting from the beakhead bulkhead. A number of portraits of the *Charles* are known, but all show slightly different gunport arrangements. This is the only highly finished drawing of her and is probably the most accurate.

NMM No 534. Elder, c1675. Inscribed 'de hiarles'.

ing ceremony in March of 1668 occasioned much excitement, with the royal family and many other dignitaries in attendance. Pepys recorded the event in his Diary, and, with the nightmare of the Medway still in mind, added 'God send her better luck than the former'.

Her official name was supposed to be the *Charles the Second*, but this pun was usually disregarded in favour of the shorter version. In addition, she was occasionally called *Royal Charles* until 1673 when another ship was given that title. This must have been confusing, but of course no one cared to mention it while the royal namesake was alive. Finally, in 1687, the *Charles* was renamed *St George* when the famous old 2nd Rate of that name was made a hulk.

From the design point of view, the *Charles* seems to have been a slightly enlarged repetition of the successful *Loyal London*. This is only to be expected since the latter was also a Deptford product. Shish had previously been one of the assistants there, and he must have been involved in the *Loyal London*'s design and construction. The *Charles* was about a foot longer and a few inches greater in beam, but the proportions were approximately the same. She had 15 gunports in the lower tier, 14 in the middle, and probably 13 in the upper. The intervals between the ports were very short, and there must have been some inconvenience in operating the heavier guns.

Her decoration was tasteful and not at all extravagant, with a simple lion sufficing for a figurehead. She did have distinctive quarter-galleries, with sharply defined vertical divisions which were vaguely reminiscent of a gothic cathedral façade. The very deep beakhead bulkhead contained an unusual feature in the form of three semi-circular galleries which projected forward at the level of the upper deck.

She was somewhat smaller than the later 1st Rates and was reclassified as a 2nd Rate in 1691. After more than thirty years without major modifications, the *St George*, as she was then called, was rebuilt in 1701. It is probable that 'rebuilt' in this case meant an entirely new ship incorporating 'serviceable timbers' from the old hull. The new vessel differed so greatly that she is usually considered a separate ship. A fine dockyard model of the 1701 version, complete with original rigging, is displayed at the US Naval Academy Museum.

The 'St Michael'

The *Charles* was followed in 1669 by the *St Michael*, built in the royal dockyard at Portsmouth by Sir John Tippetts, who had been the Master Shipwright of that yard since 1650. The *St Michael* was much smaller than the other 1st Rates, and in fact was classed as a 2nd Rate until 1672. Her dimensions were only marginally greater than those of the *Royal Katherine*, and her gundeck (155ft) was over 7ft shorter than that of the *Charles*. The *St Michael* seems to have been an experimental design exploring the maximum ratio of armament to size. By using short, lightweight guns–with demi-cannon on the lower deck–the Admiralty managed to cram 98 guns into her. In this state she was somewhat overgunned, and the number was soon reduced to 90. Even this was excessive. In 1674 she received a much-needed girdling which increased the beam from 40ft 8½in to 41ft 8in, the tonnage rising from 1101 to 1154. After this she appears in some ordnance lists with up to 96 guns; but the ship was seldom commissioned in peacetime, and it is unlikely that she carried that many.

A minor but intelligent innovation which soon

105

105, 106, 107
Details of the *Charles*.

105. NMM No 496. Detail of a drawing by the Younger, c1675.

106. NMM No 543. Younger, 1676. Inscribed 'de gallerij van de karlis 1676'.

107. From a private collection. Detail of a drawing by the Younger, 1678. Inscribed 'd . . . (rubbed out) sareles 1678'.

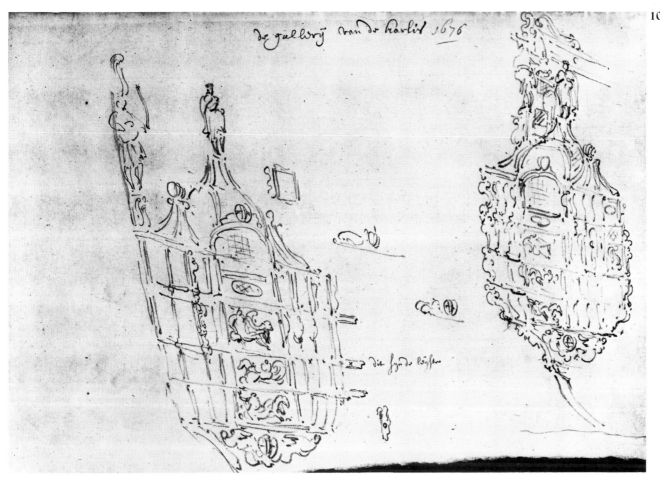

de galberÿ van de harlit 1676

dit synde løÿgten

108
Dockyard model of the *St George*
of 1701, an entirely rebuilt
version of the *Charles*.

USNA. This is one of the earliest
dockyard models with original rigging
preserved.

109, 110, 111
A portrait of the *St Michael*,
along with details of her head
and quarter-gallery.

109. NMM No 537. Elder, ?1676.

110. NMM No 545. Younger ?1676.
Inscribed 'd mighal' and 'dit is te lange'
(this is too long).

111. NMM No 544. Younger, ?1676.
Inscribed 'vand sint mighel' (of the *St
Michael*).

became a fairly standard feature of seventeenth century
English three-deckers was probably introduced in the
St Michael. This was the siting of a middle deck gunport
between the headrails. In all previous 1st Rates, the
foremost broadside gunport had been located in the
lower tier just abaft the hawseholes, where it was
intended to command the vulnerable arc off the bow.
In practice, this port was almost useless, since in all but
the most placid seas it could be opened only at the risk
of inundating the lower deck. The arrangement of the
St Michael provided firing over the same arc from a
much drier position.

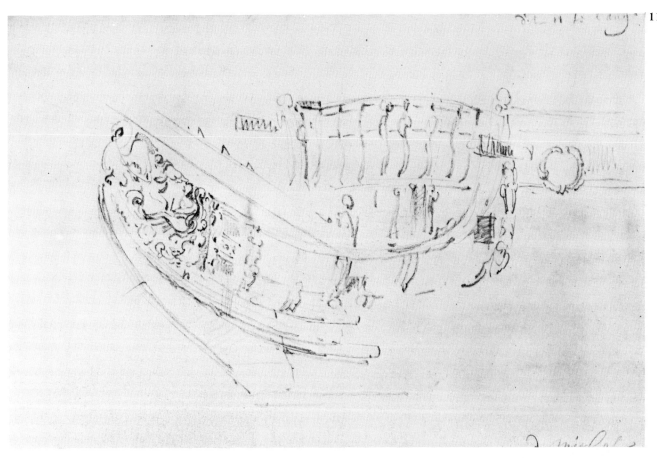

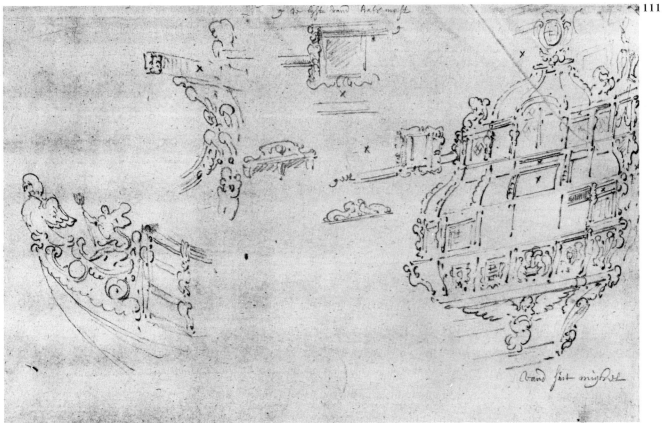

At least one of her illustrious captains, Sir Robert Holmes, thought the world of her and told anyone who would listen that the *St Michael* was a handy and economical vessel–the perfect 1st Rate. Hardly anyone agreed. The consensus was that she had no business being classed as a 1st Rate at all. She was rather small for her armament, and she must have had to carry her lower deck guns dangerously close to the water. The design was not repeated.

In 1689, after she had been greatly surpassed in size by a group of new 90-gun 2nd Rates, the *St Michael* reverted to her original 2nd Rate status. Broken up in the early years of Queen Anne's reign, her usable timbers were incorporated in a new 90-gun ship, the *Marlborough*, which was launched in 1708.

Despite the faults of the *St Michael*'s extreme design, one thing was undeniable: she could outgun any foreign ship of comparable size. Consequently she was a valuable unit in any battle line. Engaged in all of the battles of the Third Anglo-Dutch War, the *St Michael* also fought the French at Barfleur, and she returned from every fight with a grisly casualty list. In the seventeenth century there was no higher compliment.

The 'London'

In addition to building new ships, the Admiralty did not neglect the possibility of rebuilding the three-deckers which had been fired by the Dutch in 1667. Almost before the waters of the Medway had quenched the flames, the surveyors from Chatham Dockyard had examined the remains. On 19 July they reported to the Navy Board that since the underwater parts of the *Royal James*, *Loyal London* and *Royal Oak* appeared to be intact, it seemed worthwhile to attempt their repair.

Unfortunately, when the ships were raised it was found that the *Royal Oak* was too far gone to be of any use. Although the *Royal James* was drydocked at

Woolwich, it was eventually decided that the expense of rebuilding her would be too great. She was broken up in August 1670. The *Loyal London* fared better; placed in the hands of old Jonas Shish at Deptford, she emerged as an almost entirely new 96-gun ship on 25 July 1670.

By that time she was no longer known as the *Loyal London*. The repairs turned out to be more expensive than expected, and Charles II appealed to the merchants of the City to provide the necessary funds, pointing out that she was, after all, 'their' ship. Many of those gentlemen were in serious financial straits due to the Great Fire and the Dutch blockade of 1667. In fact the payments to Captain Taylor for the original vessel were behind schedule. When they came up empty-handed, the King petulantly struck the word 'Loyal' from her name, and she was just plain *London* thereafter.

It is not certain whether Shish actually broke up the remains of the *Loyal London* and started afresh, or simply built on the surviving frames as they stood; but the new *London* was slightly longer and over 2ft broader than her predecessor. Like the *Charles* she was given a leonine figurehead and three-turreted 'cathedral-front' quarter-galleries. With simple square port-wreaths and a complete absence of 'gingerbread' on her hull, the

112
The *St Michael* fought under Rear-Admiral Sir Robert Holmes at the Smyrna Convoy action of 1672 and the Battle of Solebay. The officer at left is Holmes' protégé Captain Sir Frescheville Holles. Sir Frescheville was killed commanding the *Cambridge* at Solebay.

NMM. Painting by Sir Peter Lely.

London appears from Van de Velde drawings to have been rather more businesslike in appearance than some of the other 1st Rates.

Like many other seventeenth century warships, the *London* lasted a long time and survived many battles. She was broken up in 1701, but some of her timbers were used in a new 100-gun *London* which appeared in 1706.

114

115

114, 115
The rebuilt *London*.

114. Boymans No 333. Elder, c1675.
Inscribed 'London' in a hand other than
the artist's.

115. Boymans No 441. Elder, c1675.
Inscribed 'de Londen'.

The 'St Andrew'

In the same year that the rebuilt *London* appeared, an entirely new 1st Rate was launched at Woolwich. This fine ship was the 96-gun *St Andrew*. She had been designed and laid down by Christopher Pett, but Pett had died in 1668. The construction of the *St Andrew* was taken over and completed by his successor at Woolwich, a little-known shipwright named Edward Byland.

The *St Andrew* was very similar to the *London* in tonnage and dimensions, though she differed in appearance and gunport arrangement. Both were highly successful ships. More care was evidently taken to ensure stability in these vessels than in most other three-deckers of the period: their proportions were unusually beamy relative to length, neither requiring girdling, and they were able to carry a very heavy weight of ordnance for their tonnage. A group of large 2nd Rates were later designed with similar dimensions, and the resulting vessels were equally satisfactory.

In addition to several drawings, two excellent Van de Velde paintings of the *St Andrew* are known, one attributed to the Elder and the other to the Younger.

117

The pictures differ in some details such as the location of the entry port and hancing pieces, but they do agree on the gunport arrangement and the decorative scheme. In none of the portraits is the figurehead clearly visible. However, the ship can be seen in the distance in several Van de Velde battle scenes, and in these the figurehead seems to be a lion. The *St Andrew* and *London* were, as far as is known, the last English warships to be ornamented with square port-wreaths. All ships built after 1670 received circular wreaths until such decoration was finally discontinued in the early eighteenth century.

Seventeenth century 1st Rates were fitted out and committed to battle much more frequently than their descendants in the next century. The *St Andrew* was no exception. She fought with distinction throughout the Third Anglo-Dutch War under the flag of Sir John Kempthorne, the hero of the celebrated *Mary Rose* action of 1669. Later she was in the line at Beachy Head in 1690, and also at Barfleur in 1692. The *St Andrew* was eventually broken up and 'rebuilt' as the 100-gun *Royal Anne* of 1704.

117
Dockyard model of about 1670. Except for the circular port wreaths, the figurehead, and the unusual triple wale, this model strongly resembles the *St Andrew*.

NMM.

The 'Prince'

The 100-gun Prince was the third 1st Rate to appear in 1670. She was built at Chatham under the direction of Sir Phineas Pett, great-nephew of the Phineas Pett who had designed the Sovereign of the Seas two generations before.

In dimensions the Prince was only 6in shorter than the Sovereign, but her beam (44ft 9in) was a full 3ft less. Pett must have understood that the narrow hull could result in dangerous stability problems. A low centre of gravity was imperative, and her designer apparently tried to obtain this by mounting as much of the armament as possible below the upper deck. The Prince's lower and middle tiers were provided with fifteen ports each, as opposed to only thirteen each in the Sovereign. This was not a successful arrangement, since the intervals between the guns were too short.

The Prince was first commissioned in 1672, on the outbreak of the Third Anglo-Dutch War. Her lieutenant and later captain, Sir John Narbrough, called her 'a great and brave-contrived ship', finding that she 'wrought very well in staying and bearing up, and steereth mighty well.' Unfortunately, it was also found that in a full loaded state she carried her guns only 3½ft from the water and was 'a little tender-sided'; thus despite her builder's efforts the Prince had turned out to be unstable. 'Girdling the ship,' wrote Narbrough, 'would make her one of the finest ships in the whole universe, for it would make her much more floatier and carry her guns higher, and she would bear the better sail and be a better and securer ship to receive shot, and I believe it will not prejudice her sailing.' But the Prince was then fleet flagship, and she simply could not be sent off to the dockyard until after the campaign. Instead, the Duke of York found a simple and intelligent makeshift solution: he ordered her masts and lower yards shortened and the sails reduced in size accordingly. The smaller sail area must have cut her speed somewhat, but at least she could operate safely. Later, when conditions permitted, she received a substantial girdling which increased her beam to 45ft 10in.

A well-known and beautifully executed dockyard model of the Prince is displayed at the Science Museum in London. While the purpose of most seventeenth century models is not very clear, this one was probably assembled before the ship. It differed from the actual Prince in several minor but noticeable matters which are explicable only by modifications during construction. This can be known today only because very few seventeenth century ships attracted as much attention from the marine artists as the Prince, and most of her portraits show satisfyingly consistent details.

Throughout the Third Anglo-Dutch War the Prince served as a flagship for high-ranking officers, which made her a prime target for attacks. At the Battle of the Texel in 1673 she was subjected to a particularly determined assault by a concentration of Dutch ships. She barely avoided destruction with an epic defence that became legendary in the Royal Navy.

In 1691–92 the Prince was treated to a major repair at Chatham which resulted in an increase in beam to 47ft 10in. This was a much more substantial affair than a simple girdling, but it was not, as is sometimes stated, a complete rebuild. It was hoped that she would become a better match for the giant French 1st Rates with which the Navy was at that time confronted. She was renamed Royal William shortly after her reappearance and fought with that name at Barfleur.

Another 'rebuild' was performed on the Royal William in 1719, but this time the result was an entirely new ship. The new vessel, which included the usable parts of the original version, became famous for her remarkable longevity. The 'Old Billy', as she came to be affectionately known, survived until 1813, and it was said that by then her timbers were tough enough to turn the strongest nails.

Plate XIX

The St Andrew.

NMM. Painting by the Younger, c1675.

Plate XX

A royal visit to the fleet in 1672 (probably the visit of the King and Queen on 18 June). The 100-gun Prince, then flagship of the Duke of York, is in the right foreground. The three-decker in the centre background is the London, and the yachts in the centre foreground are the Cleveland (broadside) and Katherine (stern view). The King has just transferred from the Cleveland to the barge alongside; note the seaman striking the royal standard at the yacht's masthead. Sir John Narbrough's journal entry for that occasion noted that the Prince was dressed with 'all the colours and pendants flying at the yardarms, the Standard at the main-topmast head, the Anchor-standard at the fore-topmast head and the Union flag at the mizzen-topmast head.'

NMM. Painting by or after the Younger.

Plate XXI

The burning of the Royal James at the Battle of Solebay. In the right foreground is the bow of the Dutch ship Witte Olifant, flagship of Vice-Admiral Isaac Sweers. The Dutch ship in the left background with the flag at the main is the Eendracht, flagship of Lieutenant-Admiral Aert van Nes.

Nederlandsch Historisch Scheepvaart Museum. Painting by the Younger.

Plate XXII

Possibly a 'posthumous' portrait of the Royal James of 1671, shown becalmed with other warships. A drawing which appears to have been made in preparation for the painting, showing some details more clearly, is reproduced as illustration 122. The oared vessel in the centre background is the James Galley.

NMM. Painting by the Elder, 1678.

XIX

XX

XXI

XXII

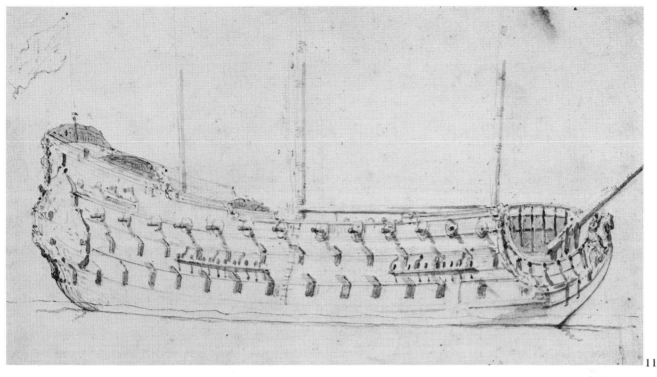

118

119

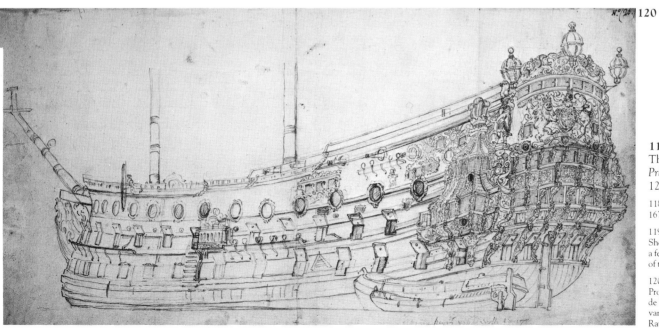

120

118, 119, 120
Three views of the 100-gun
Prince of 1670. (see also pages
125 and 126)

118. Rijksmuseum, Amsterdam. Younger,
1675. Inscribed 'de rooijal prinz 1675.

119. Boymans No 334. Elder, c1675'.
Shows a straight forecastle hancing piece,
a feature which appears in several portraits
of the ship.

120. Rijksmuseum, Amsterdam, No 6837.
Probably by an artist other than the Van
de Veldes, c1672. Inscribed 'Rojal prijns
van de eerste rang' (*Royal Prince* of the 1st
Rate).

121
Sir Anthony Deane.
NMM. Painting by Sir Godfrey Kneller.

The 'Royal James' of 1671

The programme of big ship construction after the Second Anglo-Dutch War coincided with the rise and eventual paramountcy of Sir Anthony Deane in the shipbuilding hierarchy. Deane and Pepys had long before recognised each other as rising stars, and it was on Pepys' recommendation that Deane had been appointed Master Shipwright at Harwich in 1664. After that he continued to strengthen his ties with Pepys, and as the latter rose, so did Deane. In 1668 he became Master Shipwright at Portsmouth, and in 1672 Commissioner of the same yard, although he still built some ships at Harwich.

It would be a mistake to assume that Sir Antony owed his success to Pepys. It is generally acknowledged today that Deane was the premier naval architect of his day. By the standards of the time his approach to the art was unusually scientific, and he introduced a number of valuable innovations. In addition, he was much more literate than most of the other shipwrights, and his treatises are highly regarded by modern researchers. By the late 1660s Deane's qualities had become evident to the higher authorities, and he was entrusted with the design and construction of three 100-gun 1st rates, all of which were built at Portsmouth.

The first of Deane's three-deckers was launched in the spring of 1671. Since it had proven impracticable to rebuild the charred hull of the old *Royal James*, Sir Anthony's ship was given that name. This unlucky vessel was lost after only one year, burned by a Dutch fireship at the Battle of Solebay in 1672. One of the victims of this catastrophe was Edward Montagu, Earl of Sandwich, who was Pepys' patron and also one of the Navy's best admirals.

From all reports the *Royal James* was an outstanding ship. She was an unusually weatherly sailer, with none of the instability that was so characteristic of most seventeenth century 1st Rates. The *Royal James* also incorporated an important improvement in shipbuilding techniques. In a daring innovation Deane fitted her with iron pillars and knees as a way around the increasingly serious shortage of compass timber. Unfortunately the ship's untimely loss prevented sufficient evaluation. Sir Anthony apparently did not repeat the experiment, and the Royal Navy had to wait another century before iron knees were successfully reintroduced.

Mainly because of her abbreviated career, no portraits of the *Royal James* were apparently produced 'from life'—at least, none is known to have survived. The appearance of the ship has been best known from a painting by Van de Velde the Younger showing her fiery destruction. This picture, of which the artist and his studio prepared many similar versions, gives a good view of the head and quarter-gallery, but the midships area is obscured by flame and smoke. Another painting, signed by Van de Velde the Elder and dated 1678, may be a 'posthumous' portrait of the *Royal James*; all the details are the same as those in the Solebay picture. Paintings were frequently commissioned by seventeenth century naval officers and shipwrights to show the ships they had served in or worked on, and this may be of that type. It is, of course, impossible to be certain of the accuracy of the two paintings, but most of the Van de Veldes' customers were important officers who should have been able to give them the details they needed. The Navy's official artists might well have been provided with a model or draught.

The 'Royal Charles'

The second of Deane's 1st Rates was the *Royal Charles*, completed in March 1673. It is reasonable to expect that the design of the *Royal James*, which was considered particularly successful, would have been repeated: in fact the *Royal Charles*, was almost identical in size with the *Royal James* and, if the portraits of the latter can be trusted, they had the same gunport arrangement as well. It is possible, although there is no documentary evidence to confirm it, that the two ships were built from the same set of draughts.

In the superficial matter of outward appearance, the *Royal Charles* seemed quite different from her predecessor. Her figurehead was most unusual. It depicted a helmeted warrior being drawn in a two-horse chariot, accompanied by driver and armed escort. The ship marked a new fashion in sternpiece decoration, with the royal arms diminished in importance in favour of three rows of windows and open projecting galleries. The last-mentioned feature was a normal part of Deane's style in the 1672–75 period. He, and also the King, had greatly admired a French squadron which had visited Portsmouth in 1672. Deane's *Swiftsure* and

Harwich—3rd Rates launched in 1673 and 1674 respectively—were built, in the words of Harwich Dockyard official Silas Taylor, 'with Balconies and Galleries, partly imitating the setting off of some of the French Men of War'. In the *Royal Charles*, a tiny 'balcony' also projected forward from the quarter-gallery.

She was unquestionably a magnificent-looking vessel, and like her late sister she turned out to be unusually speedy. Unfortunately, there were some teething troubles. Despite Deane's scientific approach the calculations necessary for determining metacentric height were beyond the knowledge of any seventeenth century shipwright, and the *Royal Charles* proved to be a sickeningly deep roller. It was hoped that this could be corrected by adjusting the ballast; but at the First Battle of Schooneveld in 1673, where Prince Rupert commanded the fleet from her decks, she was unable to open her lower ports at all. Afterwards, Rupert disgustedly shifted his flag to the *Sovereign*, and the *Royal Charles* spent the remainder of the Third Anglo-Dutch War as a private ship.

125

124

124, 125
The quarter-gallery and the French-inspired stern of the *Royal Charles.* The quarter-gallery is a detail of an engraving made in 1796 after a now-lost Van de Velde drawing. The stern is a crude sketch by neither Van de Velde.

124. Mariner's Museum, Newport News, Va. Detail of an engraving of 1796 after a Van de Velde drawing. Titled 'Side View of the *Royal Charles* built 1673'.

125. NMM No 1110. Detail of an anonymous drawing.

126

126
The *Royal Charles,* portrayed by Isaac Sailmaker with the flags the ship wore at the First Battle of Schooneveld in 1673. The red flag at the fore was the signal to engage the enemy.

Photo: Bristol Museum and Art Gallery. Original last noted in the collection of the late L J Culverwell. Attributed to Isaac Sailmaker.

At the end of the war she was taken in hand and administered a girdling which increased her beam from 44ft 8in to 46ft. This evidently cured her rolling tendency; at least no further complaints are known. The *Royal Charles* was further modified in 1693, after which she was renamed *Queen*. Exactly what was done to the ship at that time is not certain. Since the repair took only one year she is not likely to have been completely rebuilt; that normally took about two years and sometimes much more. The dimensions changed slightly but this is not necessarily significant. The *Queen* was ultimately taken apart and 'rebuilt' as the *Royal George* of 1715.

In the late seventeenth century a model of the *Royal Charles* is known to have been displayed in a public house at Ratcliffe called the Three Pigeons. Unfortunately the model has not been noted since.

The 'Royal James' of 1675

The third and last of Deane's three-deckers was launched on 29 June 1675, and it was on this occasion that the King bestowed a knighthood on his favourite shipwright. To the new 1st Rate the seemingly luckless name of *Royal James* was once again assigned. Oddly enough this vessel, like the two previous ships with the same name, was destined to be destroyed by fire, though not until she had recorded 46 years of service and three name changes.

Although all the new 1st Rates had been very welcome additions to the fleet, the Third Anglo-Dutch War had revealed several defects. The 1675 *Royal James* was the only one to have been planned with the benefit of war experience, and her design embodied several modifications.

One of these was in the gunport distribution. In response to complaints from the fleet, the Admiralty had directed on 16 October 1673 that it should become 'an established rule that all ships to be built hereafter are to have one port fewer on each side, the handling of the guns being much impeded by the nearness of the ports to one another'. This evidently meant one port fewer per deck, since one port per side would have had but minimal effect. The *Royal James* had her gunports arranged in a 13-13-12 pattern, in contrast to the 14-14-13 configuration of Sir Anthony's earlier 1st Rates.

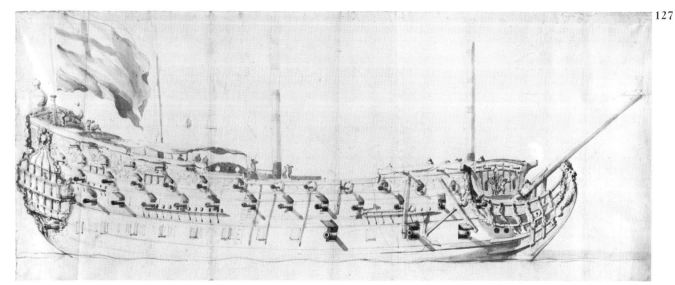

127

128

127, 128
Two portraits of the *Royal James* of 1675, probably drawn about 1678.

127. NMM No 567. Younger, ?1678. Inscribed 'Roijal Jems blaue gront daer d ornemt op hange ent schilt' (*Royal James*, blue ground where the decoration hangs).

128. Boymans No 350. Elder, ?1678.

129, 130
Dockyard model of a 1st Rate of
the 1670s. Its dimensions and
gunport arrangement do not
correspond to any known ship. It
was at one time thought to
represent the *Albemarle* of 1680,
but that ship is now known to
have been very different. Earlier
the model had been called from
tradition the *Royal James* of
1675. There is good reason to
believe that the design of Sir
Anthony Deane's final 1st Rate
had to be modified after the
Admiralty's order of October
1673 increasing the intervals
between gunports, and it is
therefore quite possible that the
model represented his original
design for the ship.

Photos: USNA Museum. Model formerly
displayed at the Royal United Services
Institution Museum, London.

The reduction in the number of gunports gave her
designer a chance to avoid the instability which had
afflicted the *Royal Charles*. This was accomplished by
reducing the length by about 4ft, bringing the proportions into line with those of the reasonably stable
London and *St Andrew*. This still permitted the intervals between the guns to increase by about 1ft. The
only problem was that the Admiralty required that her
armament be the same as that of the *Royal Charles* and
Prince. With fewer gunports on her battery decks, this
meant that an excessively high proportion of her
armament had to be mounted in the upperworks. Since
the *Royal James* was somewhat smaller than the other
100-gun ships, she was certainly overgunned.

That this was eventually recognised is shown by an
armament establishment originating from the Ordnance Office in 1685 (see Appendix V). This proposed
to reduce the lower deck armament of the *Royal James*
to demi-cannon in place of the cannon-of-seven that
had been her original equipment. Apparently this was
to be accomplished by administratively exchanging
guns with the elderly *Victory*, which was too worn-out
and rotten to have been of further use. However, since
the ships were in ordinary at the time, it is unlikely that
the change was implemented immediately.

The *Royal James* had a number of interesting features. Unlike other 100-gun 1st Rates, she was given a
simple lion figurehead. Her namesake, the Duke of
York, was in eclipse at the time of her construction,
and it must have seemed politically unwise for his effigy
to be shown trampling his enemies. In other respects
the Portsmouth wood-carving crew seem to have surpassed themselves, with the upper parts of the hull and
the space between the upper headrails covered with
intricate carvings. The quarter-galleries and stern,
equipped with projecting galleries, bore a marked family resemblance to the *Royal Charles*'. Another feature
seems to have been unique: the bowsprit rested directly
on the whorl at the end of the beak, in a groove
specially designed to receive it.

The name *Royal James* was naturally unpopular after
James was overthrown in the Revolution of 1688, so
the ship was renamed *Victory* in 1691. She was in
action only once, at the Battle of Barfleur in 1692. She
was given a major repair in 1695, renamed *Royal
George* in 1714, and *Victory* again in 1715. The ship's
history came to an abrupt end in 1721 when she was
gutted by an accidental fire. The surviving timbers
were stored for many years, and were then used in the
construction of a new *Victory* which was completed in
1739. This was the ill-fated 'Balchen's *Victory*', so
called because Admiral Sir John Balchen was the most
prominent victim when the ship was wrecked with the
loss of all hands–over a thousand men–in 1744.

130

6. Continental Navies

During the reign of Charles II the most important Continental navies were the Dutch and, from the late 1660s, the French. Sweden, Denmark-Norway, and Spain ranked far behind the great powers numerically, but all possessed large and up-to-date vessels. Shipbuilding techniques were basically the same throughout Europe, but, as in every age, each country built vessels to match its own strategic needs and aspirations. In addition, artistic tastes and abilities varied from place to place so that each navy displayed characteristic decorative styles.

The Netherlands

England's principal maritime rival of the mid-seventeenth century was the Netherlands. Their navy was administered by five more or less independent admiralties: Amsterdam, The Maas (Rotterdam), Zeeland, Friesland, and the North Quarter. In terms of shipbuilding the first two were by far the most important. Each admiralty built its own ships, and because of this Dutch battle fleets frequently included vessels with duplicate names.

Until 1666 the Republic bolstered its fleet with units of the Dutch East India Company, which had what amounted to a private navy. Some of the Indiamen carried well over 70 guns, and in 1665 most of the biggest Dutch vessels were Company ships. Indiamen looked little different from warships, but they were not as heavily timbered and their guns tended to be lighter. They sometimes gave a good account of themselves, as at Bergen in 1665, but their officers and crews were poorly trained for open-sea battles. A disproportionate percentage of the Dutch losses at Lowestoft were Indiamen. After that their use in the battle line became less common, and after 1665 they were dispensed with almost entirely.

Dutch warships differed from their English counterparts in a number of ways. The shoals of the Dutch shorelines and harbours made shallow draught a primary consideration. This limitation meant that their ships had to be relatively flat-bottomed and somewhat squarish in section. That was the only way the displacement necessary for a strong armament could be obtained without making the hulls excessively beamy.

131
A grisaille by Van de Velde the Elder showing Dutch warships assembled for a council of war in 1665. The vessel in the foreground is the 76-gun *Eendracht*, flagship of Jacob van Wassenaer, Earl of Obdam. The *Eendracht* was blown up in action at the Battle of Lowestoft.

Museum Prins Hendrik, Rotterdam. Grisaille by the Elder, c1666.

Other structural differences were in the design of the bow and stern. The Dutch, and for that matter most other navies, did not adopt the rounded English stern until the eighteenth century. The Continental 'square tuck' was structurally weaker and hydrodynamically less efficient than the English system. A flat stern, however, was easier to construct and less expensive since it did not require the curved transom timbers of the English ships. Forward, the cutwater which supported the head extended all the way to the keel in English ships, while the Dutch preferred to fair it into the stem only a few feet below the waterline. Dutch ships dating from before 1670 had long, graceful heads, but in later ships they gradually became shorter and angled more towards the vertical. Catheads were located lower than was customary in England and usually projected over the headrails. The figurehead was nearly always a red lion.

One obvious external characteristic of Dutch ships was the almost complete absence of hull decoration, except for the stern. Gunport wreaths were never employed, and the upper sides had plain clinker-laid, or overlapped, planking. The waist often had high bulwarks pierced with loopholes for musketry. These were of dubious value, since they afforded little or no protection and also provided an unnecessary source of deadly splinters. Quarter-galleries seldom exhibited the fantastic spires and cupolas of the English ships. They normally served only the great cabin on the upper deck, but sometimes a cylindrical turret projected upwards to accommodate the quarterdeck cabin as well.

The decoration of the stern was the only real concession to vanity. Until late in the century the Dutch used only one row of stern windows in even the biggest ships, leaving a large area above–the taffrail–on which the main ornamental efforts were concentrated. This space, which was always surrounded by various carved figures, was usually dominated by a coat of arms appropriate to the ship's name. However, many ships were named after castles (*Slot Honingen*), palaces (*Huise Te Swieten*), or words expressing republican sentiments (*Vrijheid*, or liberty). In such cases a painted scene was frequently employed. Famous artists were sometimes commissioned, and some ships may have displayed genuine masterpieces.

In 1665 the Dutch entered their second conflict with England with a numerically strong but badly outgunned fleet, just as they had in the 1652–54 war. Except for a few outsized Indiamen there were no ships larger than the smallest English 2nd Rates, whilst the bulk of the fleet consisted of vessels corresponding to the English 4th Rates. Lowestoft quickly proved the hopelessness of this situation. The Dutch commanders complained bitterly but the admiralties were quite aware of the deficiency, and a major building programme was already in hand.

Because of the shallow draught requirement, the Dutch had no intention of opposing the English 1st Rates with giants of their own. They preferred to neutralise them with a superior number of ships in the 80-gun range. By the end of the war eleven vessels of that size were ready, plus a dozen more with around 70 guns. None had more than two complete tiers, but the largest Amsterdam ships–the *Gouden Dolfijn* (86) and the 82-gun *Gouden Leeuw* and *Witte Olifant*–had decked-over waists and so were actually three-deckers. They were approximately 154ft on the gundeck and 41ft in beam–about the same as the English *Royal Katherine*. De Ruyter's famous *Zeven Provincien* was some 7ft shorter. They were armed with 24pdrs on the lower deck (along with a few 36pdrs at times), 18pdrs on the middle deck, and 6pdrs and 4pdrs above. This was lighter ordnance than that carried in the larger English men-of-war, but a higher rate of fire compen-

132
The Dutch ship *Harderwijk*, a 40-gun two-decker equivalent to an English 5th Rate.

NMM No 159. Elder, c1665. Inscribed 'ick gelooft te zijn harderwijck' (I believe this is the *Harderwijk*).

sated to some extent. In the hands of capable leaders and well-trained crews these ships were fully able to take care of themselves in a fight. Although many of the 80-gun ships had very active careers, none was lost in battle.

At the end of the Second Anglo-Dutch War the pace of naval shipbuilding in the Netherlands slowed drastically. The next conflict, which began in 1672, was fought without the benefit of new construction because of the expense and manpower required to repel a French land invasion; large scale construction was not resumed until the early 1680s. At that point, spurred by activity in the arsenals of France and England, the Dutch again began producing large ships including–for the first time–three-deckers with over 90 guns.

133

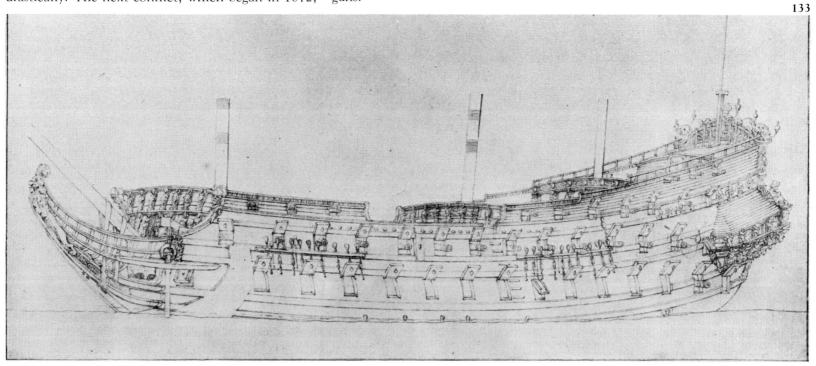

134

133, 134
Two-decked 80s: The *Hollandia* (133) and De Ruyter's famous *Zeven Provincien*.

133. Boymans. Elder c1666.

134. NMM No 321. Younger, c1670. Inscribed 'd seffen provensie gevoort bij different admirals (the Zeven Provincien commanded by various admirals).

135

136

137

135, 136, 137
Some of the largest Amsterdam
warships of the mid-1660s were
actually three-deckers. The
82-gun *Witte Olifant* (136) and
Gouden Leeuw (137) were
sister-ships, but the 86-gun
Gouden Dolfijn (135) differed
slightly.

135. NMM No 313. Elder, c1667.
Inscribed 'de dolphijn'.

136. Boymans. Elder, c1667. Inscribed 'de
oliphant visad' (the *Olifant*,
Vice-Admiral).

137. NMM No. 312. Elder, c1667.
Inscribed 'de hollantse Leeu'.

The earliest triple-tiered vessels were the *Westfriesland* and *Zeelandia* of 1682, and the *Admiraal Generaal* and *Prinses Maria* of 1683. Seven more units with identical dimensions were completed between 1687 and 1690. These ships were natural developments from the 'semi-three-deckers' of 1666–67. The new vessels differed only in that they could accommodate upper deck guns in the waist; no forecastle was provided, and there was no advance in dimensions. The size of the ordnance was also unchanged. From all reports their design was unsatisfactory: the lower deck ports could rarely be opened, and for fear of excessive heeling they had to shorten sail in even moderate breezes. The instability was caused by the very narrow beam which

the authorities foolishly imposed upon the shipwrights. Despite their shortcomings the *Westfriesland* and *Prinses Maria* fought nobly at Beachy Head in 1690.

Dutch shipbuilding in the seventeenth century was admired throughout Europe, and most Continental navies bought Dutch ships or employed Dutch shipwrights at one time or another. It should be remembered, however, that the Dutch almost always had to face larger and stronger ships than their own. It was not ships, but the skill and courage of their seamen–De Ruyter, the Tromps, the Evertsens, and their illustrious lieutenants, along with many thousands of forgotten heroes from the lower deck–which accounted for the Dutch successes.

138
One of the few large Dutch ships built in the 1670s was the 76-gun *Steenbergen*, completed in 1671.

NMM No 346. Elder, c1672. Inscribed 'steenbergen'.

138

139

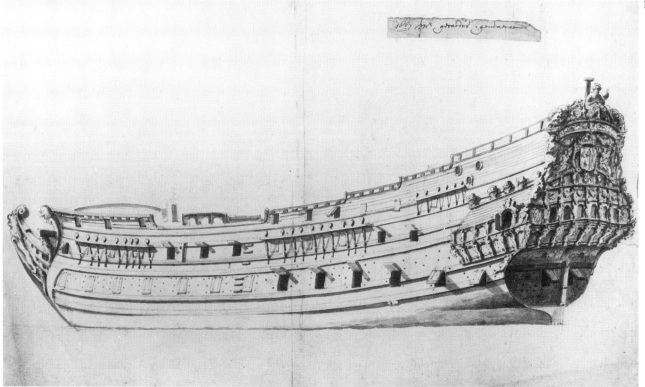

139
One of the six Dutch-built French ships of 1667. As completed they were pierced for 74 guns, but they may have carried over 80 in the French service.

Museum Prins Hendrik, Rotterdam. Younger, 1667. Inscribed 'aallicsander' (*Alexander*) and '1667 mr gerardus gemaeckt' (built in 1667 by Mr Gerardus). The French ships built in the Netherlands were *Le Conquérant*, *La Courtisan*, *L'Intrépide*, *L'Invincible*, *Le Neptune*, and *Le Normand*; but some may have borne different names before delivery. The name *Alexander* is suggestive of *Le Conquérant*.

140

141

140, 141, 142
Le Royal-Louis (140), *Le Dauphin-Royal* (141) and *Le Monarque* (142) – all Toulon-built 1st Rates – bore the fantastic statuary of sculptor Pierre Puget. One of the greatest French admirals, Abraham Duquesne, so despised *Le Royal-Louis* that he flatly refused to take her to sea until directly ordered to do so by the King himself.

140. Musée de la Marine, Paris, Pierre Puget, probably around 1690.

141. Musée de la Marine, Paris. Pierre Puget, date unknown.

142. Musée des Beaux-Arts, Marseilles. Anonymous, but probably after Puget.

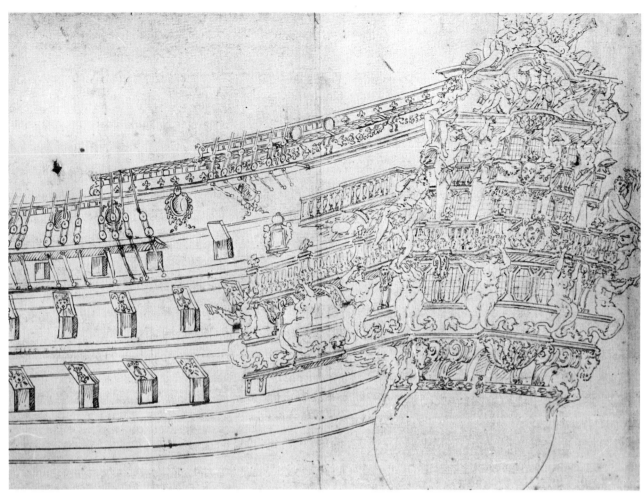

France

In the time of Cardinal Richelieu, France had possessed one of the most impressive fleets in Europe. After Richelieu's death in 1642 this powerful force was allowed to deteriorate; ships rotted at their moorings, harbours silted over, and shipwrights and seamen sought other occupations. By the time Louis XIV assumed control in 1661, there remained only one vessel capable of carrying as many as 60 guns.

Louis himself was not especially interested in naval affairs, except as a matter of prestige. However, his Intendant of Finance, Jean-Baptiste Colbert, was most definitely interested. Colbert planned an extensive expansion of French overseas commerce, and a strong navy was necessary to protect the merchant fleets. In 1663 he obtained the title of Intendant de la Marine, and immediately set out to rebuild the Navy.

Although a few new ships were constructed almost immediately, most of the early years were spent in building up the necessary support organization. The arsenals at Brest and Toulon were enlarged, and a new facility was opened at Rochefort. Preparations for a really large-scale shipbuilding programme were not ready until 1667, so in the meantime Colbert shopped abroad for his warships. Orders were placed in foreign dockyards for ten men-of-war of about 74 guns, two from Denmark and eight from the Netherlands. Two of the Dutch ships were cancelled, but the rest were delivered in 1666. At the time the sale of these vessels

must have seemed like good business to the penny-wise Dutch, but only six years later most of the same ships were in a French battle line facing De Ruyter.

The appearance of the Danish vessels is not certain. One was smaller than the other, and it is known that both originally had a deck over the waist which was removed when they arrived in France. The Van de Veldes drew portraits of all of the Dutch-built ships. In most respects they were very similar to the Amsterdam Admiralty's *Gouden Leeuw* and *Witte Olifant*. The French ships had fewer ports in their upperworks, and their decoration was slightly more ornate, but there were no other significant differences. In fact, it is tempting to suggest that the *Gouden Leeuw* and *Witte Olifant* might have had their origins in the two undelivered units.

By 1667 the French dockyards were ready for major efforts of their own. Colbert imported Dutch and Venetian shipwrights, and Louis provided vast sums of money. Within three years, before the rest of Europe realised what was happening, France had become a great naval power—at least in terms of ships.

The core of the fleet was a series of three-deckers which were completed at Toulon and Brest in 1668–69. The largest were the biggest ships in the world, but they did not outclass their English counterparts by nearly as much as is sometimes claimed. The 2000-ton figures usually quoted for the French 1st Rates of this period are not even remotely consistent

143
French shipwrights in Atlantic dockyards were much influenced by the Dutch, and their products had relatively simple decorations. This Brest-built 1st Rate is *La Reine*, the Comte d'Estrées' 110-gun flagship at the Battles of Schooneveld and the Texel in 1673.

NMM No 418. Elder, 1673.

144, 145, 146
Le Royal-Thérèse (144), the Toulon-built 70-gun flagship of the Marquis Martel, the French second-in-command at the Texel. She is shown just after Charles II, visiting the ship, has 'caused the bow guns to be fired three times because they carried so far.' Note the smoke issuing from the muzzle of the starboard bow chaser. The ship was built as *Le Paris* in 1670, with decorations by Puget (146). She became *Le Royal-Thérèse* (145) in 1671 and was redecorated accordingly. For some reason Van de Velde called this ship the 'World's Wonder'.

144. Worcester, Mass., Art Museum. Elder, 1673. An inscription translates as follows: 'The King was here forward on the half-deck (?) of this ship called The World's Wonder. She was, I believe, the second square Rear-Admiral of the French on which the King caused the bow guns to be fired three times because they carried so far.' A second inscription reads 'The King was here forward on this ship called the World's Wonder, the French Rear-Admiral.' Possibly drawn during Charles II's visit to the French fleet on 9 July 1673.

145. NMM No 424. Detail from a drawing by the Elder, 1673. Inscribed 'ditad van achteren' (?details aft).

146. Musée des Beaux-Arts, Marseilles. Pierre Puget, ?1670.

with their known dimensions. The accompanying tables gives data (in English measurements) for these vessels, with tonnages based on an approximation of the English 'calculated' method.

The French 1st Rates seem to have been built mainly for propaganda purposes. Despite the high reputations they enjoyed, there are indications that they were not entirely satisfactory. Like many English three-deckers, *Le Royal-Louis* had to be girdled before proceeding to sea, and none of the larger units was frequently commissioned. *Le Soleil-Royal* and *Le Dauphin-Royal* saw no action until 1690, and as far as is known *Le Royal-Louis* never fired her guns in anger. Her only commission was an uneventful cruise in 1678. The only one that took

French three-deckers completed in 1668-9

Name	Year Launched	Dockyard	Guns	Stem to Sternpost Length (ft in)	Estimated Gundeck Length (ft)	Beam Outside Planking (ft in)	Calculated Tonnage
Royal-Louis	1668	Toulon	104-120	174 10	169	48 0	1675
Soleil-Royal	1669	Brest	98-120	175 4	170	46 11	1610
Dauphin-Royal	1668	Toulon	90-110	170 0	165	46 5	1530
Royal-Duc	1668	Brest	100-110	166 4	161	44 10	1390
Monarque	1668	Toulon	80- 94	?	?	?	?
Couronne	1668	Brest	76- 92	153 6	149	41 7	1110

The English formula for tonnage determination in the second half of the seventeenth century was $B^2K/188$, where B is the beam (usually measured outside the planking) and K is the keel length. The keel for tonnage used in the above table is 18 per cent of the gundeck length. The same calculation applied to English 1st Rates yields a figure within a few inches of the keel determined by the normal 'harping' method (see Appendix 1). The gundeck of a French ship was usually about 3 per cent less than the stem-to-sternpost figure.

146

part in the North Sea battles against De Ruyter was *Le Royal-Duc* (renamed *La Reine* in 1671), which fought at Schooneveld and the Texel in 1673.

After 1669 the French built no more genuine 1st Rates until 1690, with one exception. That was *Le Victorieux*, of 100 guns and about 1700 tons, built at Rochefort in 1677. Something must have been badly wrong with that ship, because she had to be broken up after only eight years.

Colbert's great programme of the late 1660s and early 1670s also produced about twenty ships of 60–80 guns and another two dozen or so in the 50–60 gun range. These were usually larger than English ships of the same number of guns. As with the 1st Rates, the size advantage was not as great as is often stated. After 1672 the French dockyards were not nearly as active as before, but construction at least matched the fleet's attrition rate until 1689, when the next major expansion began.

French ships varied markedly in appearance depending on where they were built. Those from the Atlantic ports—mainly Brest and Rochefort—showed a strong Dutch influence. The decoration was an elaboration on the forms usually seen in Dutch ships, with the exception that the French favoured open, projecting quarter and stern galleries. Nearly every vessel seems to have had them. The effect was rather formal and angular, but not unpleasing.

147

147, 148
These very large two-deckers
were flagships in the Third
Anglo-Dutch War. The 74-gun
ship (147) is probably *Le
Terrible*, which wore the flag of
Hector Des Ardens, the French
second-in-command at
Schooneveld and
third-in-command at the Texel.
The 84-gun ship (148) may be
L'Orgueilleux, the flagship of the
Marquis de Grancey,
third-in-command at
Schooneveld.

147. NMM No 421. Elder, 1673.
Inscribed 'schout bij nacht met de 4 kante
vlag' (Rear-Admiral with the square flag).
In the third Anglo-Dutch War the French
Commander-in-Chief wore a square flag at
the fore. His Vice-Admiral wore a square
flag at the mizzen and the Rear-Admiral a
cornet at the mizzen. In 1673 the French
ships with a square flag at the mizzen were
Le Terrible (at Schooneveld) and *Le
Royal-Thérèse* (at the Texel). Since *Le
Royal-Thérèse* has been identified in other
drawings, this should be *Le Terrible*.

148. NMM No 422. Elder, 1673.
Inscribed in a cornet 'schout bij nacht'
(Rear-Admiral).

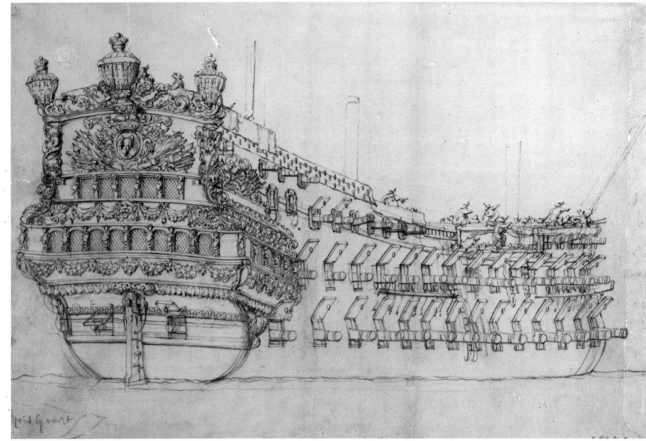

148

Plates XXIII, XXIV, XXV
The dockyard model of the *Prince*, preserved in the Science
Museum in London, is one of the finest and most famous still in
existence. This model differed slightly from the actual ship. In the
completed vessel an extra middle tier gunport was worked into the
long interval that appears abaft the headrails on the model.
Another port was added on each side of the quarterdeck, and a
small projecting gallery was fitted to the stern at upper deck level.
Both the model and the ship had a middle deck gunport disguised
as a quarter-gallery window, and there was an undecorated
quarterdeck port hidden abaft the quarter-gallery. The latter
feature, though present on the model, is not easily visible in these
photographs. (See page 104).

Crown Copyright. Science Museum, London.

Plate XXVI
A Dutch two-decker firing a salute. All navies expended
prodigious amounts of powder in this way, but it provided useful
exercise for the gun crews.

Rijksmuseum, Amsterdam. Painting by the Younger.

Plate XXVII
Shipping in the Ij at Amsterdam, with the stern of the 82-gun
Gouden Leeuw shown prominently in the foreground.

Rijksmuseum, Amsterdam. Painting by the Younger.

XXIII

XXIV

XXV

XXVII

149
This unidentified French two-decker of about 60 guns was probably built in one of the Atlantic dockyards. The projecting stern galleries of such vessels were much admired by the English.

V&A No 4693. Elder, 1673.

At Toulon, where from 1668 sculptor Pierre Puget was employed, the decoration tended to the fantastic. The sterns displayed all the elaborate architectural forms of the French Baroque, and larger-than-lifesize statuary clung to every possible perch. Puget's attitude was that the ship should be built to fit the decoration, and not the other way around. Colbert had to repeatedly remind the dockyard officials to keep him under control. *Le Furieux*, a 60-gun vessel of 1671, apparently had decoration so monumental that it affected the sailing qualities of the ship. Her captain is said to have had much of it chopped away as soon as the ship was at sea.

Denmark-Norway

In the 1600s Sweden and the combined kingdom of Denmark-Norway were not the peace-loving nations they are today. Their monarchs were intensely jealous of each other's lands and powers, and savage conflicts erupted frequently. The period corresponding to the reign of Charles II of England was a golden age for the Danish Navy. Commanded by Niels Juel–the Nelson of the North–and Cornelis Tromp, the great Dutch 'sailor of fortune' whose services they were lucky enough to obtain, the Danes inflicted two crushing defeats on larger but ill-led Swedish fleets in the Skåne War of 1675–79.

The Danish fleet was never strong numerically. There were seldom more than fifteen men-of-war of over 60 guns afloat at any one time, and since their ships had long life-spans some were always old and unserviceable. The Danes never hesitated to enlist shipwrights from other powers. They tried a wide variety of designs, ranging from three-deckers with under 70 guns to two-deckers with more than 90. Some ships were decorated according to spartan Dutch traditions, while others were covered with spectacular English-style 'gingerbread'.

One characteristic common to many Danish warships was an unusually wide gangway–actually a boat deck–joining the forecastle and quarterdeck. Most English and Dutch ships had only a narrow, lightweight platform made of extra spars and usually terminating forward of the mainmast.

Danish vessels were smaller and carried lighter ordnance than English ships of the same nominal force. The Danish flagship at the battles of Öland (1676) and Köge Bugt (1677) was the *Christianus Quintus*, the largest of a group of five 'semi-three-deckers' built in 1664–65. Both she and the English *Royal Katherine* of 1664 were rated for 84 guns in 1677. However, the *Katherine* was actually 10–15 per cent larger and had a 33 per cent superiority in weight of broadside, as can be seen from the table.

A comparison of the armament of the 'Christianus Quintus' and the 'Royal Katherine'

Christianus V	Katherine
14-24pdr	26-32pdr
24-18pdr	26-18pdr
12-12pdr	24- 6pdr
20- 8pdr	8- 5pdr
10- 4pdr	
4- 3pdr	
Weight of broadside: 562lb	Weight of broadside: 742lb

The *Christianus Quintus* was built as the *Prins Christian* and renamed in 1674. Her name was again changed, to *Elefanten*, in 1684. She should not be confused with the *Christianus Quintus* of 1683, a conventional three-decker of 90-100 guns.

For much of the last half of the century the most powerful unit in the Danish fleet was the 86–100 gun *Sophia Amalia* of 1650. This great three-decker was built by an Englishman, James Robbins, at the Christiana yard in Norway. Robbins was obviously influenced by the *Sovereign of the Seas*. The *Sophia Amalia* had many English features and may have had a round tuck; Van de Velde portraits do not make this clear. She was nearly 165ft long on the gundeck, and her burden would probably have worked out to about 1200 tons. Her fantastic decoration was every bit the equal of the *Sovereign*'s. There is no reason to think that there was anything wrong with the *Sophia Amalia*'s design, but her deep draught—about 20ft—must have been an embarrassment in the treacherous Baltic shoals. She was seldom commissioned, never saw a battle, and spent nearly all of her 39 years resting peacefully in reserve.

Another big Danish ship from the same period was the *Fredericus Tertius* (86) of 1649. In contrast to the ornate but conventional *Sophia Amalia*, the *Fredericus Tertius* was one of the strangest warships ever built. She was a three-decker, complete with a forecastle and a towering aftercastle. Her armament was distributed on four levels fore and aft, but on only two in the waist. This curious configuration was not in itself unique; several other Danish vessels were similarly arranged, including the *Christianus Quintus* of 1665. The really startling feature of the *Fredericus Tertius* was the design of her quarter-galleries. These took the form of life-sized elephants, one to each side, which perched precariously on the lower wales. When Van de Velde the Elder drew her portrait, in about 1658, she had accidentally lost her figurehead, and the overall effect was decidedly bizarre.

150, 151
The Danish ships *Hannibal* (150) and *Tre Løver* (151). The *Hannibal* is portrayed probably in 1659 and the *Tre Løver* in 1667. A topgallant poop and a very wide gangway, or spar deck, were typical features of even medium-size Danish warships.

150. NMM No 58. Elder, ?1659. Inscribed '. . . deense anijbul Visadr' (Danish *Hannibal*, Vice-Admiral). In 1658 the *Hannibal* was renamed *Svan*, but in 1659 she was the flagship of Niels Juel, who served as a Vice-Admiral in that year.

151. NMM No 165. Elder, 1667. Not inscribed, but easily identified from the figurehead. Probably drawn in 1667, when the *Tre Løver* and several smaller Danish ships escorted a convoy to the Texel.

150

151

152

153

154

152, 153, 154
Two views of the 86-gun *Sophia Amalia* of 1650 (152, 153). She was obviously inspired by the *Sovereign of the Seas* and may have had an English-style round tuck. Like many Early Stuart English ships her coach was detached from the rest of the after castle. The third drawing (154) depicts the outlandish *Fredericus Tertius* of 1649 with a towering stern and an elephant for a quarter-galley.

152. Boymans No 360. Elder, ?1658.

153. V&A No 4685. Elder, ?1658.

154. Boymans No 301. Elder, ?1658.

Sweden

Sweden, like Denmark, frequently sought the services of foreign shipwrights, and these must have produced many interesting designs. Unfortunately the Van de Veldes had little chance to portray Swedish men-of-war. As a result most Swedish ships of the mid-century are known today only as bare statistics in official lists and ordnance establishments.

Before 1660 most Swedish vessels were similar to those of the Dutch, except that the decoration was more extensive. In the late 1650s there was a strong influx of English influence in the form of a shipwright named Francis Sheldon. Sheldon apparently arrived in Sweden around 1658, and he soon convinced the authorities of his ability to build large warships. His 84–90 gun *Riks-Äpplet*, launched at Goteborg in 1661, was one of the largest ships to have been built in Sweden up to that time.

A model believed to have been made by Sheldon is displayed at the Statens Sjöhistoriska Museum in Stockholm. It had traditionally been described as the English *Naseby* of 1655 (the *Royal Charles* of Medway misfortune), but Van de Velde portraits of that ship make the identification unlikely. It seems far more probable that it represents the design for Sheldon's *Riks-Äpplet*. The *Äpplet* went aground and was lost in

1676 following the Battle of Öland, and many artifacts from the wreck were recovered in the early twentieth century. Some of the preserved decorations appear to correspond directly to carvings on the model.

Another of Sheldon's projects was the mighty *Riks-Kronan*, completed in 1672. At 128 guns she was the most heavily armed warship of the entire seventeenth century. The *Kronan* must have been a magnificent sight, but no reliable portraits of her are known. She is said to have had seventeen ports to a tier, with 36pdrs on the lower deck and 24pdrs on the middle. She was lost at the Battle of Öland–or more correctly, before the battle–when a blunder by the admiral caused her to heel deeply while her lower deck ports were open. The water rushed in, and the ship rolled on to her beam ends and then blew up, killing 801 people.

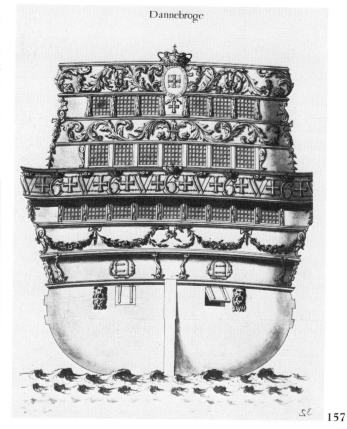

155

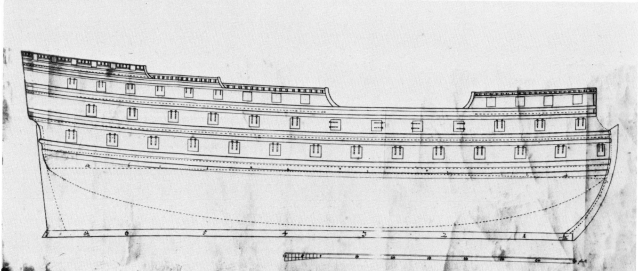

156

157

155, 156, 157
From the mid-1660s Danish shipwrights built reasonably conventional men-of-war. The dockyard model (155) shows the design of the 70-gun *Tre Løver* of 1689, which was little different from other European warships except for the wide spar deck over the waist. There were, however, highly unusual designs. The draught (156, 157) shows the *Dannebrog* of 1692, a two-decker of over 90 guns.

Royal Naval Museum, Copenhagen.

Although this mishap was caused by inexcusable negligence, the *Kronan*'s margin of stability cannot have been very great. She was about 168ft long on the gundeck (174ft from stem to sternpost), and her beam was around 44ft. These dimensions are similar to those of the English *Prince* of 1670 and *Royal Charles* of 1673, both of which were found to be unstable with 100 guns. With 128 guns the *Kronan* must have been dangerously overloaded.

Öland cost Sweden another 1st Rate, the 94-gun *Svardet* of 1662, which was destroyed by the error of a Dutch fireship commander who did not realise she had surrendered. Only 51 were saved out of a crew of 670.

The destruction of the three-deckers at Öland and another disastrous defeat at Köge Bugt in 1677 left the Swedish Navy badly depleted in big ships. After the end of the Skane War in 1679 their dockyards worked at full capacity to make up the deficit, and a number of ships of 80–90 guns were produced. Little information is available on the exact layout and appearance of most of these vessels. However, it is known that Swedish shipwrights were in close touch with the French in those days, and some of the largest vessels were built and decorated from designs prepared in France. At the same time Sheldon's sons, Francis and Charles, had risen to important dockyard positions. All the Sheldons maintained contact with England, and their ships probably had many English features. By 1700 the various foreign influences had been entirely absorbed, and in the eighteenth century Swedish shipbuilding eventually came to be admired in its own right.

158

159

158, 159
Swedish ships of the seventeenth-century are known mainly from dockyard models. One (158) is probably Francis Sheldon's design for the 86-gun *Riks-Äpplet* of 1661. Its layout is similar to the original design of the English *London* of 1656, which Sheldon helped to build before emigrating to Sweden. Note the complex deck arrangement aft. The other model (159) shows the 70-gun *Victoria* of 1683, a conventional two-decker.

158, 159. Statens Sjöhistoriska Museum, Stockholm.

Spain

Spain was not a great naval power in the second half of the seventeenth century. Her shipbuilding industry, however, was highly advanced. The primary function of the Spanish Navy was the protection of the lines of communication with the far-flung and vulnerable overseas dominions. Their ships were expected to operate in the open Atlantic and the Caribbean, which sometimes meant hurricanes. To ensure stability in heavy seas they were usually larger for their armament and more heavily timbered than other European warships. Although in those days few of their men-of-war carried more than 80 guns, a Spanish '80' was nearly as big as an English 1st Rate. Some of the best galleons (for some reason the word 'galleon' has always been reserved for Spanish ships) were built of exotic tropical hardwoods in the great arsenal at Havana.

One of the few reliable portraits of large Spanish warships of this period is a Van de Velde drawing from the mid-1660s. The unnamed vessel had two tiers and apparently a decked-over waist. She appears to have been pierced for only 60–64 guns, although in English or Dutch hands the same ship would likely have packed in 70–80. Her taffrail was decorated with a religious painting. The quarter-galleries were of an old-fashioned wrap-around 'catwalk' type which had ceased to be used in other European ships by about 1650. It is surprising to find this style still in use as late as the 1660s.

160
A Spanish 'galleon' of about 64 guns, shown in the 1660s. The height of the gunwale amidships indicates that the waist was probably decked over.

NMM No 303. Younger, c1666.

7. The Middle Restoration Period
1668-1676

On 12 March 1672 an English squadron in the Channel made an unprovoked attack on a Dutch convoy homeward bound from the Mediterranean. This ambush–a costly failure–marked the start of the Third Anglo-Dutch War. While openly professing friendship with the Dutch, Charles II had made a covert agreement with Louis XIV to assist the French in the destruction of the Netherlands. In return he was to receive generous subsidies and a share of the conquered territories. The alliance was roundly despised by the English people, most of whom were sympathetic to the Dutch. Charles convinced a hostile Parliament to vote funds for fitting out the fleet only by playing on the members' fear of another Medway raid.

Louis planned an invasion of the Netherlands from the south and east. This was to be accompanied by an amphibious assault from England as soon as the combined Anglo-French fleet could sweep De Ruyter's squadrons aside. The Dutch, though hard-pressed, stalled the land invasion by opening their dykes. This meant that victory or defeat depended largely on the outcome of the naval campaign.

The Dutch Navy, though larger than either the English or the French, could not match its opponents' combined forces. Had Louis committed his entire fleet the issue would never have been in doubt. As it was he sent the English 26 ships of over 40 guns under Vice-Admiral Jean d'Estreés, an incompetent ex-army officer. Overall command of the Allied fleet was granted to the Duke of York.

For the Anglo-French plans to succeed it was necessary to have full control of the North Sea. The invading army would have to be transported safely and then supplied from the sea until its work was complete. Before any large-scale landing could be attempted the opposing navy would have to be eliminated. Merely blockading it in its ports would be insufficient, since a strong east wind could drive the Allied ships off station, leaving the Dutch fleet free to cut the army's communications. The only way to keep De Ruyter from interfering was to destroy him in a decisive battle. Unfortunately for Charles and Louis, the wily Dutch admiral obstinately refused to give battle–except on his own terms.

Battles of the Third Anglo-Dutch War

De Ruyter's performance in this war was nothing short of brilliant. He began by charging boldly across the North Sea, catching the unsuspecting Allies lying at anchor. This resulted in the Battle of Southwold Bay, or Solebay, fought off the Suffolk coast on 28 May 1672. Tactically it was a draw, but the outnumbered Dutch gained most of the glory. They had only 62 ships of over 40 guns, while the Allies had 74, including seven English 1st Rates.

De Ruyter meant to get his fireships into the Allied fleet while it was still in confusion. This plan was foiled by the lightness of the wind, which did not allow the Dutch to close quickly enough. The English and French had time to cut their cables and get under way, but the behaviour of d'Estreés removed the Allies' chances for victory. To the disgust of his own captains, he took the French squadron out on a heading almost opposite from that taken by the English. He was then content to engage in a long range cannonade with the squadron De Ruyter sent after him. The Dutch were

161
James, Duke of York, the Lord High Admiral.

NMM: Greenwich Hospital Collection.
Painting by Henri Gascar, c1672.

The final stages of the Battle of
Solebay, viewed from the east.
The English (foreground) have
at last gained the wind by
breaking through the Dutch
centre. At left centre foreground
is the *London*, with the royal
standard at the main. She had
become the Duke of York's
flagship when the *St Michael* (off
the *London*'s port quarter) had
received serious underwater
damage. He had earlier shifted to
the *St Michael* from the disabled
Prince. In the right foreground is
the *Royal Sovereign*, wearing the
flag of Sir Joseph Jordan,
Vice-Admiral of the Blue. At
centre an English two-decker,
with sails aback, trades
broadsides with the *Maagd Van
Dordrecht*, flagship of Dutch
Vice-Admiral Jan de Liefde. The
centre of the three clouds of
smoke in the middle distance
marks the site of the *Royal James*
disaster. The French (centre
background) have finally come
onto the starboard tack, but still
maintain a great distance
between themselves and the
Dutch squadron under Banckert
(left background). In the
distance, off the port bow of the
French ships, are three crippled
English vessels, including the
Henry and *Royal Katherine*. Both
had been captured but later
retaken. Van de Velde viewed
the scene from the small vessel
in the left foreground.

Rijksmuseum No 14817. Elder, c1673.
Probably drawn after the battle in
preparation for a tapestry.

able to oppose the English on nearly even terms, and
according to most observers the resulting battle was the
most violent struggle of the entire Anglo-Dutch Wars.

The principal English flagships, the Duke of York's
Prince and the Earl of Sandwich's new *Royal James*,
worked their way deep into the Dutch fleet. Then the
wind dropped completely, leaving the two ships
unsupported. Help eventually reached the *Prince*, but
the *Royal James*, after a heroic defence, was grappled by
a fireship and destroyed. The Earl of Sandwich was not
among the survivors. Towards the end of the day the

English gradually gained the upper hand. As soon as he
sensed this, De Ruyter prudently gathered his ships and
broke off the fight.

Casualties were heavy on both sides. The Dutch lost
two ships, but this was more than balanced by the
burning of the 100-gun *Royal James*. The Dutch also
captured the 2nd Rates *Royal Katherine* and *Henry*, but
both were later retaken by their own crews. For the rest
of the 1672 season De Ruyter pursued a passive
defence, lurking behind the shoals of the Dutch coast
where the English three-deckers dared not enter. The
Allies tried blockades and threatened landings, but
storms, disease and shortages of supplies defeated every
project.

In the spring of 1673 Prince Rupert was appointed to
command the Allied fleet. The Duke of York was a
victim of the Test Act, which barred Roman Catholics
from holding Crown offices. This was part of the price
exacted by a sullen Parliament for voting funds to carry
on the war.

In May the Allies, 76 ships strong, sailed to the
Netherlands to seek a decisive showdown. On the 28th
they found De Ruyter waiting patiently in the
Schooneveld, a broad anchorage on the Walcheren
coast. It was assumed that the Dutch would refuse
action, and a light squadron was sent in to draw them
out. To the surprise of the Allies, 52 Dutch ships
suddenly bolted from the Schooneveld, driving the
scouting squadron before it and assaulting the main
body so precipitously that it had no chance to get in the
proper order. After a confused 9-hour fight De Ruyter
led his squadrons back to the Schooneveld.

A week later on 4 June, the Dutch again dashed out
unexpectedly and caught the Allies unprepared. Seven
hours of broadsides followed, after which the Dutch
calmly returned to their anchorage. No ships were lost

Edward Montagu, Earl of
Sandwich, who was lost with the
Royal James at Solebay. He was
attempting to shift his flag to
another vessel when the
panic-stricken crew of his blazing
flagship tried to pile into the
boat, swamping it. His body was
later found and identified from
the decorations on his coat.

NMM: Greenwich Hospital Collection.
Painting by Sir Peter Lely.

in either of these engagements, and casualties were nearly equal. However, the damage of two major battles forced both fleets into port, which was in itself a significant victory for the Dutch. The invasion was postponed, while the army slowly ate its way through the English treasury.

The Anglo-French fleet was not ready for sea until mid-July. This time they had 56 English ships and 30 French against De Ruyter's 60. For a time the Dutch stayed in their secure Schooneveld anchorage, but in early August the need to cover an incoming East Indies convoy forced them to come out. This was against De Ruyter's wishes. As he had feared, Rupert trapped him against the shoreline, and to avoid being cut off from the Schooneveld there was no choice but to fight. The clash came on 11 August off the island of Texel at the mouth of the Zuider Zee.

This should have been the decisive battle the Allies needed but, as at Solebay, d'Estrées ruined everything. De Ruyter, who had formed an accurate opinion of the French admiral, sent only nine ships to 'amuse' him. This squadron easily out-manoeuvered the French, and then contemptuously came about and joined De Ruyter's fight against the English. A Dutch sailor was overheard to say that the French 'have hired the English to fight for them, and they're only here to see that the English earn their wages'.

With the French standing by idly the English had to fight for their lives against the ferocious onslaught of the whole Dutch fleet. The commander of the Blue Squadron, Sir Edward Spragge, was killed, and the 1st Rate *Prince* was very nearly lost. Only at the end of the day did the French show signs of renewed interest. When they did De Ruyter simply broke off and sailed home. Both the English and the Dutch suffered terrible casualties, but amazingly no ships were lost. The English contingent was too damaged to stay at sea, and a very angry Prince Rupert stormed back to England. The invasion was again postponed, this time for good.

The shameful performance of the French convinced the last doubters that England was fighting on the wrong side. Charles II made his peace with the Netherlands and laid up his fleet. The Dutch, freed from fears of a seaborne attack, went on to repulse the French, though this required four more years of hard fighting. To the embarrassment of many excellent French officers, it turned out that Louis had privately instructed d'Estrées' to see to it that the English did most of the fighting. D'Estrées' incompetence was, however, no act. On a later occasion he destroyed most of a French fleet by negligently running it on to a reef.

The failure of the Royal Navy in the Third Anglo-Dutch War could not be blamed entirely on the French. The fleet's efficiency was definitely not up to the standards of the previous conflicts: the ships were undermanned throughout; most of the seamen had little enthusiasm for harming the Dutch; and besides, they remembered having been put ashore without their pay in 1666. The ships' crews had to be supplemented by soldiers trained for a different kind of war. In addition the old problems of logistical support were not yet solved, and the fleet wasted many weeks waiting in

164
English ships at sea in 1673. The three-decker at centre is probably the *Charles*, flagship of Sir John Chicheley, Rear-Admiral of the Red. The only other English three-decker with a Rear-Admiral's flag in 1673 was the *St Michael*, which looked considerably different from this ship. The Union at the mizzen peak is the signal for forming line of battle. The ship at right may be the *Victory*, a 2nd Rate which was in Chicheley's division throughout the campaign of 1673.

NMM No 1077. Elder, 1673.

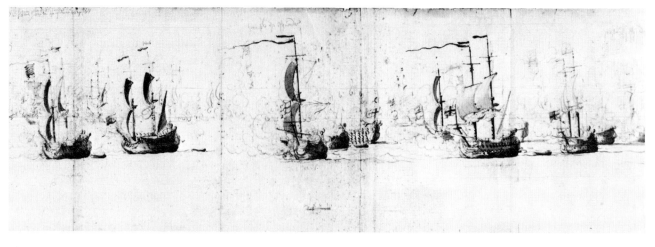

165

An eyewitness view of the early stages of the First Battle of Schooneveld, by Van de Velde the Elder. In this scene the van and centre divisions of Prince Rupert's Red Squadron sail by in considerable confusion, intermingled with the White (French) Squadron and even some units of the Blue Squadron. At left the *Resolution* and another two-decker lead the van division. Astern of them are several vessels which should have been in the Blue Squadron, including the 2nd Rate *St George* (viewed nearly head-on). At right centre the French second-in-command, Des Ardens, is just out of sight beyond the English ships *French Ruby, Anne* and *Constant Warwick*. The three-decker astern of them is Vice-Admiral Sir John Harman's *London* (flag at the fore). The *London* is trailed by *La Reine*, d'Estrées' flagship (white flag at the fore), in a clump of English and French ships sailing four and five abreast. This clump is followed by Rupert's *Royal Charles* (Union at the main) along with the ships of the Red Squadron's centre division. In the right background is the Blue Squadron. The flags of Vice-Admiral Sir John Kempthorne (*St Andrew*) and Admiral Sir Edward Spragge (*Prince*) are visible above the *Royal Charles*. Van de Velde is in one of the ketches in the right foreground.

Boymans No 93. Elder, 1673. Part of a ten-part series of views which the Elder sketched during the battle and presumably worked up later. This is No 3.

port for supplies. As a result Dutch overseas commerce was never entirely stopped.

The most important factor was simply the skill of the opponents. De Ruyter's strategy was carefully thought out, and in action his leadership and judgment were superb. Except at the Texel, he risked battle only when surprise gave him a temporary advantage. On every occasion he quickly disengaged as soon as the advantage was lost. He was well served by the tactical ability of his lieutenants, particularly Adriaan Banckert and Cornelis Tromp. The survival of the Dutch is even more remarkable when it is realised that the English leaders were all experienced veterans.

The Royal Navy was reasonably well led, but there were mistakes. The Duke of York was overconfident, while Prince Rupert's strategy was too cautious and unaggressive. It was when battle was joined that the English commanders-in-chief came into their own.

The Duke carried out remarkable manoeuvres to turn the tide at Solebay, and Rupert handled the dangerous situation at the Texel very well. Sandwich and the independent-minded Spragge allowed personal feelings to draw them into taking fatal risks, the former because of an insult by the Duke and the latter through a strange vendetta with Cornelis Tromp. Most of the English junior flag-officers performed with great skill. Sir John Harman, Sir John Kempthorne and the Earl of Ossory all added to already illustrious reputations.

The war did confirm the Admiralty's confidence in its big three-deckers. Although the Dutch were not defeated their ships were repeatedly mauled by the heavy guns of the English 1st Rates. At the Texel the disabled *Prince* was besieged for hours by numerous opponents, but she never yielded. The burning of the *Royal James* was by no means a cheap victory for the Dutch. One ship which dared to exchange broadsides with her lost 200 men out of a crew of 300.

166

166

Thomas Butler, Earl of Ossory, the Rear-Admiral of the Blue in 1673. His flagship was the *St Michael*.

NMM. Engraving after Sir Peter Lely.

167

Prince Rupert

NMM. Painting by Sir Peter Lely.

167

New Construction 1668–1672: The 'Edgar'

The Royal Navy's concentration on expensive three-deckers in the late 1660s and early 1670s made it difficult to finance the construction of 3rd and 4th Rates. With one exception, every project was dropped with the litany-like refrain: 'there being no money'. Among the cancelled vessels was a large 3rd Rate which Sir Thomas Strickland had laid down in 1668 at Pill of Foudre in Lancashire. In the same year it was proposed to build a 3rd Rate on the slipway at the Forest of Dean, but the project was dropped and the slipway sold. In 1670 three more 3rd Rates were authorised and later cancelled. Two of these were to have been built at Hull and the other at Bristol. In the next year the Admiralty resolved to build three 3rd Rates and six 4th Rates in the port of London for £69,000, but the funds were simply not available. None of the ships was ever built.

The lone exception was a 3rd Rate which was laid down at Bristol near the end of the Second Anglo-Dutch War, possibly as a part of the 'ten great ships' programme of 1666. This was the *Edgar*, built on contract by Francis Bayley and launched in 1668. With a gundeck of 153ft 6in and a beam of 39ft 8in, the *Edgar* was much larger than any previous 3rd Rate. She could carry 72–74 guns, with demi-cannon on the lower deck and either culverins or 12pdrs on the upper deck. No portraits of this important vessel have been identified, and nothing is known of her appearance. Pepys saw the *Edgar* shortly before her launching, and noted that 'she will be a fine ship'. In fact she proved to sail exceptionally well. This perplexed the royal shipwrights, since the illiterate Bayley never even used draughts and built his ships entirely by eye. What had happened was that this shrewd old carpenter had discovered a major flaw in the Royal Navy's ship designs. He had obtained his excellent results simply by stepping the *Edgar*'s masts some 10 to 12ft farther aft than normal. Sir Phineas Pett was the first of the royal shipwrights to suspect the reason for Bayley's success. When the 1st Rate *St Andrew* at first sailed badly despite fast lines, Sir Phineas tried moving her masts 6ft aft. The improvement was remarkable.

168
De Ruyter, with the *Zeven Provincien* in the background.
NMM. Painting by Ferdinand Bol.

Bayley was asked to build another 3rd Rate in 1670, but this was one of the projects that later had to be cancelled. The *Edgar* had a long history, taking an honourable part in seven fleet actions before being entirely rebuilt in 1700.

Third Rates of 1673–1675

The start of the Third Anglo-Dutch War brought little improvement in the Navy's finances, but it did stimulate the construction of several 3rd Rates. The first project began in January 1672, when Sir Anthony Deane, the Commissioner at Portsmouth, proposed to build a pair of 3rd Rates in the government's facility at Harwich. The Admiralty accepted the proposal and Deane agreed to produce the ships for £9 per ton. The first unit, the *Swiftsure*, was launched in 1673. The other, completed in 1674, was named *Harwich* at the request of the citizens of the town.

Much has been claimed for these vessels. A tradition started by Pepys says that the dimensions of the *Harwich* were copied from a French ship and that she

169
A moment of drama at the Battle of the Texel. The commander of the Blue Squadron, Sir Edward Spragge, pushes off in a boat from the damaged *St George* (right foreground) attempting to shift his flag to the *Royal Charles* (right centre). But all was not well in the *Royal Charles;* her captain was dead and everything was in confusion. She sailed majestically past, leaving Sir Edward's helpless barge to fend for itself. Before the admiral could reach safety a cannon shot struck the boat, and Spragge was killed. At left the *Prince,* Spragge's first flagship, makes her famous defence against the determined assault of Dutch Admiral Cornelis Tromp. Tromp is alongside the *Prince*'s starboard side. Spragge had earlier sworn to the King that he would kill Tromp or die himself. Note the booms extended from the English vessels to fend off fireships, one of which burns out harmlessly at the extreme left.

NMM No 409. Elder, ?1673. A drawing made after the battle, possibly for a tapestry.

170
Deane's *Swiftsure.* The corner of one of the 'balconies' across the stern is visible beneath the after end of the quarter-gallery.

NMM No 417. Elder, 1673. Inscribed 'de . . . te harwits dat nade nieue swifsiuer' (the launch of the new *Swiftsure* at Harwich).

170

became a model for later English shipbuilding. There is a grain of truth in this, but not much more. It should be kept in mind that Pepys consistently promoted his friend Deane's reputation at the expense of other shipwrights.

It is true that the alliance with Louis XIV provided the opportunity for a close examination of the latest examples of French naval architecture. Charles II visited the French fleet when it arrived at Spithead in the spring of 1672. He was particularly impressed with the appearance of *Le Superbe*, a two-decker of 74 guns. Deane was summoned, and the King directed him to make his new ships like *Le Superbe*. Deane was unquestionably impressed by the size of the French vessel and Pepys wrote:

'This ship was greatly commended, both by the French, and English that went on board her. She was 40 foot broad, carried 74 guns and 6 months provision. And but 2½ decks; our frigates, being narrower, could not stow so much provision nor carry their guns so far from the water. Which Sir A.

D. observing, measured the ship and gave his Majesty an account thereof, who was pleased to command A. D. to build the Harwich as near as he could of the Superbe's dimension; which was done according, with such general satisfaction as to be the pattern for the 20 3rd-rates built by the late Act of Parliament, which is generally agreed to be without exception, and the highest improvement that is known to this day'.

Pepys' claim simply cannot be supported. The *Harwich*–and the nearly identical *Swiftsure*–were very successful ships, but the evidence indicates that they were influenced by *Le Superbe* only in the French-style 'balconies and galleries' across their sterns. The ships were outstanding in neither size nor proportions. The *Edgar* was larger, and several earlier 3rd Rates–particularly the *Warspite* of 1666–were beamier relative to length.

The height of the batteries could have been raised and the stowage capacity increased by employing the full lines favoured by the French. There is nothing to indicate that Deane did so. The *Swiftsure* easily outsailed a Dutch squadron that chased her in 1673, and Pepys wrote that 'the *Harwich* carries the bell from the whole fleet both great and small'. Their reputation for fast sailing is a strong indication that they were quite fine-ended. The vessels described as having been 'built by Act of Parliament' are the subject of the next chapter. It suffices here to point out that although the 3rd Rates of that programme were first planned to be about the same size as Deane's ships, it was the King himself who insisted that the new ships be enlarged to match the French standards.

The fact is that the French custom of mounting the armament as far above the water as possible was not the policy of the Royal Navy. As a matter of routine, the English crammed in as many guns as a ship could bear without sinking. If a vessel was found to carry her armament abnormally high, the Admiralty simply increased the ordnance—and for the sake of stability the ballast—until she sat as low as the rest of the fleet. This may be one reason why the *Loyal London*'s establishment was increased from 80 to 92 guns within a month of her completion. Another example is *Le Rubis*, a prize taken from the French in 1666. At the time of her capture she mounted only 54 guns, but the English authorities noted that she could 'be well made to bear 60 odd guns'. In fact they gave her 66. This was soon increased to 76, and even after that she was deemed capable of carrying more: in 1672 the *French Ruby*, as she was called, was modified to carry 80 guns, apparently in three complete tiers.

If there was a copy of *Le Superbe*, it is most likely to have been the *Royal Oak*, which was completed in 1674 by Jonas Shish in the royal dockyard at Deptford. Like the French ship—and unlike the *Harwich*—she was '40 foot broad' (40ft 6in to be exact) and carried 74 guns. This great 3rd Rate remained the largest and most powerfully armed two-decker in the Royal Navy until the 1690s. With demi-cannon in the lower tier and culverins in the upper, she could fire a heavier broadside than many 2nd Rates. The *Royal Oak* eventually became the prototype for a class of 80-gun two-deckers built in the reign of William III.

A much smaller 3rd Rate was launched in 1675.

171
An unidentified 3rd Rate with stern decoration appropriate for the *Harwich* or *Swiftsure*. The carved taffrail makes it unlikely that this is one of the twenty 3rd Rates of 1678-1680, which had smooth taffrails. The ship probably dates from between 1673 and 1675. It is not the *Royal Oak*, but could be the *Harwich*, *Swiftsure* or the *Defiance* of 1675.

British Museum. Younger, ?1680s.

This was the 64-gun *Defiance*, built at Chatham by Sir Phineas Pett. She was about the same size as the *Defiance* of 1666, and was presumably intended as a replacement. No portraits of her have been definitely identified, although there are a few 'possibles'.

Incidentally, *Le Superbe* was apparently not as successful as the English believed. After the 1672 campaign she was sent back to France to have her waist decked over. This was a procedure which was later employed by the English to correct ships which were found to be weak in their upperworks. *Le Superbe* was seldom commissioned afterwards and was sold to the breakers in 1687, only sixteen years after her launching.

172
The *Royal Oak*. Note the equestrian figurehead, unique among seventeenth century 3rd Rates. Another feature unusual for a two-decker is the presence of a topgallant poop.

Collection of the late Dr R C Anderson. Mrs Anderson has loaned this drawing to the National Maritime Museum, London. Elder, c1675.

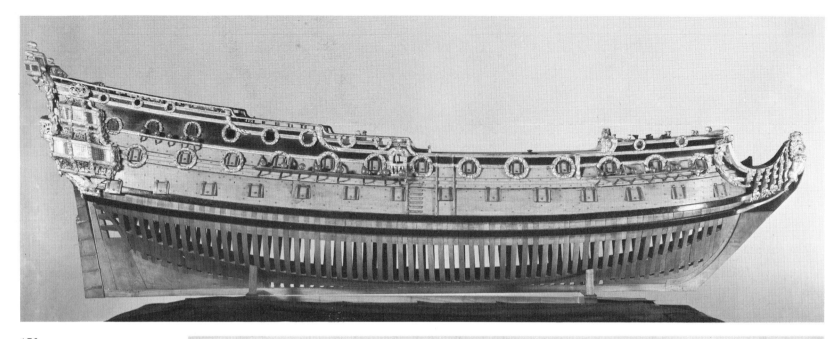

173
Dockyard model of an
unidentified 80-gun two-decker
of about 1692. Such vessels were
designed along the lines of the
successful *Royal Oak,* but the
Admiralty overloaded their hulls
with heavy ordnance and they
became notorious failures.
Because of a shipwright's initials
carved into the stand, it has
been suggested that it represents
the *Sussex.*

USNA Museum.

174
A large 3rd Rate at sea, probably
the *Royal Oak.* Tentatively
identified on the basis of the
similarity of the gunport
arrangement to that shown in
proven portraits of the *Royal
Oak.*

V&A No 4660. Younger, date unknown.

Fourth Rates, 1668–1685

Fourth Rates were very useful ships. They were regularly employed in the battle line until after the end of the century; they were also found to be the right size for opposing the North African corsairs with which the Royal Navy was almost continually at war. Because of their relatively shallow draught 4th Rates could go places that a 3rd Rate could not. In addition their smaller complements made them more economical, and many were consequently left in commission in peacetime while their larger sisters were laid up.

176

Nevertheless few ships of this class were built in Charles II's reign, the reason being that the many remaining 4th Rates of Commonwealth and earlier vintage were sufficient to satisfy most of the Navy's needs. It was cheaper to rebuild or repair these vessels than to build new ones.

New 4th Rates were planned on two occasions in the early 1670s, but none was laid down. The first group were the six 4th Rates included in the cancelled 'port of London' programme of 1670. Another plan arose when Admiral Sir Edward Spragge suggested in 1673 that new ships might be obtained inexpensively in Ireland. To test this idea the Admiralty granted Spragge a contract to have four 4th Rates built at Waterford for £8 6s 3d per ton. The Admiral's agent–Sir Nicholas Armorer–began purchasing materials immediately, but the plan was dropped when Sir Edward was killed at the Battle of the Texel.

Not counting four upgraded 5th Rates–and several unusual variants–the Royal Navy built only two genuine 4th Rates between 1668 and 1685. These were the *Oxford* of 1674 and the *Woolwich* of 1675. The former was built on contract by Francis Bayley of Bristol, while the latter was produced at Woolwich by Phineas Pett (the grandson of 'old' Phineas, not the same person as Sir Phineas Pett). Both ships were

equipped with 54 guns. For reasons which remain obscure Pett's vessel was encrusted with carvings of almost unbelievable intricacy, rivalling the decorations of the greatest 1st Rates. This might have been because of an intended role as a peacetime flagship, or perhaps the artisans of Woolwich simply wanted the ship named after their town to be the most magnificent of all. In any event this remarkable vessel became a favourite subject of many marine artists, and eight portraits of her are currently known. By contrast the appearance of the *Oxford* is a complete mystery, as is that of every one of Bayley's products.

One fine 4th Rate, the 48-gun *Mordaunt*, was acquired by purchase in 1683. She was originally what could only be described as a private man-of-war. The *Mordaunt* was built in 1681 at Captain Castle's yard at Deptford, for a syndicate led by Lord Mordaunt, later Earl of Peterborough. An international incident arose over the ship shortly after her completion. The Spanish Ambassador heard that she was to be commissioned by the Elector of Brandenburg to prey on Spanish treasure ships. After much argument Lord Mordaunt was compelled to leave a bond to guarantee the ship's peaceful occupation. The Navy finally bought the ship after Mordaunt defaulted on the crew's wages.

175, 176
Two views of the fantastically decorated *Woolwich* of 1675. Note the old-fashioned catwalk forward of the quarter-gallery, an Early Stuart feature which was briefly resurrected in the mid-1670s. The second drawing shows the ship at her launching.

175. NMM. Engraving after a now-lost Van de Velde drawing.

176. Charles Gore Collection, Goethe Museum, Weimar. Elder, 1675.

177
Port quarter view of the *Woolwich* by an unknown artist. Note that the royal arms no longer dominated the stern; and also that there were four lower deck stern ports, unusual in a 4th Rate.

British Museum. Not drawn by either Van de Velde, but possibly by one of their students.

Plate XXVIII
The 54-gun *Woolwich*, built in 1675. The square tuck is a mistake made either by one of Van de Velde's students or by a later restorer.

NMM: Greenwich Hospital Collection. Painting probably after the Elder.

Plate XXIX
The early stages of the Battle of Solebay, seen from the shore. The English are in reverse order with the Blue Squadron sailing Northward across the left-hand page. The division of Vice-Admiral Sir Joseph Jordan (*Royal Sovereign*) is in the lead at extreme left, followed by the divisions of the Earl of Sandwich (*Royal James*) and Rear-Admiral Sir John Kempthorne (*St Andrew*). The *Royal James* is already in trouble, with Dutch Captain Jan van Brakel's *Groot Hollandia* across her bow. Midway between Sandwich and Kempthorne the *Henry* has narrowly avoided a fireship. The inscription here reads 'Capt Digby kild and the shipp afterward taken.' The Red Squadron is at centre and centre right, with Rear-Admiral Sir John Harman (*Charles*) in the leading division. The *Charles* has had her foretop yard brought down. Next comes the Duke of York's *Prince*, hotly engaged with De Ruyter and Rear-Admiral Jan van Nes. The Duke is followed closely by Sir Robert Holmes' *St Michael*, while the division of Vice-Admiral Sir Edward Spragge (*London*) is further to the right. Just forward of the *London*, Sir John Chicheley's *Royal Katherine* (seen from astern) is boarded and taken. The French squadron sails off the page in the distance at extreme right.

Mariner's Museum, Newport News, Va. Anonymous engraving.

Plate XXX
The Dutch close in on the damaged *Prince* at the Battle of the Texel, with Cornelis Tromp's *Gouden Leeuw* leading the way, with the *Prince* at right. Prince Rupert's *Royal Sovereign* is visible in the centre distance, while the flag of Sir John Harman (*London*) can be seen beyond the falling mizzen topmast of the *Prince*. Partly obscured by the smoke of the *Gouden Leeuw*'s port broadside is Rear-Admiral Sir John Chicheley's *Charles*, losing her mizzen topmast. The other Dutch ships are (left to right) the *Witte Olifant* (flag at the fore), (*Hollandia* flag at the mizzen), *Comeetster*, and (erroneously) the *Woerden*. De Ruyter's flag is visible above the *Woerden*'s bowsprit. Van de Velde included the *Woerden* in several representations of the Battle of the Texel, but actually she was not there. The artist was working for the English in 1673 and was probably unaware of the changes in the Dutch order of battle.

NMM. Painting by the Younger, 1687.

Plate XXXI
The Battle of the Texel, showing the wild mêlée which developed around the disabled *Prince*, in the centre, with Tromp along her starboard side and de Haen off her starboard quarter. Spragge has shifted to the *St George*, the ship at right centre without a figurehead. The three-decker in the right foreground is the *Royal Charles*. At the extreme left, Kempthorne's *St Andrew* is partly hidden by an English two-decker, while Ossory's *St Michael* is in the middle distance at centre.

Felbrigg Hall, a property of the National Trust. Painting by the Younger.

Plate XXXII
The *Charles Galley*. Like the *Woolwich*, she had a short catwalk extending forward from the quarter-gallery.

NMM. Painting by or after the Elder.

XXVIII

XXIX

XXX

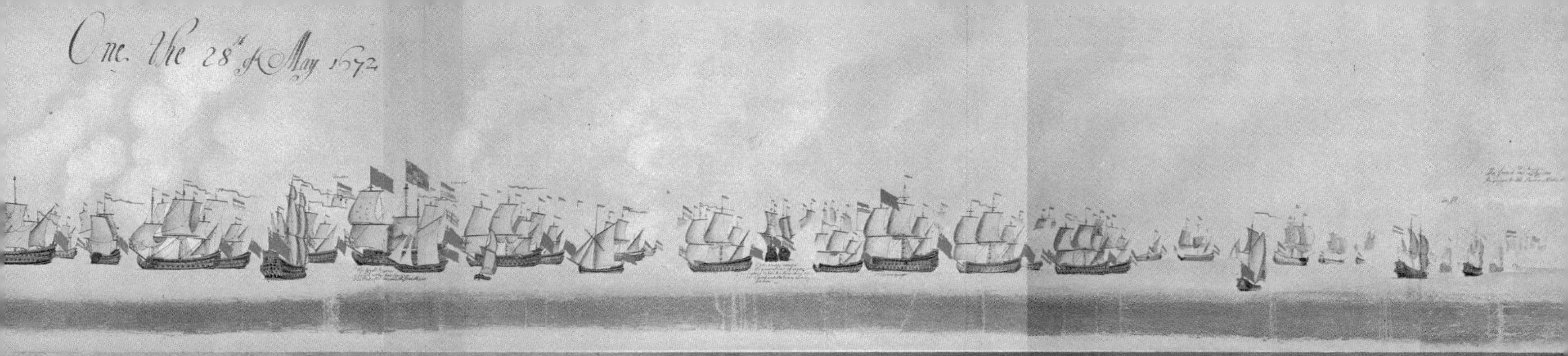
One. the 28th of May 1672

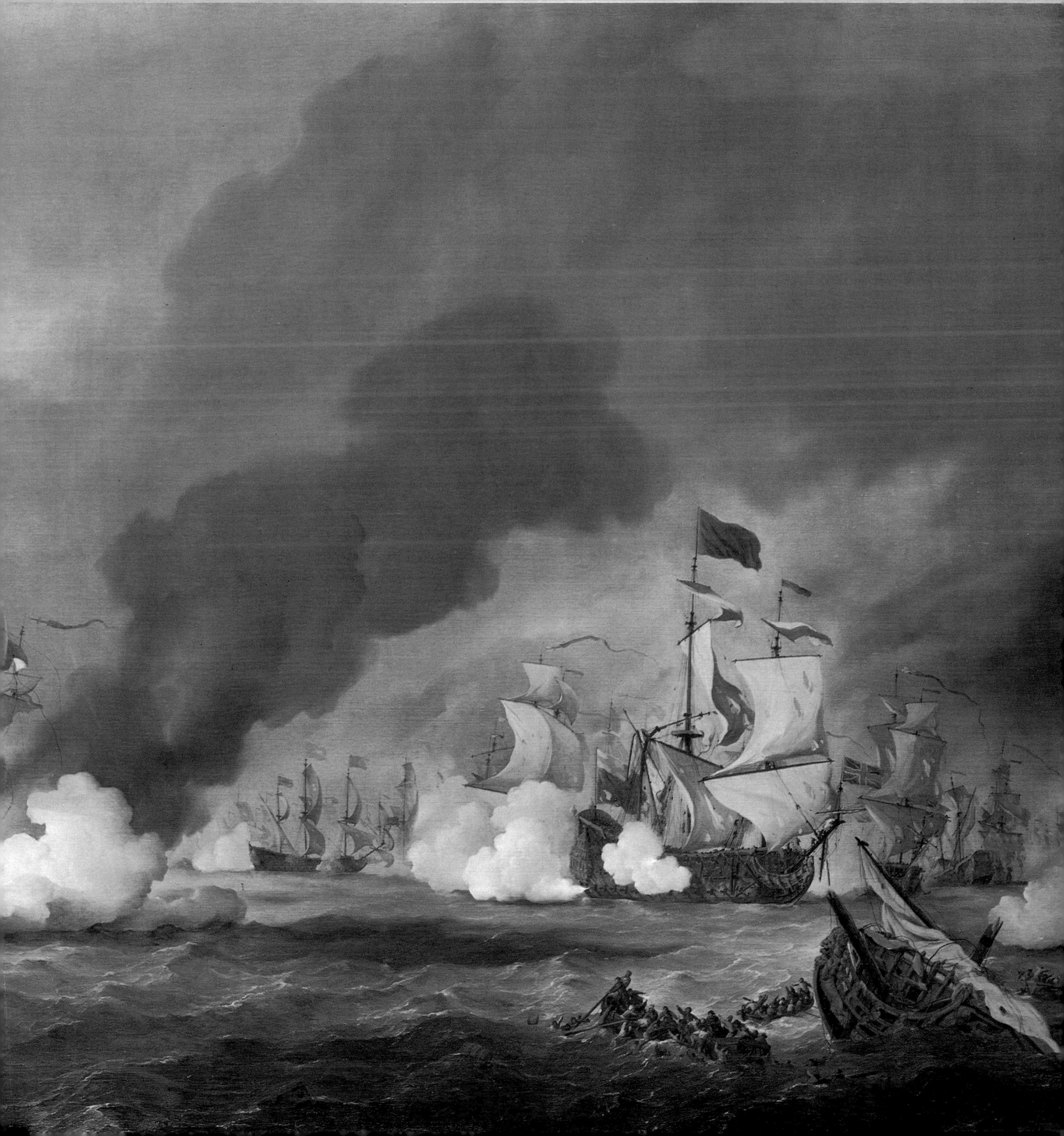

XXXI

XXXII

178
The *Mordaunt*, originally a privateer. NMM No 598. Elder, ?1681. Inscribed 'mordhent'.

Variant Fourth Rates

As noted in Chapter 3, the Navy had experimented in the 1640s with auxiliary oar propulsion for some of the smaller 4th Rates. There is no reason to doubt the success of the vessels so equipped, but the provision of sweep ports became rare after about 1650. In the mid-1670s Charles II heard about a French oared vessel of a new type–probably *La Bien-Aimée*, 24 guns, built at Toulon in 1672. At the King's request Deane investigated and in due course obtained the details of the design. Based on this the Navy produced in 1676 the 32-gun *Charles Galley* and the 30-gun *James Galley*. The *Charles* was built at Woolwich by Phineas Pett (grandson of 'old' Phineas), whilst the *James* was built at Blackwall by Deane's son, also named Anthony. In these ships everything was sacrificed for speed. They were very narrow for their length and had unusually fine lines. They were ship-rigged two-deckers, but only the upper deck had a full tier of guns. Except for a single broadside port aft (two in the *Charles*) and another forward, the lower tier was reserved exclusively for sweep ports. Despite their rather light armament (all sakers, except for 3pdrs on the quarterdeck) they were classed as 4th Rates.

The construction of the galley-frigates caused hardship for the Thames Watermen's Company, 160 of whose members were impressed to work the oars. Because of the requirement for rowers they were rather uneconomical to operate. Even so they were highly successful ships. Under sail they showed up well against the yacht *Katherine* in a specially staged race, and in combat they proved very effective against the Mediterranean corsairs.

Through several intermediate stages the *Charles Galley* and *James Galley*–with credit to *La Bien-Aimée*–were the ancestors of the famous frigates of Nelson's day. The key feature became the location of the main armament on the upper deck. The sweeps which had been the *raison d'être* of the original versions became rare after the mid-1700s. One of the last of the true galley-frigates was the American *Confederacy*, 32 guns, built in 1778 and captured by the Royal Navy in 1781.

Another unusual 4th Rate was the 46-gun *Kingfisher* built in 1675. She was intended to masquerade as a merchantman to lure unsuspecting Algerine corsairs to their destruction. Her upper deck guns were hidden behind false bulwarks which could be dropped in a few seconds. She was provided with various means of changing her appearance, including a removable figurehead. In World War I the Royal Navy used a similar scheme–the Q-ships–to entrap German U-boats. Like the Parliamentary and early Commonwealth frigates, the *Kingfisher* was initially built without a forecastle. This omission turned out to be no less of a nuisance than it had been in the earlier vessels, but a forecastle was not added to the ship until 1685.

The *Kingfisher* was engaged against the corsairs on several occasions. The most notable came in 1681,

when under the command of Captain Morgan Kempthorne she was attacked by seven Algerine men-of-
war. After a twelve-hour fight in which her captain was
killed, the *Kingfisher* drove off her assailants. Kemp-

thorne's father was Admiral Sir John Kempthorne. By
an odd coincidence Sir John had himself defeated
seven Algerines while commanding the *Mary Rose* in
1669.

179

179, 180
The galley-frigate *James* (179)
and the slightly larger *Charles*
(180). The cook is evidently at
work on the *Charles*; note the
wisp issuing from the galley
chimney on the forecastle.

175. Boymans No 345. Elder, c1676.

176. NMM No 538. Elder, c1676.
Inscribed 'd sarles galeij'.

181, 182
The success of the *Charles Galley*
and *James Galley* led the
Admiralty in 1681 to rebuild the
old 4th Rate *Tiger* as a
galley-frigate.

181. NMM No 1220. Elder, 1681. This
and many other drawings of the *Tiger* were
probably made during the King's visit to
the ship shortly after she was launched.

182. Boymans No 356. Elder, 1681.
Inscribed by the Elder 'de nieu theiger',
and by the Younger 'de Nieuw theijger'.

180

181

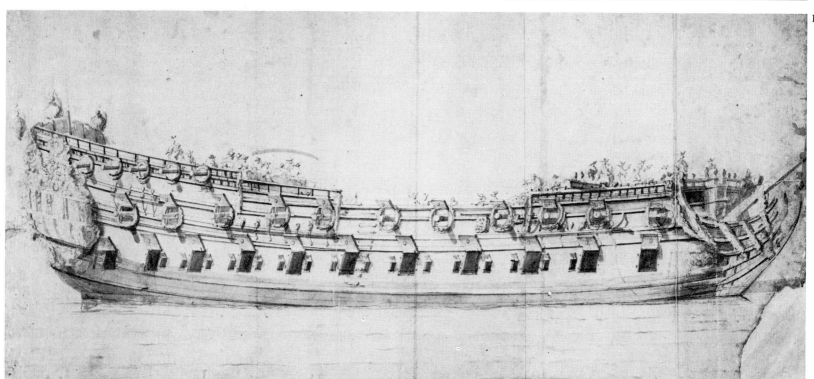

Fifth Rates

In Charles II's reign 5th Rates became somewhat anomalous. They were poorly suited for commerce raiding for the simple reason that they were outgunned by many of the merchantmen worth taking. Their 'popgun' ordnance contributed next to nothing to the battle line, and their former use as advice boats for relaying orders was better accomplished by the more nimble 6th Rates and yachts. Most of the 5th Rates acquired by capture were converted to fireships, and the few English-built units were usually employed for patrolling distant stations in India, North America, and the Caribbean.

If many of the 2nd Rates could be described as 'three-deckers spoilt' then most of the 5th Rates were 'two-deckers spoilt'. They had a complete lower tier, but the upper deck was unarmed in the waist. Of the seven built in the reign of Charles II, four–the *Falcon* (1666), *Sweepstakes* (1666), *Nonsuch* (1668), and *Phoenix* (1671)–were found to be capable of bearing 4th Rate armament and were reclassified within a few years of their completion.

Fifth Rates were often used as testbeds for new ideas. One of these was a strange shipbuilding theory proposed by Sir Lawrence Van Heemskirk and John de Morelyn, two foreigners in the King's service. They claimed that they could design a ship which would be 50 per cent faster than any other in the fleet. The much-publicised plan, however, turned out to involve nothing more than the orientation of the grain of the timbers. Even so the King ordered Sir Anthony Deane to build a ship to test the idea, and the *Nonsuch* of 1668 was the result. She did prove to be very speedy, but almost everyone realised that it was because of Deane's skill and not the theory. Heemskirk and de Morelyn never received more than a fraction of the £20,000 they had been promised for a successful test.

In a more sensible experiment the bottom of Deane's *Phoenix* was sheathed with lead to provide further improvements in speed and to protect the hull against

183
A typical 5th Rate, the 36-gun *Garland*, or *Guardland* (ex-*Grantham* of 1654). She eventually became a fireship.

V&A No 4699, c1673. Inscribed 'fergadt Garland' (frigate *Garland*).

wood-boring marine organisms. This was initially considered successful and sheathing was applied to a number of other vessels. However, the treatment had to be abandoned when it was found that the electrolytic action of seawater dissolved the iron fastenings. The English had better luck in the eighteenth century using copper sheathing with copper fastenings. The Spanish, by using lead fastenings, had successfully employed lead sheathing since the mid-1500s. The *Phoenix* was also famous for her performance at the Battle of Solebay. When the 3rd Rate *Cambridge* was disabled and forced to fall out of the line, the brave little *Phoenix* took her place although she had already exhausted her ammunition.

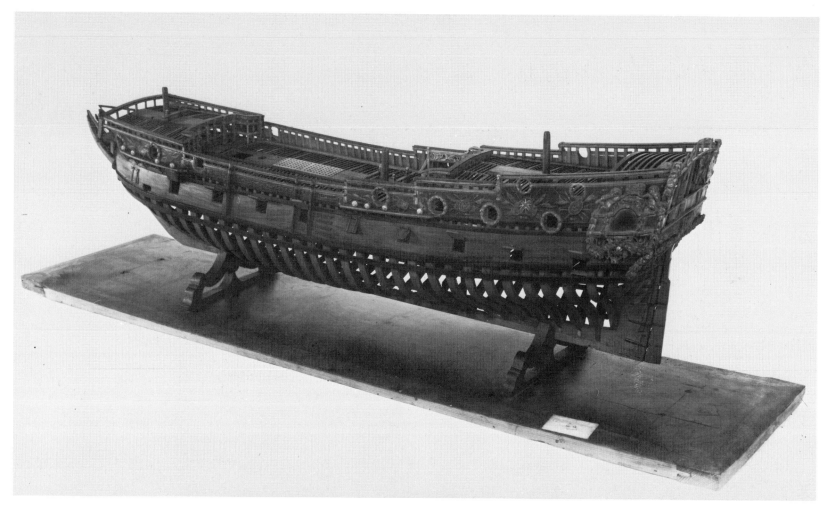

184
Dockyard model of a large 5th Rate of about 1670, showing an incomplete upper tier. This could be a design for the *Falcon, Sweepstakes, Nonsuch,* or *Phoenix.*

NMM

185
The *Phoenix,* shown as a 4th Rate in 1675 with a complete upper tier. The *Falcon, Sweepstakes,* and *Nonsuch* were similarly modified.

NMM No 489. Younger, 1675. Inscribed 'd feenicx 1675'.

8. The Thirty Ships
1678-1685

186, 187
The *Lenox* (186) and *Hampton Court* (187). Among the new 3rd Rates they were unusual in having only twelve gunports in the upper tier. In these drawings the ships are pierced for only 60 guns, but in wartime additional pieces were mounted on the forecastle and poop. Another ship, the *Captain*, had the same configuration.

186. Boymans No 364. Elder, 1678. Inscribed 'Leonoox'.

187. Goethe Museum, Weimar. Elder, 1678. Inscribed 'hamptkort'.

As the unpopular Third Anglo-Dutch War ground to a close in 1674, there was a strong desire throughout the country for economy. At first this feeling was shared even by the King and the Admiralty. The Navy's debts were so great that a large shipbuilding programme seemed out of the question. After all, was not the fleet, with six new 1st Rates afloat and another on the stocks, at the greatest level of strength it had ever attained? With the other sea powers at each other's throats, what could England have to fear anyway?

There were some in the naval administration who found this attitude disturbing. Chief among them were Pepys and Deane. They both realised that the Royal Navy, however strong on paper, had never overcome the numerical superiority the Dutch had obtained in 1667. Colbert had so enlarged the French Marine–and was continuing to do so–that England had actually fallen to third place. The deficit was not in numbers alone. Fully half of the King's ships were at least twenty years old, and many were in a poor state of repair, whilst most of the Dutch vessels and nearly all of the

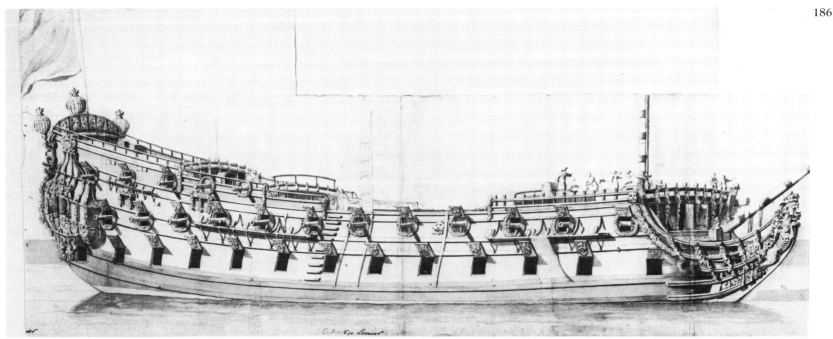

186

187

French were of quite recent vintage. The late war had already demonstrated that it had become impossible to defeat either power without the assistance of the other.

Deane, the Commissioner at Portsmouth, was too far from London to exert much influence. Pepys, however, had gained the full confidence of the King. In 1673 he had been given the job of Secretary of the newly appointed Admiralty Commission and, of equal importance, he had a seat in the Commons. Thus fortified, he set out to restore the power of the Navy. The first step was to win over the King and the Admiralty. This was accomplished without much difficulty by the end of 1674; but the Commons, dominated by powerful anti-Stuart forces, was another matter. It met in April of 1675. Pepys boldly requested funds to build no less than two 1st Rates, seven 2nd Rates, twenty-seven 3rd Rates and four 4th Rates. The Opposition blandly suggested that the money be taken from the Customs receipts. Pepys patiently explained that the under-strength fleet was already using every penny from the Customs. Before the hopeless argument could proceed any further the Lords and Commons became embroiled in an internal dispute, and Charles prorogued the Parliament until the autumn.

The next session, opening in October, was a frustrating one for Pepys. After three weeks of debate, £300,000 was grudgingly voted for the construction of one 1st Rate, five 2nd Rates and fourteen 3rd Rates. But nothing came of it. In the next week the Opposition fought back, amending the bill to require the funds to be obtained from Customs. In the face of such obstinance on this and other issues, the King had no choice but to prorogue the Houses. No Parliament met for fourteen months, during which time the Navy was reduced to a skeletal force, with only a few small ships in commission even in the summer.

Parliament met at last in February 1677, and Pepys renewed his campaign. By then many of the members were finally becoming aware of the growing power of France, and some appropriation seemed likely. Every-thing fell into place when the leaders of the Opposition, the Duke of Buckingham and the Earl of Shaftesbury, made a serious political blunder. Emboldened by their earlier successes and certain of their control of the electorate, they dared to demand new elections. Quoting an ancient statute, they claimed that the Commons was automatically dissolved because of the lengthy recess. Even their own political friends were outraged at the suggestion that the House was sitting illegally. The two were unceremoniously flung into the Tower. With the Opposition divided and softened by fear of the French, the King's forces carried the day. After a convincing speech by Pepys on 22 February, Parliament authorised on 5 March a sum of nearly £600,000 for one 1st Rate of 1400 tons, nine 2nd Rates of 1100 and twenty 3rd Rates of 900. All were to be completed within two years.

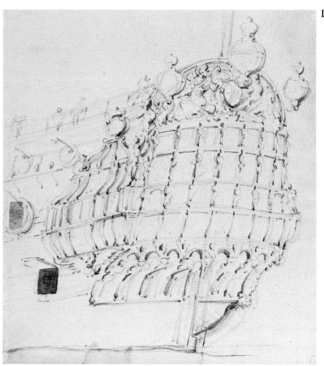

188

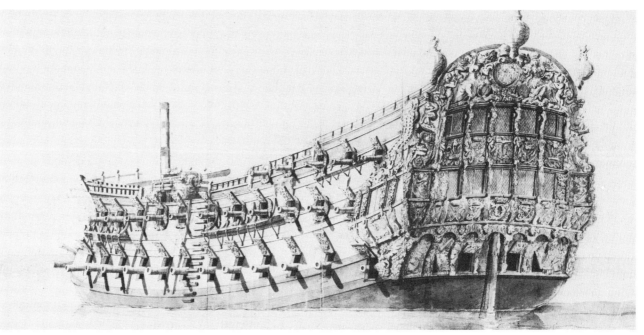

189

188, 189, 190
Port quarter details of the *Captain* (188), *Lenox* (189), and *Hampton Court* (190). Even when ships were planned as sisters, individual designs were prepared for stern decoration and quarter-galleries.

188. NMM No 1236. ?Elder, c1685.

189. Boymans No 362. Detail from a drawing by the Elder, c1678.

190. Boymans No 359. Detail from a drawing by the Elder, c1678. Inscribed 'hamptkoordt'.

191, 192
The 3rd Rate *Hope* (191) and
the very similar *Elizabeth*. When
seventeenth century two-deckers
had the same number of gunports
in both tiers, the upper deck
ports were usually crowded
towards the bow. These two
ships were unusual in that the
crowding occurred aft.

191. Boymans No 365. Elder, *c*1680.
Inscribed '. . . op'.

192. Boymans No 366. Elder, *c*1680.
Contains a partially cut-off inscription
with a double-letter combination which
can be read either as 'ff' (as in *Suffolk*) or
'ss' (as in *Essex* or *Elissabets*, as Van de
Velde might have spelled *Elizabeth*). The
ship is so similar to Captain Castle's *Hope*
that it seems most likely to be his other
3rd Rate, the *Elizabeth*. Van de Velde
included a very distant view of the *Suffolk*
in a drawing in the British Museum, and
spelled the name 'sudtfolck'.

191

192

The credit for the passage of this appropriation belongs almost entirely to Samuel Pepys. It is unlikely that the ships could have been obtained without his efforts, and in later years he considered their acquisition the greatest achievement of his career.

Planning and Design

The Royal Navy had never attempted to build on such a large scale. The Admiralty Commission itself–under the *de facto* leadership of Pepys–co-ordinated the planning for the programme. It met frequently during the spring with the King and the Navy Board sitting in most of the time. Despite everyone's desire to complete the ships as soon as possible, it was prudently decided to give equal attention to the needs of the existing fleet before it became too late. Accordingly, thirty decayed ships were docked for repairs during the summer and autumn. For some ships it was already too late. The 3rd Rate *Revenge* and the 4th Rate *Princess* and *Yarmouth* were found to be entirely rotten and were broken up.

The 1677 programme entailed great demands on the nation's manpower, timber resources, and transportation facilities. To obtain extra carpenters and dockyard workers, press warrants were issued for compulsory service. The Navy's normal suppliers of oak were able to provide only a fraction of the required compass timber, and the Navy Board's purveyors were empowered to search private parks and estates throughout the country for additional supplies. Larger orders were also placed for East Country plank and deals from the Baltic. For transportation the Crown invoked the right to requisition animals and wagons wherever it chose. Many of these measures were unpopular, but the blows were much softened by the Navy Board being able–for once–to pay in hard cash rather than credit.

The design of the new ships was much influenced by Charles himself. Noting that the tonnages specified by Parliament compared unfavourably with French warships, he ordered the dimensions to be increased. When told that this would entail more expense than the Act authorised, he promised that 'he would make it good out of his own purse rather than hazard the wronging of the ships for want of it'. The King also insisted that all masts, spars, rigging, and fittings be standardised for each rate to simplify maintenance. At Pepys' urging, standardisation was also extended to cover the ordnance establishments. While there was no intention of making the decoration uniform, its style and application were carefully controlled. These very sensible policies marked the first serious efforts on the part of the Admiralty to take naval architecture out of the sometimes capricious hands of the master-shipwrights.

193

193, 194
Dockyard model of an unidentified 3rd Rate showing upper deck ports crowded aft in the manner of the *Hope* and *Elizabeth*. The stern contains Charles II's cipher and the date 1684 is carved in the stand. The rigging is not original and contains several mistakes. The decoration cannot be linked to any known ship, but both the gunport arrangement and the unusual quarter-gallery supports are suggestive of the *Hope* and *Elizabeth*.

Photos: USNA museum. Model last noted in the Vienna Museum of Technology.

Specifications of the 1677 Programme

Rate	Gundeck Length (ft)	External Beam (ft in)	Depth in Hold (ft in)
1st	165	46 0	19 2
2nd	158	44 0	18 2
3rd	150	39 8	17 0

Ordnance Establishments of the 1677 Programme

1st Rate

Lower Deck	26 cannon-of-seven
Middle Deck	28 culverins
Upper Deck	28 sakers
Quarterdeck	12 light sakers
Forecastle	4 light sakers
Poop	2 3pdrs
Total	**100**

2nd Rates

Lower Deck	26 demi-cannon
Middle Deck	26 culverins
Upper Deck	26 sakers
Quarterdeck	10 light sakers
Poop	2 3pdrs
Total	**90**

3rd Rates

Lower Deck	26 demi-cannon
Upper Deck	26 12pdrs
Quarterdeck	10 light sakers
Forecastle	4 light sakers
Poop	4 3pdrs
Total	**70**

Construction

Because of the competing maintenance requirements of the older vessels, only fifteen of the new ships were laid down immediately. Of these, three 2nd Rates and eleven 3rd Rates were assigned to the royal dockyards. One more 3rd Rate was ordered on contract from Francis Bayley, the elderly Bristol shipwright who had built the *Edgar* of 1668. The Admiralty had originally intended that none of the ships be built by contract. It was felt that the private builders – especially those in the Thames – would be in competition with the royal dockyards for desperately needed manpower and materials, driving up prices. Besides, the prevailing view in the naval administration was that a contractor would 'perform his work as slightly as he can' to increase the profits. Bayley's contract was granted only because his facility was too distant from the royal yards to pose any threat. He also had an excellent reputation, and his price of £9 per ton was too good to pass up. Bayley's ship, the *Northumberland*, was launched in 1679, but her designer died before she was completed.

The Admiralty ordered that the first group of ships be launched as soon as they would float. They could then be finished alongside—in Continental fashion – while other hulls could be laid down on the vacated slips. Even so it was becoming apparent by late 1677 that the royal dockyards were falling behind schedule. The second instalment was to include one 1st Rate, six 2nd Rates and eight 3rd Rates. The construction of the three-deckers, especially, placed heavy demands on the dockyards' resources. Furthermore, space and materials still had to be reserved for the maintenance needs of the existing vessels. In January the Admiralty reluctantly directed the Navy Board to arrange contracts for four 3rd Rates to be built by Sir Henry Johnson at Blackwall and two more by Captain William Castle at Deptford. Castle and Johnson would not agree to a price below £10 10s 0d per ton (exclusive of masts and spars) but this was finally accepted. Their work was closely supervised by Sir John Tippetts (Surveyor of the Navy) and Commissioner Deane. The construction of the contract vessels proceeded smoothly. Castle completed the *Hope* before the end of the year and the *Elizabeth* in the next, while Johnson's *Essex* and *Kent* were launched in 1679 and the *Exeter* and *Suffolk* in 1680.

All the 3rd Rates and five of the 2nd Rates were afloat by the end of 1680, but by then dockyard activity had slowed markedly. This was largely due to the political and civil disturbances caused by the so-called 'Popish Plot' which erupted in 1678. Although this had nothing to do with the Navy, its reverberations undermined the King's Parliamentary position. Feeding on the Plot, the Opposition became strong enough in 1679 to force Charles to dismiss the entire Admiralty Commission. Pepys actually spent several weeks in the Tower on false charges of popery and treason. The new and inexperienced Commission was pathetically inept, and the last ship was not ready until 1685.

The Third Rates

The twenty 3rd Rates of the 1677 programme were the most numerous class of seventeenth century warships to be built to a single set of specifications, although this does not mean that the ships were identical. Restoration shipwrights understood specifications to be minimums, and most of the new 3rd Rates were larger than the establishment required. They averaged about 151ft on the gundeck and most were between 40 and 41ft in beam.

Many portraits of these vessels were produced by marine artists, including Van de Velde drawings of almost photographic quality. At present, representations of at least seventeen of the 3rd Rates are known, of which ten can be satisfactorily matched with names. The drawings show that the Admiralty actually allowed the shipwrights a certain amount of experimentation in designing some features. One ship, the *Berwick*, built by Sir Phineas Pett at Chatham, is known to have had a triple lower wale, whilst only a few of the vessels had their gunports arranged in the establishment pattern, most having non-standard numbers of ports in the upperworks. In addition, three of the early units–the *Lenox*, *Hampton Court*, and *Captain*–had only twelve ports in the upper tier. Of these, the first two were built by John Shish in the King's yard at Deptford, while the third was produced by John's brother Thomas at Woolwich. The three vessels were so similar that it seems probable that the brothers–sons of Jonas Shish–used the same draughts.

The 3rd Rates of 1678–80, as portrayed by the Van de Veldes, must rank among the best-looking warships ever built. Their hulls appeared lean and graceful, and the carvings, while elaborate, were harmonious and attractive. There were a number of new decorative features. In earlier vessels the headrails had joined in a whorl beneath the bowsprit, but from 1678 they terminated separately in the back of the figurehead. The latter was still a lion, but it was now accompanied by various cherubic figures. The taffrail, or upper margin of the stern, was no longer broken by carving but formed a smooth lunate curve. All the two-deckers had two rows of large stern windows and most, but not all, had open stern galleries. The Stuart arms were usually to be found somewhere on the stern, but often without the traditional lion and unicorn. The decorative patterns used in the Thirty Ships were also adapted to the older vessels that were under repair at the same time. The close stylistic similarities among the ships decorated and redecorated in this period points strongly to some centralised control. The authors of the new style remain unknown, but their influence was so great that no significant changes in fashion occurred for the next quarter of a century.

The 3rd Rates were all tested against the French in the reign of William III. The *Pendennis* and *Elizabeth* fought at Bantry Bay in 1689, the *Elizabeth* serving as a flagship. Fourteen were in the line at Beachy Head in 1690 and sixteen were present at Barfleur in 1692. The *Anne* was badly damaged at Beachy Head and had to be run ashore after the battle, being finally destroyed by fireships. In later years both of Captain Castle's ships suffered the indignity of being captured by the French, the *Hope* in 1695 and the *Elizabeth* in 1704. Three other losses were due to mishaps. The *Pendennis* was wrecked in 1689, and accidental explosions claimed the *Breda* in 1690 and the *Exeter* in 1691. Between 1699 and 1702 the surviving units were rebuilt (except for the *Captain*, whose rebuilding was delayed until 1708, and the *Elizabeth*). After this they continued to gain battle honours; several were at Vigo and Malaga, and the *Expedition* became famous as Sir Charles Wager's flagship at Cartagena. It should be noted, however, that the rebuilt versions actually had little in common with the original vessels, except their names. In the case of the *Hampton Court*, which was probably typical, the dockyard was ordered to 'take down and remove all the old decayed materials . . . and from the bottom or any part so remaining make a new ship of the same size'.

195
Dockyard model of the *Grafton*, photographed in its unrestored state in the early 1900s, with the sternpiece and head missing, along with the wreath around the foremost upper deck gunport. The positions of the gunports, hances, and upper wales correspond exactly to those in the Van de Velde drawings of the *Grafton*. Indeed, except for a different quarter-galley and a few extra gunports on the forecastle, poop, and the forward end of the quarterdeck, the completed ship was almost identical to the model. The model was first identified as the *Grafton* on the basis of a medallion at the break of the quarterdeck containing the arms of Admiral Lord Dartmouth. The *Grafton* was Dartmouth's flagship in 1683-84. It must have been after that time that the Admiral obtained the model and placed his arms on it. The model was probably made in 1677-78 as a preliminary design. Before the model was obtained by the Naval Academy it was unfortunately restored almost beyond recognition.

USNA Museum

196

This may be Sir Henry Johnson's *Suffolk* or *Essex*. Note the two-level quarter-gallery which was fitted to several of the new 3rd Rates.

NMM No 606. Younger, *c*1685. Contains a cut-off inscription with a double-letter combination which could be either 'ss' or 'ff'.

197, 198

The 3rd Rates built by Thomas Shish of Woolwich differed noticeably from each other in both decoration and gunport arrangement – the *Burford* (197) and the *Grafton* (198).

197. Boymans No 363. Elder, *c*1685.

198. NMM No 1209. Younger, *c*1685. Inscribed 'd grafton'.

199
A 3rd Rate at sea, probably the
Stirling Castle.

British Museum. ?Elder, c1685.

The Second Rates

The dimensions planned for the nine 2nd Rates appear to have been copied directly from those of the 96-gun *St Andrew* of 1670, whilst the armament was arranged on the logical pattern of the *St Michael*. Both the *St Andrew* and the *St Michael* were classed as 1st Rates,

and the 90-gun ships of the 1677 programme would certainly have been called 1st Rates a few years earlier. In fact they, like the new 3rd Rates, were given greater dimensions than the establishment required. In some cases the increase was considerable. The *Neptune*, with a gundeck of 163ft 1in and a beam of 45ft, was actually larger than the 100-gun *Royal James* of 1675.

160

200

The *Stirling Castle,* showing gunports arranged on the 'establishment' pattern. This drawing was made at her launching in 1679.

NMM No 571. Elder, 1679. Inscribed 'de Lense vande sterlings kastell' (the launching of the *Stirling Castle).*

201, 202

The *Anne* (201) and *Restoration.*

201. Boymans No 327. Younger *c*1685. Inscribed 'de Anna'.

202. Boymans No 408. Elder, *c*1685. Inscribed 'de Restoratijon'.

201

202

203

203, 204
Two unidentified 3rd Rates of
the 1677 programme. These very
similar vessels display a not
uncommon gunport
arrangement, with provision for
up to 74 guns. Both ships appear
in several Van de Velde works,
but never with inscriptions.

203. NMM No 1243. Younger, *c*1685.

204. V&A No D138-1888. Younger,
*c*1685.

204

205

205, 206, 207
Among the earlier 2nd Rates to
be completed were the *Windsor
Castle* (205, 207) and the
Duchess (206). Note the
differences in gunport
arrangement. The configuration
of the *Duchess* was the most
common, with thirteen ports in
each tier and six a side on the
quarterdeck.

205. Boymans No 367. Elder, *c*1678.
Inscribed 'Windsor Kastoll'.

206. NMM No 605. Younger, *c*1680.
Inscribed 'd dusses'.

207. NMM No 1231. Elder, *c*1678.

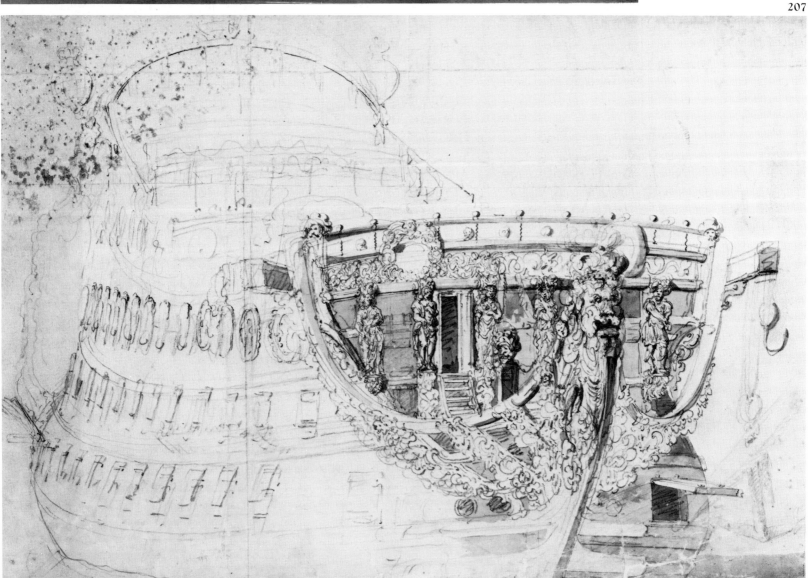

The '90s' also carried a greater weight of ordnance than some of the earlier 1st Rates, but despite this their broadsides were less powerful. The reasons for this seemingly backward step are not certain. Part of the explanation may be that earlier three-deckers had been at least partly equipped with brass ordnance. Cast iron guns such as those ordered for the 1677 programme were only one-eighth as expensive as brass, but they were somewhat brittle. To prevent bursting they had to be fortified with extra-thick metal, and were consequently much heavier. The guns of the new ships were, however, unusually massive even for iron ordnance. It may be that they were early examples of the more reliable 'double-fortified' pieces which became standard in the next century. Whatever the reason, the penalty was that to avoid excessive topweight the

90-gun ships had to be equipped with smaller calibres than earlier vessels of comparable tonnage: demi-cannon on the lower deck in place of cannon-of-seven, and sakers instead of demi-culverins on the upper deck. This represented a substantial drop in firepower, but since the ships were only classed as 2nd Rates it does not seem to have been criticised.

Weight of ordnance of the new '90's compared with the 'Charles' and the 'St Michael'

	Weight of Ordnance (tons)	Weight of shot (lb)*
Charles (96)	155	1902
St Michael (90)	138.75	1590
'90's of 1678-85	159.30	512

*The data for this and the following table were taken from the Establishment of 1677. See Appendix IV.

All of the 2nd Rates were produced by the royal dockyards; no one even considered having such impor-tant ships built by contract. The *Windsor Castle* and *Duke* were built at Woolwich by Thomas Shish, while John Shish of Deptford built the *Duchess* and *Neptune*. The *Ossory*, *Vanguard*, and *Coronation* were built at Portsmouth, the first two by Daniel Furzer and the *Coronation* by Isaac Betts. Betts also built two others, the *Albemarle* and *Sandwich*, at Harwich. Although five were completed in good time, the others were long delayed. The *Ossory* and *Duke* were completed in 1682 and the *Neptune* in 1683. The *Coronation*, held up by shortages of money and materials, was not launched until 1685.

The Van de Veldes produced drawings of at least six of the 2nd Rates. With lion figureheads, lunate taffrails and ornate circular port-wreaths, they were consistent with the 3rd Rates in decoration, and they seem to have been more uniform than the smaller class in design. They generally followed the prescribed arma-ment distribution, except that most had an extra port on either side of the quarterdeck. All the 2nd Rates had space for extra armament on the forecastle and poop, and most were armed with 96 guns in later years. One of the earliest units, the *Windsor Castle*, was somewhat different from the others. She was lacking the usual luff port between the headrails and thus had only twelve gunports in the middle tier. Instead, her beakhead and rails were dropped low enough to allow a clear field of fire for a pair of middle deck bow chasers pointing through ports in the bulkhead. This arrange-ment had been common in earlier three-deckers, but by the 1670s it had become an anachronism.

Every unit was in action at either Beachy Head or Barfleur, the *Windsor Castle*, *Sandwich*, *Albemarle*, and *Duchess* contributing their broadsides on both occa-sions. None was lost in battle, but the *Coronation* was wrecked in 1691 and the *Windsor Castle* suffered the same fate in 1693.

The *Vanguard* became one of the many victims of the Great Storm of 1703. Accompanied by gales of tornado force, this storm raked southern England on the night of 26/27 November. It killed over 1500 of the Navy's seamen and claimed many important Restora-tion and Commonwealth warships. Among the vessels wrecked were the rebuilt 3rd Rates *Resolution*, *Stirling Castle*, *Restoration*, and *Northumberland*, plus the battle scarred old *Mary* (ex-*Speaker* of 1650). Several smaller ships were also destroyed, including the rebuilt Com-monwealth 4th Rates *Newcastle* and *Reserve*. The *York* of 1654, a near-sister of the *Mary*, had been lost two days earlier in a forerunner of the main gale. The *Vanguard* was in ordinary off Chatham and simply sank at her mooring; thus by an odd coincidence her resting place was only a short distance from where the previous *Vanguard* had been sunk in 1667. Thanks to prompt salvage efforts she was successfully raised and restored to service, but the other unlucky ships were caught at sea and lost forever.

Plate XXXIII
A 3rd Rate in a storm, possibly the *Hampton Court*. Identified on the basis of similarity to Van de Velde drawings of the *Hampton Court*, but the very similar *Captain* remains a possibility as well. The often reproduced painting at Greenwich called '3rd Rates in a storm' is a copy of this picture and its now-missing mate.

Birmingham Museums and Art Gallery. Painting by the Younger.

Plate XXXIV
English warships becalmed. In the foreground is an unidentified 3rd Rate of the 1677 programme, while one of the nine 2nd Rates is in the middle distance on the right.

NMM. Painting by the Elder.

Plate XXXV
A very fine dockyard model of a 90-gun ship of the 1677 programme. This model bears James II's ciphers, and for that reason it has been traditionally identified as the *Coronation*, the only unit not yet launched at the time of Charles II's death. However, it may be that only the decoration dates from James' reign, while the original hull could have been made as early as 1677 to show the preliminary design for the entire class. Evidence for this is that the gunports are arranged in the 'establishment' pattern, with five ports a side on the quarterdeck. All Van de Velde portraits of units completed after 1678 show six quarterdeck ports.

Kriegstein Family Collection, Roslyn, New York.

Plate XXXVI
The *Lenox* (right) and an old 4th Rate passing Greenwich in the early morning light.

Los Angeles County Museum of Art. Painting by Jan van Beecq.

Plate XXXVII
The *Britannia*. An accurate painting by Isaac Sailmaker showing both broadside and stern views.

From a private collection. Painting by Isaac Sailmaker, c1685.

XXXV

XXXIV

XXXVI

XXXVII

In Charles II's reign the magnitude of the disaster would have been far smaller since in his time no large vessels would have been in commission so late in the year. Admiral Sir Clowdisley Shovell had cautioned that 'an admiral would deserve to be broke who kept great-ships out after the end of September, and to be shot if after October'. Proving his own point, Sir Clowdisley was killed in 1707 when his flagship, the 96-gun *Association*, was wrecked with the loss of all hands in a late-October storm.

All the remaining 2nd Rates of the 1677 programme were broken up in the early 1700s and rebuilt as entirely new ships. One of these, the *Neptune*, was renamed *Torbay* in 1750. With her upper deck removed she became the first English-built example of the famous '74s' that formed the backbone of the fleet in the time of Rodney, Howe, and Nelson.

The 'Britannia'

The only 1st Rate of the 1677 programme was laid down at Chatham in June 1679. Christened *Britannia*, she was launched three years later amid much fanfare. Her builder was Sir Phineas Pett, who had previously produced the *Prince* of 1670.

Many of the earlier 1st Rates, including the *Prince*, had suffered from instability caused by a combination of excessive topweight and inadequate beam. The rest of the Thirty Ships are said to have carried their lower tier higher than had been previously customary, and the *Britannia* was no exception. To provide the extra stability–and more–required by the increased height of the batteries, Pett gave his new design much beamier proportions than he had allowed for his earlier 1st Rate. While he made the *Britannia* only 2in longer than the *Prince*, he provided an increase of 3½in in beam. This was 16in in excess of the specifications. With such a generous beam the *Britannia* should have been the masterpiece of Restoration naval architecture. Unfortunately, it was not to be.

The 'Britannia's' armament compared with that of the 'Prince' and the 'Royal Sovereign'

	Weight of Ordnance (tons)	Weight of shot (lb)
Prince	173	1930
Royal Sovereign	177	2098
Britannia	187.40	1850

Although Sir Phineas had stretched the specifications as far as he could, there was still insufficient allowance for the massive weight of ordnance the authorities expected the ship to bear. As was true of all the Thirty Ships, the *Britannia* was assigned guns which were unusually heavy for their calibres. As a concession her upper tier was lightened by the substitution of sakers for the standard demi-culverins, but beyond that the Admiralty was not willing to go. With her weak upper deck armament she already compared poorly in offensive power with the existing 1st Rates, and any further sacrifices might place her at a disadvantage against the French. Her cannon-of-seven weighed 6500lb apiece, almost 20 per cent more than those of the *Charles* of 1668. The lower deck armament alone

weighed more than the entire establishment of many 3rd Rates. The result was that the *Britannia*, like so many other 1st Rates, turned out to be a top-heavy 'slug'.

The defects did not become apparent at first, because the ship was not commissioned for several years after her completion. The *Britannia*'s full wartime armament was not loaded aboard until 1690, when the long-expected trial of arms with the French finally materialised. She was found to be so unstable that no one dared to risk her at sea without major modifications. The Admiralty sadly ordered her to be docked, and she consequently missed the first of the great clashes in the Channel. The ship received a thick girdling, of fir, for some reason, increasing the beam to 48ft 8in.

By 1691, the *Britannia* was again ready for sea. The following year she served as Lord Russell's flagship at Barfleur, where she was matched against the Comte de Tourville's mighty *Soleil-Royal*. Both ships were crippled in the encounter, but the outnumbered French fleet was eventually forced to retire. Tourville's reluctance to abandon his shattered flagship was an important factor in the success of the Anglo-Dutch pursuit, leading to the destruction of the French 'great ships' at La Hogue and Cherbourg.

The *Britannia* gained enough glory at Barfleur to secure a place among the Navy's most famous warships, but she was never in action again. Even after the girdling in 1690 the ship's overloaded hull continued to give trouble. A great repair was administered in 1700–01, but she finally had to be broken up in 1715, the serviceable timbers being used in the construction of a new *Britannia* which was launched in 1719 and survived until 1749.

210, 211
A famous – and controversial – dockyard model of the *Britannia*. Some authorities have doubted its identification, but recent measurements based on the normal 1:48 scale show that its dimensions match with the *Britannia* with remarkable precision. The problems appear to stem from the fact that such models were usually preliminary designs, with further complications in this case since the present decorations date from 1701, when the *Britannia* received a great repair. The model originally had the *Britannia*'s gunport arrangement of 14 ports in the lower and middle tiers and 13 in the upper. However, the 1701 quarter-gallery covered up the aftermost middle tier port, while the foremost middle tier port – between the headrails – was blocked up so that its outline is now visible only on very close examination. The absence of gunports on the poop is not significant; they seldom appeared on Restoration ship models. The only real anomaly was that in the completed ship the model's foremost upper tier gunport was deleted and replaced by another at the after end of the tier. Incidentally, one highly unusual feature of the *Britannia* was shared with the model: an entry port on both sides.

USNA Museum.

The Final Years

The Thirty Ships returned the Royal Navy to at least parity with its principal Continental rivals. In the final years of Charles II's reign, however, the advances were very nearly undone. The Dutch and French naturally responded to the English programme with major ship-building efforts which were not answered in England. Even worse, the incompetent Admiralty Commission of 1679 allowed the brand new ships to lie unattended in ordinary. The results were appalling. The King finally dismissed the bumbling commission in 1684 and personally assumed the position of Lord High Admiral. To direct affairs he recalled Pepys, made him Secretary of the Admiralty, and gave him greater powers than he had ever held before. Pepys surveyed the Thirty Ships and, in his words, 'with my own hands gathered toad-stools growing in the most considerable of them, as big as my fists'. Some were found to be in imminent danger of sinking.

Before much could be done Charles II died in February 1685. He was succeeded by his brother, the Duke of York, who became King James II. The latter quickly established a 'Special Commission for the Recovery of the Navy', with Pepys as the principal executive. The efforts of James's commission succeeded in repairing the damage only to have the fleet turned against him after his fall in the Revolution of 1688. This upheaval brought William of Orange, an implacable foe of Louis XIV, to the English throne, sparking the confrontation with the French.

212
Bow of the *Britannia*.

NMM No 603. Elder, c1685. Inscribed 'De Britage' in a hand other than the artist's.

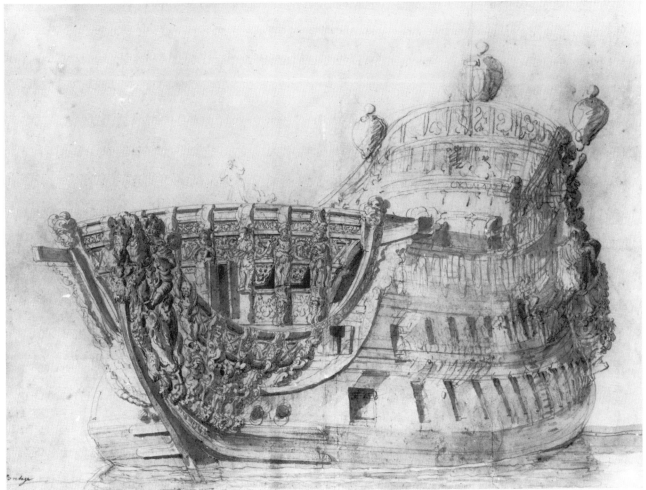

The battles of King William's War were a part of the history of the Restoration Navy every bit as much as Lowestoft and the Four Days. Of the eighty-odd English ships that took part in at least one of the three general actions of the war, only four–all 4th Rates–were built after the reign of Charles II.

The last great concentration of Restoration warships was the campaign of Barfleur and La Hogue in 1692. Many famous old veterans were in the line. Among the 1st rates were the *St Andrew*, *London* and the 55-year-old *Royal Sovereign*. The *Prince* was there as well, but by then she was known as the *Royal William*. For the *St Michael* it was the sixth battle, and for the *Royal Katherine* the ninth. There were Commonwealth 'frigates' like the *Monck*, *Lion* and *Ruby*, the last facing her twelfth–but not her final–fleet action. The *Lion*'s history could be traced through three rebuildings all the

way to the reign of Mary I. Also present were Sir Anthony Deane's *Resolution*, *Rupert* and *Swiftsure*, as were the products of Jonas Shish and whole generations of Petts. Pepys' Thirty Ships were the mainstays of the fleet: of the twenty-five that were still afloat, all took part, and they contributed nearly half the English firepower.

Since the Anglo-Dutch fleet at Barfleur had an overwhelming numerical advantage, it was not the complete victory it could have been. But it was decisive. It established the pattern for over two centuries of dominance by the Royal Navy. James II, who watched the grim events of La Hogue from the shore, had himself led many of the same English ships into battle. It is said that, despite his own misfortune, he could not help cheering their success.

213
The burning of the French 'great ships' off La Hogue.

NMM. Painting by Adriaen Van Diest.

Appendices

Appendix I: List of Ships in Service, 1660-1685

On 16 January 1668, Samuel Pepys wrote: 'My work this night with my clerks till midnight at the office was to examine my list of ships I am making for myself and their dimensions, and to see how it agrees or differs from other lists, and I do find so great a difference between them all that I am at a loss which to take, and therefore think mine to be as much depended upon as any I can make out of them all.' Anyone attempting to compile data on Restoration warships will find that the situation has changed but little since Pepys' time.

Variations in figures from list to list are due to a number of factors. These include outright errors, but the most important is that some dimensions could be measured in several ways which did not yield identical figures. Most earlier lists – including those compiled by the Admiralty itself – do not distinguish figures obtained by different methods. In the list below, every effort has been made to use consistently obtained data. However, in many cases the figures are all but impossible to verify.

Many sources were used to compile this list. The most important were Pepys' *Register of Ships,* preserved at Magdalene College, Cambridge; and the late Dr R C Anderson's *List of Men-of-War, 1650-1700, Part I (English Ships),* issued by the Society for Nautical Research as *Occasional Publication No 5.* In addition, some use was made of a Dimensions Book for 1701 in the possession of the author.

The list is arranged chronologically by Rate and type of craft. Ships obtained by capture are listed separately, but no attempt has been made to include the large number of vessels employed as fireships. In all likelihood some small craft have been omitted, while the dimensions of many ships – particularly those of the Early Stuart period – are of doubtful accuracy. Much of the data requires explanation:

Name: Shows only the name by which the ship was known in the reign of Charles II.

Date: In most cases the year of launching. The letter B indicates that the date is the year of purchase, and the letter G indicates the year a vessel was given to the Navy. The letter R indicates a rebuilding or major repair. For ships built before 1660 only the latest

known rebuilding or major repair is listed. Several vessels may have received repairs or rebuildings for which documentation is lacking.

Dockyard: The letter P following 'Deptford' in several cases indicates that the ship was built not in the royal dockyard but in a private facility.

Shipwright: The numbers following some entries distinguish shipwrights with identical names.

Gundeck: The length of the lower deck, from the rabbet of the stem to the rabbet of the sternpost.

Keel: In Charles II's reign two types of keel measurement were used for determining tonnage. The 'touch' figure was the length of the actual keel, measured from the point at which it abutted the stem. The other measurement was the 'harping' or 'calculated' keel, which was adopted in the 1660s or possibly a little before. This was the perpendicular length of the lower wale, or 'harping', minus three-fifths of the beam. For the larger vessels the calculated keel was some three to five feet longer than the touch measurement. To make length and tonnage comparisons more meaningful, an attempt has been made to provide separate listings for the two types. For vessels smaller than 3rd Rates there was not enough data to make the distinction possible, and for these ships all keel lengths have been arbitrarily listed under the 'touch' column. In any event the variation would not have been very great in these cases. Even with many large ships it was difficult to be certain in which column the 'traditional' keel lengths and tonnages belong. These have been indicated by italics.

Keels determined by yet a third method are listed by many authorities for ships built between 1678 and 1685. This was the 'tread' length, or the total distance from the foot of the sternpost to the angle formed by the cutwater. This resulted in an inflated tonnage which is useless for comparative purposes. It has not been listed here.

Beam: Normally measured outside the planking, but not including the wales. The letter G indicates a girdled beam.

Depth: Usually the perpendicular distance from the lowest point of the breadth line to the upper surface of the keel. No attempt has been made to list draught, a figure much too variable to be meaningful. For a large ship the fully loaded draught would be two or three feet greater than the depth, while for small vessels the draught would be slightly less than the depth.

Burden: The seventeenth century formula for burden was $B^2K/188$, where B is the beam and K is the keel. Many lists show 'traditional' tonnages which are inconsistent with the known dimensions of some ships. In cases in which the dimensions are firmly established the burdens have been recalculated.

Note that burden was a measure of capacity, and not displacement. The fully loaded displacement of a large seventeenth century ship would be around 25% more than the burden.

Guns: Armament for 'war at home' between 1660 and 1685. For most vessels smaller than 4th Rates, the figures are maximums.

Name	Built	Dockyard	Shipwright	Gundeck Length	Keel length Touch	Keel length Calc	Beam	Depth	Burden Touch	Burden Calc	Guns	Fate
First Rates												
Royal Prince	1641R	Woolwich	Peter Pett I	–	115-0	–	44-0	–	1187	–	86-92	Taken and burned by Dutch 1666
	1663R	Chatham	Sir Phineas Pett II			132-0	45-2	18-10		1432		
Royal Charles	1655	Woolwich	Peter Pett I	–	–	131-0	42-6	18-0	–	1258	80-86	Taken by Dutch 1667
Royal Sovereign	1660R	Chatham	Capt John Taylor	167-9	127-0	–	47-10	19-2	1545	–	92-102	Burned by accident 1696
	1684R	Chatham	Robert Lee	167-9	131-0	135-6	48-0	19-2	1605	1661		
Charles	1668	Deptford	Jonas Shish	162-6	128-0	131-0	42-6	18-6	1229	1257	96	Renamed St George 1687; made a 2nd Rate 1691, rebuilt 1701
St Andrew	1670	Woolwich	Edward Byland	158-9	–	128-0	44-4	18-8	–	1308	96-100	Rebuilt as Royal Anne 1704
London	1670R	Deptford	Jonas Shish	160-8	–	129-0	44-0	19-0	–	1328	94-96	Broken up 1701; rebuilt 1706
Prince	1670	Chatham	Sir Phineas Pett II	167-3	131-0	136-0	44-9 G45-10	19-0	1395 1463	1448 1520	100	Great repair and renamed Royal William 1692; rebuilt 1719
Royal James	1671	Portsmouth	Sir Anthony Deane	–	–	136-0	45-0	18-5	–	1465	100	Burned in action 1672
Royal Charles	1673	Portsmouth	Sir Anthony Deane	–	–	136-0	44-8 G46-0	18-3	–	1443 1531	100	Great repair and renamed Queen 1693; rebuilt as Royal George 1715
Royal James	1675	Portsmouth	Sir Anthony Deane	163-1	–	132-0	45-0	18-4	–	1422	100	Renamed Victory 1691; great repair 1695; renamed Royal George 1714, Victory again 1715. Burned by accident 1721
Britannia	1682	Chatham	Sir Phineas Pett II	167-5	–	136-0	47-4	19-7½	–	1620	100	Girdled 1691; great repair 1701; broken up 1715 and rebuilt 1719
Second Rates												
Rainbow	1617R	Deptford	Mr Bright	–	114-0	–	37-10	15-0	866	–	56-64	Ordered sunk at Sheerness 1680
Victory	1620	Deptford	William Burrell I	–	108-0	–	37-6	16-6	808	–	60-64	Rebuilt 1666
St Andrew	1622	Deptford	William Burrell I	–	116-0	–	38-0	15-0	891	–	66	Wrecked 1666
St George	1622	Deptford	William Burrell I	–	117-0	–	38-0	14-10	898	–	66-70	Hulk 1687; last mentioned 1697
Triumph	1623	Deptford	William Burrell I	–	117-0	–	38-0	15-6	898	–	70-74	Sold 1688
Vanguard	1631R	Chatham	John Bright		112-0		38-0	14-0	860		60	Sunk in the Medway 1667; raised and sold
Unicorn	1634	Woolwich	Edward Boate	–	110-0	–	37-6	15-1	823	–	60-68	Sold 1688
Old James	1634	Deptford	Peter Pett II	138-0	110-0	–	39-0	16-0	890	–	70	Made a 3rd Rate 1677; sold 1682
Swiftsure	1653R	Woolwich	Christopher Pett	–	118-0	–	37-10	16-0	898	–	66	Taken by Dutch 1666
Henry	1656	Deptford	Manley Callis	–	120-0	124-0	G40-6	17-0	1047	1082	72-82	Burned by accident 1682
London	1656	Chatham	Capt John Taylor	–	–	123-6	G41-0	16-6	–	1104	72-80	Blown up by accident 1665
Royal James	1658	Woolwich	Christopher Pett	–	–	124-0	41-0	18-0		1108	82	Made a 1st Rate 1660; burned by Dutch 1667; remains broken up 1670
Royal Katherine	1664	Woolwich	Christopher Pett	153-1	120-0	124-0	39-8 G41-0	17-2	1004 1073	1038 1108	76-86	Rebuilt 1702
Royal Oak	1664	Portsmouth	Sir John Tippetts	–	121-0	–	39-10	17-1½	1021	–	76	Burned by Dutch 1667
Loyal London	1666	Deptford	Capt John Taylor	–	127-0	–	41-9½	17-0	1180	–	80-92	Burned by Dutch 1667; rebuilt as London 1670
Victory	1666R	Chatham	Sir Phineas Pett II	–	121-0	–	40-0	17-0	1029	–	76-84	Broken up 1691
St Michael	1669	Portsmouth	Sir John Tippetts	155-2	122-6	125-0	40-8½ G41-8	17-5	1079 1131	1101 1154	90-98	Made a 1st Rate 1672; 2nd Rate again 1689; rebuilt as Marlborough 1708
Vanguard	1678	Portsmouth	Daniel Furzer	160-0	126-11	132-0	44-10	18-5	1357	1411	90	Sunk in the Medway 1703; rebuilt 1710
Windsor Castle	1678	Woolwich	Thomas Shish	162-0	125-7	–	44-6½	18-3	1325	–	90	Wrecked 1693

Name	Built	Dockyard	Shipwright	Gundeck Length	Keel length Touch	Keel length Calc	Beam	Depth	Burden Touch	Burden Calc	Guns	Fate
Duchess	1679	Deptford	John Shish	162-8	126-2	131-8	45-1	18-4	1364	1423	90	Renamed Princess Anne 1701, Windsor Castle 1702, Blenheim 1706; rebuilt 1709
Sandwich	1679	Harwich	Isaac Betts	161-6	126-10	132-6	44-8	18-3	1346	1406	90	Rebuilt 1710
Albemarle	1680	Harwich	Isaac Betts	162-0	126-6	131-0	44-4	18-3½	1322	1369	90	Rebuilt 1704
Duke	1682	Woolwich	Thomas Shish	162-10	126-2	131-6	45-1	18-9	1364	1421	90	Rebuilt as Prince George 1701
Ossory	1682	Woolwich	Thomas Shish	161-0	124-1	132-0	44-6	18-2	1307	1390	90	Renamed Prince 1705; rebuilt 1711
Neptune	1683	Deptford	John Shish	163-11	127-10	134-6	45-0	18-6	1377	1448	90	Rebuilt 1710
Coronation	1685	Portsmouth	Isaac Betts	160-4	126-4	–	44-9	18-2	1346	–	90	Wrecked 1691

Third Rates

Name	Built	Dockyard	Shipwright	Gundeck Length	Keel length Touch	Keel length Calc	Beam	Depth	Burden Touch	Burden Calc	Guns	Fate
Mary	1650 ?R	Woolwich	Christopher Pett	143-3	116-0	–	34-4 G35-6 36-8	14-6	727 777 829	–	58-64	Wrecked 1703
Dunkirk	1651	Woolwich	William Burrell II	141-5	112-0	–	33-4	14-0	662	–	56-60	Great repair 1692; rebuilt 1704
Fairfax	1653	Chatham	Capt John Taylor	–	118-0	–	34-9 G36-0	14-4	756 813	–	60-62	Wrecked 1682
Plymouth	1653 ?R	Wapping	Capt John Taylor	139-6	116-0	–	34-8 36-9	14-6	742 833	–	58-60	Rebuilt 1705
Essex	1653	Deptford	Sir Phineas Pett II	–	118-0	–	32-3	14-0	652	–	56	Taken by Dutch 1666
Resolution	1654	Ratcliffe	Sir Phineas Pett II	–	117-3	–	35-2	14-5	771	–	58	Burned in action 1666
Henrietta	1654	Horselydown	John Bright	–	116-0	–	35-7	14-4	781	–	58-62	Wrecked 1689
Gloucester	1654	Limehouse	Matthew Graves	–	117-0	–	34-10	14-6	755	–	58-62	Wrecked 1682
Revenge	1654	Limehouse	Matthew Graves	–	117-6	–	35-0	14-5	766	–	58-62	Broken up 1678
Montagu	1654 1675R	Portsmouth Chatham	Sir John Tippetts Sir Phineas Pett II	145-0	117-0	–	35-2 36-6	15-0	769 829	–	58-62	Rebuilt 1698
Anne	1654	Deptford	Mr Chamberlain	–	116-9	–	34-7	14-2	743	–	58	Blown up by accident 1673
Dreadnought	1654	Blackwall	Sir Henry Johnson	–	116-0	–	34-6	14-2	732	–	58-62	Foundered at sea 1690
York	1654	Blackwall	Sir Henry Johnson	139-0	115-0	–	35-0	14-2	749	–	58-60	Wrecked 1703
Lion	1658R	Chatham	Capt John Taylor	130-0	108-0	–	35-4	15-6	717	–	58-60	Sold 1698
Monck	1659	Portsmouth	Sir John Tippetts	136-0	108-0	–	35-0	13-11	703	–	58-60	Rebuilt 1702
Cambridge	1666	Deptford	Jonas Shish	–	121-0	–	37-10	16-4	921	–	64-70	Wrecked 1694
Warspite	1666	Blackwall	Sir Henry Johnson	142-0	117-0	–	38-0	15-6	898	–	64-70	Rebuilt 1702
Defiance	1666	Deptford P	Capt Wm Castle	–	117-0	–	37-3	15-3	863	–	64	Burned by accident 1668
Rupert	1666	Harwich	Sir Anthony Deane	144-1	119-0	–	36-3	15-6	832	–	64-66	Rebuilt 1703
Resolution	1667	Harwich	Sir Anthony Deane	148-2	120-6	–	37-2	15-6	885	–	64-70	Rebuilt 1698
Monmouth	1667	Chatham	Sir Phineas Pett II	148-5	118-9	–	36-10	15-3	856	—	64-66	Rebuilt 1700
Edgar	1668	Bristol	Francis Bayley	153-6	124-0	–	39-8	16-0	1038	–	72-74	Rebuilt 1700
Swiftsure	1673	Harwich	Sir Anthony Deane	149-3	–	123-0	38-8	15-6	–	978	66-70	Rebuilt 1696
Harwich	1674	Harwich	Sir Anthony Deane	–	–	123-9	38-10	15-8	–	993	66-70	Wrecked 1691
Royal Oak	1674	Deptford	Jonas Shish	157-6	127-0	–	40-6	18-3	1107	–	70-74	Great repair 1690; rebuilt 1713
Defiance	1675	Chatham	Sir Phineas Pett II	143-10	117-0	–	37-10	15-10	890	–	64	Rebuilt 1695
Lenox	1678	Deptford	John Shish	151-6	120-0	–	39-10	17-0	1013	–	70	Rebuilt 1701
Hampton Court	1678	Deptford	John Shish	150-6	121-3	–	40-1	17-0	1036	–	70	Rebuilt 1701
Captain	1678	Woolwich	Thomas Shish	149-6	119-10	–	40-5	17-2	1041	–	70	Rebuilt 1708
Anne	1678	Chatham	Sir Phineas Pett II	150-10	122-0	–	40-3	17-0	1051	–	70	Burned by French 1690
Restoration	1678	Harwich	Isaac Betts	150-6	120-7	124-0	39-11	17-0	1022	1051	70	Rebuilt 1702
Hope	1678	Deptford P	Capt Wm Castle	151-5	121-7	124-5	40-4	16-9	1052	1076	70	Taken by French 1695
Elizabeth	1679	Deptford P	Capt Wm Castle	151-8	120-0	124-8	41-0	16-8½	1073	1114	70	Taken by French 1704
Burford	1679	Woolwich	Thomas Shish	152-4	121-6	–	40-4	17-3	1051	–	70	Rebuilt 1699
Grafton	1679	Woolwich	Thomas Shish	150-0	120-8	–	40-6	17-2	1052	–	70	Rebuilt 1700
Stirling Castle	1679	Deptford	John Shish	151-2	120-11	–	40-7	17-3	1059	–	70	Rebuilt 1699
Berwick	1679	Chatham	Sir Phineas Pett II	150-10	121-4	–	40-2	17-0	1041	–	70	Rebuilt 1700
Pendennis	1679	Chatham	Sir Phineas Pett II	150-10	121-9	–	40-3½	17-0	1051	–	70	Wrecked 1689
Breda	1679	Harwich	Isaac Betts	151-3	120-7	124-6	39-11	16-9	1022	1055	70	Blown up by accident 1690
Eagle	1679	Portsmouth	Daniel Furzer	151-6	120-8	–	40-6	17-0	1053	–	70	Rebuilt 1699
Expedition	1679	Portsmouth	Daniel Furzer	152-1	121-0	–	40-9	17-0	1069	–	70	Rebuilt 1699
Northumberland	1679	Bristol	Francis Bayley	151-11¾	121-4	–	40-2	17-0	1041	–	70	Rebuilt 1702
Essex	1679	Blackwall	Sir Henry Johnson	150-2	120-9	124-0	40-1	16-9½	1032	1064	70	Rebuilt 1700
Kent	1679	Blackwall	Sir Henry Johnson	151-0	121-5	124-7	40-1½	16-9½	1040	1067	70	Rebuilt 1699
Exeter	1680	Blackwall	Sir Henry Johnson	150-2	120-0	124-5	40-2½	16-9½	1032	1070	70	Blown up by accident 1691
Suffolk	1680	Blackwall	Sir Henry Johnson	150-10	121-4	124-3	40-2	16-9½	1041	1066	70	Rebuilt 1699

Name	Built	Dockyard	Shipwright	Gundeck Length	Keel length Touch	Keel length Calc	Beam	Depth	Burden Touch	Burden Calc	Guns	Fate
Fourth Rates												
Expedition	1637	Bermondsey	Mr Franckmore	–	90-0	–	27-4	11-0	357	–	34-40	Sold 1667
Providence	1637	?	Matthew Graves	–	90-0	–	27-0	11-0	349	–	34-40	Wrecked 1668
Constant Warwick	1645	Ratcliffe	Peter Pett II	–	85-0	–	26-5	12-0	315	–	34-42	Privateer bought in 1649;
	1666R	Portsmouth	Sir John Tippetts		90-0		28-2	12-0	379			taken by French 1691
Nonsuch	1646	Deptford	Peter Pett II	–	98-0	–	28-4	12-0	418	–	38-40	Wrecked 1664
Assurance	1646	Deptford	Peter Pett II	–	89-0	–	26-10	11-0	340	–	38-42	Sold 1678
Adventure	1646	Woolwich	Peter Pett I	–	94-0	–	27-9	12-0	385	–	38-44	Sold 1688
Phoenix	1647	Woolwich	Peter Pett I	–	96-0		28-6	12-0	414	–	38-40	Wrecked 1664
Tiger	1647	Deptford	Peter Pett II	–	99-0	–	29-4	12-0	453	–	38-44	Rebuilt 1681
Elizabeth	1647	Deptford	Peter Pett II	–	101-6	–	29-8	12-0	475	–	38-40	Burned by Dutch 1667
Dragon	1647	Chatham	Henry Goddard	–	96-0	–	28-6	12-0	414	–	38-46	Rebuilt 1690
Amity	1650B			–	90-0	–	28-0	12-0	375	–	38	Sold 1667
Assistance	1650	Deptford	Sir Henry Johnson	121-5½	102-0	–	31-0	13-0	521	–	48-50	Rebuilt 1699
Reserve	1650	Woodbridge	Peter Pett I	118-4	100-0	–	31-1	12-4	513	–	48	Rebuilt 1701
Advice	1650	Woodbridge	Peter Pett I	118-6	100-0	–	31-2	12-3	516	–	48-50	Rebuilt 1698
	?R	?	?				32-0		544			
Portsmouth	1650	Portsmouth	Thomas Eastwood	–	100-0	–	29-6	12-6	463	–	44-46	Blown up in action 1689
Foresight	1650	Deptford	Jonas Shish	121-2	102-2	–	31-1	12-9	524	–	48	Wrecked 1698
Centurion	1650	Ratcliffe	Peter Pett II	–	104-0	–	31-0	13-0	531	–	48-50	Wrecked 1689
Bonaventure	1650	Deptford	Peter Pett II	124-10	100-0	–	29-6	12-4	462	–	48	Rebuilt 1699
	1663R	Chatham	Sir Phineas Pett II		102-9		30-8		514			
	1683R	Portsmouth	Isaac Betts		102-6		32-2		564			
Sapphire	1651	Ratcliffe	Peter Pett II	–	100-0	–	28-10	12-0	442	–	38-40	Wrecked 1670
Diamond	1651	Deptford	Peter Pett II	127-4	105-4	–	31-3	13-0	548	–	48-50	Taken by French 1693
Ruby	1651	Deptford	Peter Pett II	125-7	105-6	–	31-6	13-0	556	–	46-48	Taken by French 1707
Kent	1652	Deptford	Sir Henry Johnson	–	107-0	–	32-7	13-6	601	–	46-52	Wrecked 1672
Portland	1653	Wapping	Capt John Taylor	–	105-0	–	32-11	13-0	605	–	48-50	Burned to avoid capture 1692
Bristol	1653	Portsmouth	Sir John Tippetts	130-0	104-0	–	31-1	13-0	534	–	48-54	Rebuilt 1693
Swallow	1653	Pitch House	Thomas Taylor	–	100-10	–	31-10	13-0	543	–	48-50	Wrecked 1692
Antelope	1653	Woodbridge	Mr Carey	–	101-0	–	31-0	13-0	516	–	48-52	Sold 1693
Hampshire	1653	Deptford	Sir Phineas Pett II	118-0	101-9	–	29-9	13-0	479	–	46-48	Sunk in action 1697
Newcastle	1653	Ratcliffe	Sir Phineas Pett II	131-0	108-0	–	33-1	13-2	629	–	50-56	Rebuilt 1692
Yarmouth	1653	Yarmouth	Mr Edgar	–	105-0	–	33-0	13-3	608	–	52-54	Broken up 1680
Happy Return	1654	Yarmouth	Mr Edgar	–	104-0	–	33-2	13-0	609	–	50-54	Taken by French 1691
Jersey	1654	Maldon	Mr Starling	–	101-10	–	32-2	13-1	560	–	48-50	Taken by French 1691
Mary Rose	1654	Woodbridge	Mr Monday	–	102-0	–	32-0	13-0	556	–.	48-50	Taken by French 1691
Dover	1654	Shoreham	Capt Wm Castle	–	104-0	–	31-8	13-0	555	–	48-54	Rebuilt 1695
Crown	1654	Rotherhithe	Capt Wm Castle	–	100-6	–	31-8	13-0	536	–	48-50	Rebuilt 1689
Breda	1654	Bristol	Francis Bayley	–	100-0	–	31-0	12-8	511	–	48	Wrecked 1666
Leopard	1659	Deptford	Jonas Shish	–	109-0	–	33-9	15-0	660	–	54-58	Hulk at Gibraltar 1686; sunk for foundation at Sheerness 1699
Princess	1660	Forest of Dean	Daniel Furzer	–	104-0	–	33-0	14-3	602	–	52-54	Broken up 1680
St Patrick	1666	Bristol	Francis Bayley	–	102-0	–	33-10	14-6	621	–	48	Taken by Dutch 1667
Greenwich	1666	Woolwich	Christopher Pett	136-0	108-0	–	33-9	14-6	654	–	54-60	Rebuilt 1699
St David	1667	Conpill	Daniel Furzer	–	107-0	–	34-9	14-8	687	–	50-54	Sunk at Portsmouth 1690; hulk 1691; sold 1713
Oxford	1674	Bristol	Francis Bayley	–	109-0	–	34-2	15-6	677	–	54	Rebuilt 1702
Woolwich	1675	Woolwich	Phineas Pett III	138-3	110-0	–	35-7	15-0	741	–	54	Rebuilt 1702
Kingfisher	1675	Woolwich	Phineas Pett III	136-0	110-0	–	33-8	13-0	663	–	46	Rebuilt 1699
Charles Galley	1676	Woolwich	Phineas Pett III	–	114-0	–	28-6	8-7	493	–	32	Rebuilt 1693
James Galley	1676	Blackwall	Anthony Deane, Jr	–	104-0	–	28-1	10-2	436	–	30	Wrecked 1694
Tiger	1681R	Deptford	John Shish	123-8	104-0	–	32-8	13-8	590	–	48	Rebuilt 1702
Mordaunt	1681	Deptford P	Capt Wm Castle	–	101-9	–	32-4½	13-0	567	–	46	Privateer bought in 1683; wrecked 1693
Fifth Rates												
Mermaid	1651	Limehouse	Matthew Graves	–	86-0	–	25-0	10-0	286	–	32	Fireship 1668; reconverted and rebuilt 1689
Nightingale	1651	Horselydown	John Bright	–	86-0	–	25-2	10-0	290	–	32	Wrecked 1672
Pearl	1651	Ratcliffe	Peter Pett II	–	86-0	–	25-0	10-0	286	–	32	Fireship 1688; reconverted 1689; sunk for foundation at Sheerness 1697

Name	Built	Dockyard	Shipwright	Gundeck Length	Keel length Touch	Keel length Calc	Beam	Depth	Burden Touch	Burden Calc	Guns	Fate
Colchester	1654	Yarmouth	Mr Edgar	–	83-0	–	25-6	11-0	287	–	28	Sunk in action 1666
Eagle	1654	Wapping	Capt John Taylor	–	85-6	–	25-8	10-0	299	–	32	Fireship 1674; sunk for foundation at Sheerness 1694
Garland	1654	Southampton	Daniel Furzer	–	80-0	–	25-0	10-0	266	–	38	Fireship 1688; reconverted 1689; sold 1698
Guernsey	1654	Walderswick	Jonas Shish	–	80-0	–	24-6	10-0	255	–	30	Fireship 1688; reconverted 1689; broken up 1693
Milford	1654	Wyvenhoe	Mr Page	–	82-0	–	24-6	10-0	262	–	28	Burned by accident 1673
Norwich	1655	Chatham	Phineas Pett III	–	80-0	–	25-0	10-6	265	–	30	Wrecked 1682
Pembroke	1655	Woolwich	Mr Raven	–	81-0	–	25-0	11-0	269	–	34	Sunk in collision 1667
Dartmouth	1655	Portsmouth	Sir John Tippetts	–	80-0	–	24-9	10-0	260	–	32	Fireship 1688; reconverted 1689; wrecked 1690
Richmond	1656	Portsmouth	Sir John Tippetts	–	76-0	–	24-0	9-9	233	–	28	Fireship 1688; reconverted 1689; sold 1698
Oxford	1656	Deptford	Manley Callis	–	72-0	–	24-0	10-0	221	–	26	Given to Governor of Jamaica 1668; blown up 1669
Speedwell	1656	Deptford	Manley Callis	–	76-0	–	24-0	9-0	233	–	28	Wrecked 1678
Forester	1657	Forest of Dean	Daniel Furzer	–	80-0	–	25-0	10-6	266	–	30	Blown up by accident 1672
Success	1658	Chatham	Capt John Taylor	–	85-0	–	25-6	10-0	294	–	36	Wrecked 1680
Little Victory	1665	Chatham	Joseph Lawrence	–	75-0	–	21-0	10-0	176	–	28	Fireship and expended 1671
Falcon	1666	Woolwich	Christopher Pett	–	88-0	–	27-4	12-0	349	–	36-42	4th Rate 1668; taken by French 1694
Sweepstakes	1666	Yarmouth	Mr Edgar	–	87-0	–	28-6	11-0	376	–	36-42	4th Rate 1668; sold 1698
Nonsuch	1668	Portsmouth	Sir Anthony Deane	–	88-3	–	27-8	10-10	359	–	36-42	4th Rate 1669; taken by French 1695
Phoenix	1671	Portsmouth	Sir Anthony Deane	–	89-0	–	27-10	11-2	367	–	40-42	4th Rate 1672; burned to avoid capture 1692
Holmes	1671B			–	80-0	–	22-9	12-9	220	–	24	Fireship 1677; sold 1682
Swan	1673B			–	74-0	–	25-0	10-0	246	–	32	Bought from Capt Anthony Young; fireship 1688; reconverted 1689; wrecked 1692
Rose	1674	Yarmouth	Mr Edgar	–	75-0	–	24-0	10-0	229	–	28	Fireship 1689; sold 1698
Sapphire	1675	Harwich	Sir Anthony Deane	–	86-0	–	27-0	11-0	333	–	32	Burned in action 1696

Sixth Rates

Name	Built	Dockyard	Shipwright	Gundeck Length	Keel length Touch	Keel length Calc	Beam	Depth	Burden Touch	Burden Calc	Guns	Fate
Drake	1652	Deptford	Sir Phineas Pett II	–	85-0	–	18-0	7-8	146	–	16	Broken up 1690
Merlin	1652	Chatham	Capt John Taylor	–	75-0	–	18-0	7-8	129	–	14	Taken by Dutch 1665
Martin	1652	Portsmouth	Sir John Tippetts	–	64-0	–	19-4	7-0	127	–	12	Sold 1667
Harp	1656	Dublin		–	51-0	–	16-8	8-0	75	–	10	Sold 1671
Lily	1657	Deptford	Manley Callis	–	50-0	–	15-6	5-6	64	–	6	Sold 1667
Cignet	1657	Chatham	Capt John Taylor	–	45-0	–	15-6	5-6	58	–	8	Last mentioned 1667
Fanfan	1666	Harwich	Sir Anthony Deane	–	44-0	–	12-0	5-8	33	–	4	Pitch-boat 1693
Francis	1666	Harwich	Sir Anthony Deane	–	66-0	–	20-0	9-2	140	–	16	Wrecked 1684
Roebuck	1666	Harwich	Sir Anthony Deane	–	64-0	–	19-6	9-10	129	–	16	Sold 1683
Leicester	1667B			–	84-0	–	24-0	11-8	257	–	24	Blockship in the Thames 1667
Saudadoes	1670	Portsmouth	Sir Anthony Deane	–	51-6	–	17-6	8-0	83	–	10	Built as a Yacht.
	1673R	Deptford	Jonas Shish	–	74-0	–	21-6	10-0	180	–	16	Taken by French 1696
Greyhound	1672	Portsmouth	Sir Anthony Deane	–	75-0	–	21-6	9-0	184	–	16	Sold 1698
Young Spragge	1673B			–	46-0	–	18-0	9-0	79	–	10	Bought from Sir Edward Spragge; fireship 1677; sunk for foundation at Portsmouth 1693
Lark	1675	Blackwall	Sir Anthony Deane	–	74-0	–	22-6	9-2	199	–	18	Sold 1698

Ketches

Name	Built	Dockyard	Shipwright	Gundeck Length	Keel length Touch	Keel length Calc	Beam	Depth	Burden Touch	Burden Calc	Guns	Fate
Nonsuch	1650	Wyvenhoe	Mr Page	–	37-0	–	15-6	7-0	47	–	8	Sold 1667
Eaglet	1655	Horselydown	Mr Higgins	–	40-0	–	16-0	7-0	54	–	8	Sold 1674
Hawk	1655	Woolwich	Mr Cooper	–	42-0	–	16-0	8-0	57	–	8	Sold 1667
Hind	1655	Wyvenhoe	Mr Page	–	41-0	–	16-0	8-0	56	–	8	Wrecked 1667
Roe	1655	Wyvenhoe	Mr Page	–	42-0	–	16-0	8-0	57	–	8	Kitchen 1661; given away 1669
Giles	1661B			–	37-0	–	15-6	6-0	48	–	2	Sold 1667
Swallow	1661B			–	40-0	–	16-0	8-0	54	–	6	Sold 1674
Colchester	1664	Colchester	John Allin	–	48-0	–	16-10	9-0	72	–	8	Taken by French 1667

Name	Built	Dockyard	Shipwright	Gundeck Length	Keel length Touch	Keel length Calc	Beam	Depth	Burden Touch	Burden Calc	Guns	Fate
Deptford	1665	Deptford	Jonas Shish	–	52-0	–	18-0	9-4	89	–	10	Wrecked 1689
Portsmouth	1665	Portsmouth	Sir John Tippetts	–	48-0	–	18-10	9-1	90	–	10	Pink 1670; taken by Dutch 1673
Roe	1665	Wyvenhoe	Mr Page	–	50-0	–	18-6	8-6	91	–	8	Wrecked 1670
Wyvenhoe	1665	Wyvenhoe	Mr Page	–	52-0	–	19-1	8-6	100	–	8	Pink 1668; fireship 1673; sold 1683
Quaker	1671B			–	54-0	–	18-2	9-0	80	–	10	Sold 1698
Kingfisher	1684B			–	47-9	–	15-6	8-5½	61	–	4	Taken by French 1690

Pinks

Name	Built	Dockyard	Shipwright	Gundeck Length	Keel length Touch	Keel length Calc	Beam	Depth	Burden Touch	Burden Calc	Guns	Fate
Blackmoor	1656	Chatham	Capt John Taylor	–	47-0	–	19-0	8-6	90	–	14	Sold 1667
Chestnut	1656	Portsmouth	Sir John Tippetts	–	45-0	–	18-6	8-9	81	–	10	Wrecked 1665
Hart or Heart	1657	Woolwich	Christopher Pett	–	50-0	–	14-6	5-6	56	–	8	Sold 1683
Rose	1657	Woolwich	Christopher Pett	–	50-0	–	14-6	5-6	56	–	6	Irish packet service 1661
Swallow	1657	Deptford	Manley Callis	–	50-0	–	14-6	7-6	56		6	Irish packet service 1661

Sloops

Name	Built	Dockyard	Shipwright	Gundeck Length	Keel length Touch	Keel length Calc	Beam	Depth	Burden Touch	Burden Calc	Guns	Fate
Spy	1666	Harwich	Sir Anthony Deane	–	44-0	–	11-0	4-0	28	–	4	Sold 1683
Emsworth	1667	Emsworth	John Smith	–	40-0	–	13-7	4-9	39	–	4	Sold 1683
Portsmouth	1667	Portsmouth	Sir John Tippetts	–	40-0	–	14-0	7-0	43	–	4	Taken by Dutch 1672
Prevention	1672	Portsmouth	Sir Anthony Deane	–	60-0	–	12-0	5-0	46	–	4	Sold 1683
Swallow	1672	Deptford	Jonas Shish	–	50-0	–	16-0	6-0	68	–	2	Lost at sea 1673
Dove	1672	Deptford	Jonas Shish	–	40-0	–	9-10	4-0	20	–	4	Sold 1683
Lily	1672	Deptford	Jonas Shish	–	52-0	–	14-6	5-6	58	–	6	Lost at sea 1673
Tulip	1672	Deptford	Jonas Shish	–	43-0	–	10-0	4-0	23	–	2	Lost at sea 1673
Whipster	1672	Deptford	Jonas Shish	–	58-0	–	14-6	5-0	64	–	4	Brigantine; sold 1683
Dolphin	1673	Deptford	Jonas Shish	–	54-0	–	14-6	5-6	60	–	2	Sunk in action 1673
Lizard	1673	Deptford	Jonas Shish	–	47-0	–	12-6	4-9	39	–	4	Taken by Dutch 1674
Vulture	1673	Deptford	Jonas Shish	–	50-0	–	16-0	6-0	68	–	4	Sold 1686
Bonetta	1673	Woolwich	Phineas Pett III	–	61-0	–	13-0	5-0	57	–	4	Sold 1687
Woolwich	1673	Woolwich	Phineas Pett III	–	61-0	–	13-0	5-0	57	–	4	Wrecked 1675
Chatham	1673	Chatham	Sir Phineas Pett II	–	57-6	–	12-10	5-0	50	–	4	Wrecked 1677
Chatham Double	1673	Chatham	Sir Phineas Pett II	–	57-6	–	12-10	5-0	50	–	4	Sold 1683
Hound	1673	Chatham	Sir Phineas Pett II	–	57-6	–	12-10	5-0	50	–	4	Sold 1686
Cutter	1673	Portsmouth	Sir Anthony Deane	–	60-0	–	12-0	5-0	46	–	2	Wrecked 1673
Hunter	1673	Portsmouth	Sir Anthony Deane	–	60-0	–	12-0	5-0	46	–	4	Sold 1683
Invention	1673	Portsmouth	Sir Anthony Deane	–	44-0	–	11-0	5-0	28	–	4	Sold 1683
Experiment	1677	Greenwich	Joseph Lawrence	–	35-0	–	11-6	6-4	24		4	Given away 1680

Hoys

Name	Built	Dockyard	Shipwright	Gundeck Length	Keel length Touch	Keel length Calc	Beam	Depth	Burden Touch	Burden Calc	Guns	Fate
Marigold	1653	Portsmouth	Sir John Tippetts	–	32-0	–	14-0	7-0	33	–	–	Broken up 1712
Harwich	1660	Harwich	John Gressingham	–	38-0	–	16-0	8-0	52	–	–	Sold 1680
Prosperous	1665	Chatham	Sir Phineas Pett II	–	50-0	–	16-0	6-0	68	–	–	Horseboat; burned by Dutch 1667
Unity	1665	Chatham	Sir Phineas Pett II	–	50-0	–	16-0	6-0	68	–	–	Horseboat; sold 1712
Samuel of Strood	1667B			–	40-0	–	16-6	8-2	58	–	–	Returned to owners 1668
Samuel of Chatham	1667B			–	40-0	–	16-6	8-2	58	–	–	Returned to owners 1668
John of Chatham	1667B			–	39-0	–	16-0	8-0	53	–	–	Returned to owners 1668
Lighter	1672	Portsmouth	Sir John Tippetts	–	38-0	–	18-0	7-6	65	–	–	Sold 1713
Transporter	1677	Sheerness		–	59-0	–	17-0	–	92	–	–	Sold 1713

Smacks

Name	Built	Dockyard	Shipwright	Gundeck Length	Keel length Touch	Keel length Calc	Beam	Depth	Burden Touch	Burden Calc	Guns	Fate
Royal Escape	1660B			–	30-6	–	14-3	7-9	34	–	4	Rebuilt 1714
Swan	1666	Chatham	Sir Phineas Pett II	–	36-0	–	11-3	5-2	18	–	–	Taken by Dutch 1673
Tower	1668			–	32-0	–	13-4	5-6	30	–	4	From Ordnance Office by exchange for Charles yacht. Sold 1674
Bridget	1672	Deptford	Jonas Shish	–	32-0	–	11-3	5-6	21	–	–	Sold 1683
Little London	1672	Chatham	Sir Phineas Pett II	–	26-0	–	11-0	5-8	16	–	–	Sold 1697
Sheerness	1673	Chatham	Sir Phineas Pett II	–	28-0	–	11-0	6-0	18	–	–	Ordered sunk at Sheerness 1695
Young Shish	1673	Deptford	Jonas Shish	–	38-0	–	11-0	4-6	24	–	–	Last mentioned 1688

Miscellaneous

Name	Built	Dockyard	Shipwright	Gundeck Length	Keel length Touch	Keel length Calc	Beam	Depth	Burden Touch	Burden Calc	Guns	Fate
towing galley	1658	Chatham		–	–	–	–	–	–	–	1	Last mentioned 1664

Name	Built	Dockyard	Shipwright	Gundeck Length	Keel length Touch	Keel length Calc	Beam	Depth	Burden Touch	Burden Calc	Guns	Fate
Margaret galley	1671	Pisa	Beneditto Carlini	153-0 (oa)	–	–	–	–	–	–	–	Given away 1677
Tangier pontoon	1680	Tangier	Sir Henry Sheer	–	70-0	–	14-0	6-0	80	–	–	?
Chatham towboat (twin hull)	1683	Pitch House	Jonas Shish	–	76-0	–	9-6 (each)	4-0	73	–	–	

Yachts

Name	Built	Dockyard	Shipwright	Gundeck Length	Keel length Touch	Keel length Calc	Beam	Depth	Burden Touch	Burden Calc	Guns	Fate
Minion	1649?			–	28-0	–	12-4	4-9	22	–	6	Sold 1669
Mary	1660G			–	52-0	–	19-0	7-7	100	–	8	Given by Dutch; wrecked 1675
Bezan	1661G			–	34-0	–	14-0	7-0	35	–	4	Given by Dutch; broken up 1687
Anne	1661	Woolwich	Christopher Pett	–	52-0	–	19-0	7-0	100	–	8	Sold 1686
Katherine	1661	Deptford	Peter Pett I	–	49-0	–	19-0	7-0	94	–	10	Taken by Dutch 1673; returned and given to Ordnance Office 1674
Jemmy	1662	Lambeth	Peter Pett I	–	31-0	–	12-6	6-0	25	–	4	Broken up 1722
Charles	1662	Woolwich	Christopher Pett	–	36-0	–	14-2	7-0	38	–	6	Exchanged for Tower smack with Ordnance Office 1668
Henrietta	1663	Woolwich	Christopher Pett	–	52-0	–	19-5	7-0	104	–	12	Sunk in action 1673
Merlin	1666	Rotherhithe	Jonas Shish	–	53-0	–	19-6	6-0	109	–	6	Sold 1698
Monmouth	1666	Rotherhithe	Capt Wm Castle	–	52-0	–	19-6	8-0	103	–	6	Sold 1698
Kitchen	1670	Rotherhithe	Capt Wm Castle	–	52-0	–	19-6	8-6	103	–	6	Bomb vessel 1692; sold 1698
Cleveland	1671	Portsmouth	Sir Anthony Deane	–	53-4	–	19-4	7-6	107	–	8	Sold 1716
Queenborough	1671	Chatham	Sir Phineas Pett II	–	31-6	–	13-4	6-6	29	–	4	Rebuilt 1718
Richmond	1672B			–	45-0	–	16-6	9-0	64	–	8	Sold 1685
Isle of Wight	1673	Portsmouth	Daniel Furzer	–	31-0	–	12-6	6-0	25	–	4	Rebuilt 1701
Navy	1673	Portsmouth	Sir Anthony Deane	–	48-0	–	17-6	7-7	74	–	6	Sold 1698
Deal	1673	Woolwich	Phineas Pett III	–	32-0	–	13-0	6-0	28	–	4	Sold 1686
Portsmouth	1674	Woolwich	Phineas Pett III	–	57-0	–	20-6	7-4	133	–	8	Bomb-vessel 1688; wrecked 1703
Katherine	1674	Chatham	Sir Phineas Pett II	–	56-0	–	21-4	8-6	135	–	8	Rebuilt 1720
Charles	1675	Rotherhithe	Sir Anthony Deane	–	54-0	–	20-4	7-9	120	–	8	Wrecked 1678
Charlotte	1677	Woolwich	Phineas Pett III	–	61-0	–	21-0	9-0	142	–	8	Rebuilt 1710
Mary	1677	Chatham	Sir Phineas Pett II	–	66-6	–	21-6	8-9	166	–	8	Rebuilt 1727
Henrietta	1679	Woolwich	Thomas Shish	–	65-0	–	21-8	8-3	162	–	8	Sold 1721
Isabella	1680	Chatham	Sir Phineas Pett II	–	46-0	–	16-0	–	52	–	–	Sold 1683
Fubbs	1682	Greenwich	Sir Phineas Pett II	–	63-0	–	21-0	9-6	148	–	12	Rebuilt 1701
Isabella	1683	Greenwich	Sir Phineas Pett II	–	60-0	–	18-11	8-11½	114	–	10	Rebuilt 1703

PRIZES

Name	Taken	Taken From	Former Name	Gundeck length	Keel length Touch	Keel length Calc	Beam	Depth	Burden Touch	Burden Calc	Guns	Fate
Second Rates												
French Ruby	1666	French	Rubis	139-7	112-0	–	38-2	16-6	868	–	66-80	Wrecked 1682
Third Rates												
House of Sweeds	1665	Dutch EI*	Huis te Zwieten	–	111-0	–	36-6	16-3	786	–	70	Blockship in the Thames 1667
Golden Phoenix	1665	Dutch EI	Vergulde Phenix	–	113-0	–	36-0	16-6	779	–	70	Blockship in the Thames 1667
Slothany	1665	Dutch EI	Slot Honingen	–	112-0	–	36-0	16-10	772	–	60	Hulk 1667; sold 1686
Helverston	1665	Dutch	Hilversum	–	103-0	–	33-0	12-8	597	–	60	Blockship in the Medway 1667
Arms of Rotterdam	1674	Dutch EI	Wapen Van Rotterdam	–	119-0	–	39-6	18-9	987	–	60	Hulk 1675; broken up 1703
Fourth Rates												
Guinea	1649	Royalists	Charles	–	90-0	–	28-0	11-4	375	–	38	Sold 1667
Convertine	1650	Portuguese	–	–	103-0	–	30-0	13-6	493	–	54	Taken by Dutch 1666
Marmaduke	1651	Royalists	Revenge	–	87-0	–	31-5	15-2	457	–	42	Blockship in the Medway 1667

*EI indicates East Indiaman

Name	Taken	Taken From	Former Name	Gundeck length	Keel length Touch	Keel length Calc	Beam	Depth	Burden Touch	Burden Calc	Guns	Fate
Welcome	1652	Dutch	–	–	82-0	–	29-0	10-7	367	–	40	Blockship in the Thames 1667; raised and made fireship; 5th Rate 1671; fireship 1672; expended 1673
Charity	1653	Dutch	Liefde		106-0	–	28-4	11-0	453	–	46	Taken by Dutch 1665
Bear	1653	Dutch	Beer	–	106-0	–	26-6	12-0	396	–	44	Given to Ordnance Office 1665
Matthias	1653	Dutch	St Mattheus		108d0	–	32-0	15-0	588	–	52	Burned by Dutch 1667
Elias	1653	Dutch	Elias	–	101-0	–	27-6	11-6	406	–	36	Wrecked 1664
Indian	1654	Dutch ?EI	–	–	114-0	–	33-8	14-0	687	–	60	Sold 1660
Clove Tree	1665	Dutch EI	Nagelboom	–	103-0	–	33-0	12-8	596	–	62	Taken by Dutch 1666
West Friezland	1665	Dutch	Westfriesland	–	102-0	–	32-0	12-0	556	–	54	Sold 1667
Seven Oaks	1665	Dutch	Zevenwolden	–	105-0	–	35-0	15-0	684	–	52	Taken by Dutch 1666
Charles V	1665	Dutch EI	Carolus V	–	102-0	–	32-0	14-0	556	–	52	Burned by Dutch 1667
Guilder de Ruyter	1665	Dutch EI	Geldersche Ruiter	–	105-0	–	35-0	15-0	684	–	50	Sold 1667
Maria Sancta	1665	Dutch ?EI	St Marie	–	106-0	–	26-6	12-2	396	–	50	Burned by Dutch 1667
Mars	1665	Dutch EI	Mars	–	106-0	–	26-6	12-2	396	–	50	Sold 1667
Delfe	1665	Dutch	Delft	–	94-0	–	24-0	9-2	288	–	48	Sold 1668
St Paul	1665	Dutch EI	St Paulus	–	84-0	–	25-6	9-8	291	–	48	Burned in action 1666
Hope	1665	Dutch	Hoop	–	103-0	–	30-0	13-6	493	–	44	Wrecked 1666
Black Spread Eagle	1665	Dutch	Groningen	–	86-0	–	28-4	12-0	367	–	44	Sunk in action 1666
Golden Lion	1665	Dutch	Gouden Leeuw	–	101-4	–	28-6	13-0	438	–	42	Given to Guinea Co 1668
Zealand	1665	Dutch	Zeelandia		93-0	–	28-6	9-0	402	–	42	Sold 1667
Unity	1665	Dutch	Eendracht	–	95-0	–	24-6	9-2	303	–	42	Taken by Dutch 1667
Young Prince	1665	Dutch	Jonge Prins	–	90-0	–	28-0	10-2	375	–	38	Fireship and expended 1666
Black Bull	1665	Dutch	Edam	–	103-0	–	30-0	13-6	493	–	36	Taken and sunk by Dutch 1666
Stathouse van Harlem	1667	Dutch	Raadhuis van Haarlem	–	90-0	–	30-4	11-6	440	–	46	Foundation at Sheerness 1690
Stavoreen	1672	Dutch	Stavoren	–	100-0	–	32-0	12-9	544	–	48	Sold 1682
Arms of Terver	1673	Dutch	Kampveere	–	96-0	–	32-0	11-9	523	–	52	Given away 1674
Marigold	1677	Algerines	–	–	100-0	–	30-6	12-6	495	–	44	Wrecked 1679
Tiger Prize	1678	Algerines	–	112-0	90-0	–	31-6	12-8	475	–	48	Foundation at Sheerness 1696
Golden Horse	1681	Algerines	–	125-8	101-0	–	36-8	14-10	722	–	46	Foundation at Chatham 1688
Two Lions	1682	Algerines	–	115-6	92-6	–	33-6	13-6	552	–	44	Sold 1688
Half Moon	1682	Algerines	–	113-1	90-0	–	34-1	13-4	556	–	44	Burned by accident 1686

Fifth Rates

Name	Taken	Taken From	Former Name	Gundeck length	Keel length Touch	Keel length Calc	Beam	Depth	Burden Touch	Burden Calc	Guns	Fate
Satisfaction	1646	Dutch	–	–	89-0	–	23-6	10-6	261	–	32	Wrecked 1662
Old Success	1650	French	Jules	–	94-0	–	30-0	11-6	450	–	38	Sold 1662
Bryer	1651	Royalists	Peter	–	70-0	–	26-0	8-10	252	–	2	Fireship 1666; given away 1667
Convert	1652	Dutch	–	–	90-0	–	26-0	10-0	323	–	34	Sold 1661
Great Gift	1652	French	Don de Dieu	–	98-0	–	30-8	12-6	490	–	40	Fireship and expended 1666; also called Gift Major
Paul	1652	Dutch	St Paul	–	84-0	–	25-6	9-8	290	–	30	Sold 1667
Sophia	1652	Dutch	–	–	90-0	–	26-0	11-0	323	–	34	Sold 1667; also called Speaker's Prize
Augustine	1653	Dutch	–	–	100-0	–	26-0	13-0	360	–	32	Foundation at Harwich 1665
Church	1653	Dutch	–	–	69-0	–	23-6	9-6	203	–	26	Sold 1660
Half Moon	1653	Dutch	Halve Maan	–	97-0	–	25-0	10-8	322	–	36	Sold 1660
Lizard	1653	Royalists	–	–	60-0	–	22-9	9-0	165	–	20	Fireship and expended 1666
Rosebush	1653	Dutch	Rozeboom	–	84-0	–	24-6	11-6	268	–	34	Hulk at Harwich 1664; sold 1668
Westergate	1653	Dutch	Westergo	–	86-0	–	24-6	–	274	–	34	Lost at sea 1664
Sorlings	1654	Royalists	Royal James	–	86-0	–	26-6	11-4	321	–	32	Wrecked 1667
Dolphin	1655	Royalists	Fleetwood	–	70-0	–	20-0	9-0	149	–	20	Fireship and expended 1665
Fame	1655	French	Renommée	–	68-0	–	24-0	10-6	208	–	30	Fireship and expended 1665
Hound	1656	Spanish	–	–	80-0	–	22-0	10-0	206	–	24	Fireship and expended 1666
Hector	1657	Royalists	Three Kings	–	71-0	–	17-2	9-0	111	–	22	Sunk in action 1665
Greyhound	1657	Royalists	–	–	62-0	–	21-0	8-6	145	–	24	Fireship and expended 1666
Happy Entrance	1658	Royalists	Patrick	–	76-0	–	24-0	9-10	233	–	24	Fireship and expended 1666
Coventry	1658	Spanish	San Miguel	–	68-0	–	23-0	9-6	191	–	26	Taken by French 1666

Name	Taken	Taken From	Former Name	Gundeck length	Keel length Touch	Keel length Calc	Beam	Depth	Burden Touch	Burden Calc	Guns	Fate
Fountain	1664	Algerines	–	–	88-0	–	28-2	11-6	371	–	34	Fireship and blown up in action 1672
French Victory	1665	French	*Victoire*	–	88-0	–	29-0	11-6	393	–	38	Taken by Dutch 1672
Little Unicorn	1665	Dutch	*Eenhoorn*	–	72-0	–	22-0	10-6	185	–	18	Fireship and expended 1666
Orange	1665	Dutch	*Oranjeboom*	–	74-0	–	25-3	9-10	251	–	32	Lost at sea 1671
Elias	1666	Dutch	*Elias*	–	78-0	–	27-0	8-0	302	–	34	Sold 1667
Algier	1671	Algerines	–	–	82-6	–	28-0	12-6	344	–	32	Wrecked 1673
Hunter	1672	Dutch	–	–	80-0	–	25-0	10-6	266	–	30	Sold 1683
Orange Tree	1677	Algerines	–	–	76-0	–	26-4	8-10	280	–	30	Sold 1687
Date Tree	1678	Algerines	–	–	–	–	–	–	–	–	28	Sunk in careening 1679
St Paul	1679	Algerines	–	–	74-0	–	25-9	11-2½	261	–	32	Fireship 1688; sold 1698. Dutch-built
Red Lion	1683	Algerines	–	92-3	–	–	25-6	–	–	–	?	Sold 1683

Sixth Rates

Name	Taken	Taken From	Former Name	Gundeck length	Keel length Touch	Keel length Calc	Beam	Depth	Burden Touch	Burden Calc	Guns	Fate
Truelove	1647	Royalists	*Truelove*	–	59-0	–	18-0	7-1	102	–	14	Fireship 1668; sunk in action 1673
Paradox	1649	Royalists	–	–	60-0	–	20-0	8-0	128	–	14	Sold 1667
Mary Prize	1654	Spanish	–	–	60-0	–	18-6	9-0	109	–	14	Taken by Dutch 1666; also called *Little Mary*
Cornelian	1655	Royalists	*Cornelius*	–	52-0	–	19-0	8-8	100	–	12	Out of lists by 1664. French-built
Bramble	1656	Ostend	–	–	59-0	–	20-0	8-6	125	–	14	Fireship 1665; expended 1667
Griffin	1656	Royalists	–	–	60-0	–	19-6	7-6	121	–	12	Wrecked 1664. French-built
Hunter	1656	Royalists	–	–	45-0	–	14-6	6-0	50	–	6	Lost at sea 1661
Kinsale	1656	Royalists	–	–	55-0	–	17-8	8-8	91	–	10	Sold 1663
Lark	1656	Royalists	–	–	52-0	–	17-6	8-6	85	–	10	Sold 1663
Vulture	1656	Dunkirk	–	–	54-0	–	17-6	9-0	88	–	10	Sold 1663
Wolf	1656	Spanish	*N S Del Socorro*	–	61-0	–	20-0	8-6	130	–	16	Sold 1663
Old Francis	1657	Royalists	–	–	59-0	–	16-6	7-0	85	–	14	Fireship 1672; sold 1674
Fox	1658	Ostend	*St Anthony*	–	72-0	–	23-0	8-6	202	–	14	Fireship and expended 1666
Gift Minor	1658	Spanish	*Bon Jesus*	–	60-0	–	20-0	8-6	128	–	16	Sold 1667
Flying Greyhound	1665	Dutch	–	–	78-0	–	23-6	11-0	229	–	24	Given away 1667
Young Lion	1665	Dutch	–	–	42-0	–	14-0	5-0	44	–	10	Sold 1667; rebought 1668; foundation at Sheerness 1673
Morningstar	1672	Dutch	–	–	52-0	–	17-0	8-6	80	–	14	Given away 1674
Two Lions	1683	Salee	–	–	52-0	–	–	–	–	–	?	Sold or broken up 1685
Rose	1684	Salee	–	–	64-0	–	23-0	10-2	180	–	16	Fireship 1688; reconverted 1689; sold 1696. Also called *Sally Rose*
Shedam	1684	Salee	–	–	–	–	–	–	–	–	?	Wrecked 1684
Swan	1684	Salee	–	–	–	–	–	–	–	–	?	Given away 1684

Flyboats

Name	Taken	Taken From	Former Name	Gundeck length	Keel length Touch	Keel length Calc	Beam	Depth	Burden Touch	Burden Calc	Guns	Fate
Crown Malago	1664	All	–	–	70-0	–	23-0	10-6	197	–	6	Given away 1667
Abraham	1665	Dutch,	–	–	69-0	–	23-6	12-0	202	–	4	English prize recaptured; returned to owners 1666
Blue Boar	1665	unless	–	–	64-0	–	23-0	10-6	180	–	4	Redelivered Prize Office 1666
Coppersmith	1665	otherwise	–	–	77-0	–	22-3	10-0	203	–	10	Sold 1667
Frankekin	1665	noted	–	–	72-0	–	24-0	11-4	221	–	8	Given away 1669
Friezland	1665	–	–	–	84-6	–	22-6	10-6	227	–	8	Given to Africa Co 1672
Good Hope	1665	–	–	–	76-0	–	21-0	10-2	178	–	6	Sold 1667
Hardereen	1665	–	–	–	65-0	–	20-0	10-9	138	–	4	Sold 1674
Horseman	1665	–	–	–	68-0	–	23-0	10-6	191	–	18	Blockship in the Thames 1667
Lamb	1665	–	–	–	64-0	–	22-0	10-0	164	–	4	Sold 1667
Milkmaid	1665	–	–	–	65-0	–	21-6	10-2	152	–	4	Given away 1667
Patriach Isaac	1665	–	–	–	67-0	–	22-0	9-8	172	–	4	Redelivered Prize Office 1666
Peter	1665	–	–	–	64-0	–	23-0	10-8	180	–	4	Sold 1668
Prince William	1665	–	–	–	90-0	–	23-0	11-0	253	–	4	Taken by Dutch 1666
Sea Rider	1665	–	–	–	80-0	–	28-8	11-0	350	–	8	Sold 1668
Swan	1665	–	–	–	66-0	–	21-6	9-6	162	–	6	Redelivered Prize Office 1666
Vantrump	1665	–	–	–	102-0	–	24-0	10-3	312	–	8	Sold 1667
Wild Boar	1665	–	–	–	67-0	–	22-0	9-6	172	–	6	Sold 1667

Name	Taken	Taken From	Former Name	Gundeck length	Keel length Touch	Keel length Calc	Beam	Depth	Burden Touch	Burden Calc	Guns	Fate
Wood Merchant	1665	–	–	–	65-0	–	21-8	10-0	162	–	4	Sold 1667
Young Hoblin	1665				67-0		22-0	9-8	172	–	6	Redelivered Prize Office 1666
Fortune	1666				64-0	–	23-0	10-6	180	–	4	Blockship in the Thames 1667
White Rose	1666	–	–	–	64-0	–	23-0	10-8	180	–	6	Redelivered Prize Office 1667
Zealand	1667	–	–	–	94-0	–	29-0	10-4	420	–	8	Sold 1668
Fortune	1672	–	–	–	90-0	–	22-0	11-0	311	–	8	Sold 1674
Nassau	1672	–	–	–	64-0	–	23-0	10-8	180	–	4	Given away 1672
Peace	1672	–	–	–	80-0	–	23-0	11-0	225	–	8	Given away 1674
Unity	1672	–	–	–	67-0	–	22-0	9-8	172	–	4	Given away 1672
White Fox	1672	–	–	–	72-0	–	24-0	11-4	221	–	8	Given away 1674
Spike	1679	Algerines	–	–	98-0	–	24-10	–	321	–	?	Exchanged 1680

Doggers

Name	Taken	Taken From	Former Name	Gundeck length	Keel length Touch	Keel length Calc	Beam	Depth	Burden Touch	Burden Calc	Guns	Fate
Good Fortune	1665	All Dutch and of the	–	–	45-0	–	17-6	8-6	73	–	6	Blockship in the Medway 1667
Casimir	1666	same									6	Given away 1668
Johanna	1666	dimensions									6	Given away 1668
John and Peter	1666										6	Given away 1668
Romery Kirk	1666										6	Given away 1668
Buck	1672										6	Sold 1674
Deal	1672										8	Sold 1674
Dove	1672										8	Wrecked 1674
Dover	1672										8	Given away 1677
Fly	1672										6	Wrecked 1673
George	1672										8	Sold 1674
Hard Bargain	1672										8	Taken by Dutch 1673
Hare	1672										6	Sold 1674
Heart	1672										8	Taken by Dutch 1673
Hind	1672										6	Taken by Dutch 1674
St Jacob	1672										6	Sold 1674
St Katherine	1672										6	Lost at sea 1673
Lily	1672										6	Sold 1674
Messenger	1672										6	Given to Hudson's Bay Co 1672
Peterman	1672										6	Sold 1674
St Peter	1672										6	Taken by Dutch 1674
Roe	1672										6	Sunk in action 1673
Rose	1672										6	Sunk in action 1673
Shellfish	1672										6	Given away 1673
Tulip	1672										6	Sold 1674
Well	1672										8	Sold 1674
William	1672										8	Sold 1674
Frog	1673										6	Sold 1674

Hulks

Name	Taken	Taken From	Former Name	Gundeck length	Keel length Touch	Keel length Calc	Beam	Depth	Burden Touch	Burden Calc	Guns	Fate
Violet	1652	Dutch	–	–	98-0	–	28-0	12-6	409	–	–	Broken up 1672
Stork	1652	Dutch	Ooievaar	–	97-0	–	27-9	12-6	397	–	–	Sold 1663
Estridge	1653	Dutch EI	Struisvogel	–	116-0	–	36-3	17-0	811	–	–	Foundation at Sheerness 1679
Elias	1656	Spanish	–	–	90-0	–	27-0	10-0	350	–	–	Sold 1684
Gallion	1656	Spanish	Jesu Maria Joseph	–	90-0	–	34-6	12-8	570	–	–	Foundation at Portsmouth 1679
Alphin	1673	Dutch ?EI	–	–	120-0	–	33-6	12-0	716	–	–	Sale list 1687; broken up 1690
Arms of Horn	1673	Dutch	Eenhoorn	–	106-0	–	30-3	12-0	516	–	–	Foundation at Sheerness 1694
Europa	1673	Dutch ?EI	–	–	113-0	–	26-0	10-4	406	–	–	Burned by accident 1675
Maria	1684	Salee	–	–	–	–	–	–	120	–	–	Sold 1690

Miscellaneous

Name	Taken	Taken From	Type	Gundeck length	Keel length Touch	Keel length Calc	Beam	Depth	Burden Touch	Burden Calc	Guns	Fate
Weymouth	1646	Royalists	Pink	–	64-0	–	19-0	9-0	123	–	16	Sold 1662. Royalist Cavendish
Sparrow.	1653	Dutch	Pink	–	50-0	–	14-9	6-4	58	–	6	Sold 1661
Dunkirk	1656	Dunkirk	Sloop	–	40-0	–	12-6	4-6	33	–	2	Sold 1660
Galliot	1664	Dutch	Hoy	–	44-0	–	14-6	7-4	49	–	4	Given away 1667
Mackler	1664	Dutch	Hoy	–	57-0	–	18-6	9-6	104	–	9	Given away 1670
Adam & Eve	1665	Dutch	Hoy	–	55-0	–	15-8	7-6	72	–	–	Foundation at Sheerness 1673

Name	Taken	Taken From	Former Name	Gundeck length	Keel length Touch	Keel length Calc	Beam	Depth	Burden Touch	Burden Calc	Guns	Fate
Black Dog	1665	Dutch	Galliot	–	54-0	–	15-6	7-2	69	–	–	Foundation at Sheerness 1673
Black Posthorse	1665	Dutch	Galliot	–	54-0	–	18-8	9-0	100	–	–	Given away 1670
James	1665	Dutch	Hoy	–	47-0	–	17-0	7-4	72	–	–	Taken by Dutch 1673
Palm Tree	1665	Dutch	Hoy	–	45-6	–	16-0	7-6	62	–	–	Sold 1667
Young King	1665	Dutch	Hoy	–	57-0	–	18-4	9-7	102	–	–	Given away 1666
Chatham	1666	Dutch	Galliot	–	53-0	–	18-0	9-0	91	–	–	Given away 1667
Hope	1666	Dutch	Hoy	–	41-0	–	14-6	6-2	46	–	–	Taken by Dutch 1672
Jeremiah	1666	Dutch	Hoy	–	39-0	–	16-0	8-0	53	–	4	Given away 1667
John	1666	Dutch	Galliot	–	47-0	–	18-0	7-8	81	–	4	Sold 1667
Maybolt	1666	Dutch	Hoy	–	54-6	–	18-8	9-4	108	–	–	Sold 1667
Tripoli	1676	Tripolitans	Saietty	–	–	–	–	–	–	–	–	Sold 1682

Appendix II: Abstract of Fleet Strength, 1659–1685

The following list shows the number of ships of each Rate or type as of 31 December of each year. The 2nd Rates have been divided into two groups because of the very wide variations in size and strength within that class. The dividing line has been placed arbitrarily at 1000 tons. In a few cases, apparent changes in strength were purely administrative as ships were shifted from one rate to another. For example, the 2nd Rate *Royal James* (ex-*Richard* of 1658) was made a 1st Rate in 1660. In other cases, the 2nd Rate *St Michael* was called a 1st Rate from 1672, the 2nd Rate *Old James* became a 3rd Rate in 1677, and four 5th Rates were reclassified as 4th Rates between 1668 and 1672.

Year	1st Rates	Large 2nd Rates	Small 2nd Rates	3rd Rates	4th Rates	5th Rates	6th Rates	Yachts	Pinks & Ketches	Smacks	Sloops	Flyboats	Doggers	Hoys & Galliots	Fireships	Hulks
1659	3	3	9	15	45	37	20	1	12	0	1	0	0	1	0	7
1660	4	2	9	15	45	35	20	2	12	1	0	0	0	2	0	7
1661	4	2	9	15	45	34	19	5	10	1	0	0	0	2	0	7
1662	4	2	9	15	45	32	19	7	9	1	0	0	0	2	0	6
1663	4	2	9	15	45	32	15	8	9	1	0	0	0	2	0	5
1664	4	4	9	15	42	31	13	8	10	1	0	1	0	4	0	6
1665	4	3	9	19	56	31	13	8	13	1	0	20	1	12	4	6
1666	3	5	7	21	49	25	14	10	13	2	1	16	5	16	25	6
1667	1	3	6	19	36	20	7	10	7	2	3	6	4	12	4	7
1668	2	3	6	19	34	19	7	9	7	3	3	3	0	9	3	6
1669	2	4	6	19	35	17	7	8	7	3	3	2	0	9	3	7
1670	5	4	6	19	34	17	7	10	6	3	3	2	0	7	5	6
1671	6	4	6	19	34	19	6	12	7	3	3	2	0	7	3	6
1672	6	3	6	19	35	14	7	13	7	5	8	4	21	7	26	5
1673	7	3	6	19	36	13	8	13	5	6	14	4	15	4	13	8
1674	7	3	6	22	36	13	7	15	3	5	13	0	1	4	5	8
1675	8	3	6	22	38	14	8	15	3	5	12	0	1	4	5	8
1676	8	3	6	22	40	14	8	15	3	5	12	0	1	4	5	8
1677	8	3	5	23	41	14	7	17	3	5	12	0	0	5	7	8
1678	8	5	5	28	42	14	7	16	3	5	12	0	0	5	14	9
1679	8	7	5	40	41	14	7	17	3	5	12	1	0	5	14	8
1680	8	8	4	42	39	13	7	18	3	5	11	0	0	4	15	9
1681	8	8	4	42	40	13	7	18	3	5	11	0	0	4	16	9
1682	9	9	3	39	41	12	7	19	3	5	11	0	0	4	15	9
1683	9	10	3	39	42	11	7	19	2	4	3	0	0	4	13	7
1684	9	10	3	39	42	11	7	19	3	4	3	0	0	4	11	7
1685	9	11	3	39	42	12	9	18	3	4	3	0	0	4	11	7

Appendix III: Ordnance Establishment of 1666

The ordnance and complement table shown below is adapted from a document dating from April of 1666 preserved in the British Museum (Add 9302). This establishment should be used with the greatest care, for the simple reason that it began to be modified almost as soon as it was issued. Complements, especially, were found to be inadequate for flagships and several other large vessels, and in May a number of revisions were authorized:

Ship	Men
1st Rates	
Royal Sovereign	700
Royal Prince	632
Royal Charles	700
Royal James	532
2nd Rates	
Victory	462
Royal Oak	462
Royal Katherine	462
Henry	452
Triumph	442
Swiftsure	392
3rd Rates	
Defiance	332
Fairfax	320
Mary	312
Monck	280

In early July the 4th Rates *Leopard* and *Matthias* both had their complements increased by 50 men. Later in the same month a great many ships were granted temporary increases 'until the next engagement is over'.

There is less evidence for changes in the ordnance allowances, but some are known. In July the *Royal Sovereign* seems to have had 102 guns (and 800 men), while as described in Chapter 4 the new 2nd Rate *Loyal London* ended up with a drastically modified armament. It should also be noted that some accounts of the Four Days' Battle mention that many English ships had more guns than the establishment authorized. This is partly borne out by the fact that the Dutch found the 2nd Rate *Swiftsure* (nominally a 66-gun ship) mounting 72 guns when they captured her. A much more disturbing discrepancy arises from Dutch reports of the ordnance found in the captured *Royal Prince*. Because of differences in Dutch weight standards it is impossible to interpret their figures with certainty, but it appears that the composition of her armament differed greatly from the establishment:

Dutch Figures	Probable English Equivalents
16–48pdrs at 7000lbs	Cannon-of-7 (42pdrs)
16–36pdrs at 5000lbs	Demi-cannon (32pdrs)
30–24pdrs at 4000lbs	Culverins (18pdrs)
16–10pdrs at 2700lbs	Demi-culverins (9pdrs)
14–6pdrs at 1400lbs	Sakers (5pdrs)

Regardless of how closely the establishment was followed, it still provides extremely useful information about the arming of ships in the 1660s. Compared with later establishments (see Appendices IV and V) most vessels carried heavier pieces, though the overall numbers of guns were somewhat fewer. Note especially the assignment of cannon-of-7 to 2nd Rates and demi-cannon to some 4th Rates.

A number of features of the establishment require explanation. It includes several ships which were still under construction in April of 1666; the 2nd Rate *Loyal London*; the 3rd Rates *Cambridge*, *Monmouth*, and *Warspite*; and the 4th Rates *Greenwich*, *St David*, and *St Patrick*. The details for the new 4th Rates were left blank. Also left blank – unaccountably – were the entries for the 4th Rates *Unity* and *Expedition*, the 5th Rate *Orange*, and the 6th Rate *Cygnet*. The document also contains discrepancies between the armament breakdown and the total for the 4th Rate *Sapphire*. The 62-gun *Clove Tree*, usually classed as a 4th Rate despite her size, is listed in the document as a 3rd Rate.

To facilitate comparisons the format, order of ships, and spellings have been modified below from those in the document. Also, ketches and pinks have here been separated from the other 6th Rates, though they are all grouped together in the document. Note that the guns described as 'sakers' were probably the same as what came to be called 'light sakers' in the 1670s; pieces throwing shot weighing about five pounds.

Name	Men	Guns	Cannon-of-7	Demi-cannon	24pdrs	Culverins	12pdrs	Demi-culverins	8pdrs	Sakers or Saker-cutts
First Rates										
Royal Sovereign	600	92	22	6	–	28	–	36	–	–
Royal Prince	600	92	22	6	–	28	–	36	–	–
Royal Charles	550	82	20	6	–	26	–	30	–	–
Royal James	500	82	–	22	–	26	–	34	–	–
Second Rates										
Loyal London	470	80	22	4	–	26	–	28	–	–
Victory	450	76	22	4	–	26	–	24	–	–
Royal Oak	450	76	22	4	–	26	–	24	–	–
Royal Katherine	450	76	10	12	–	30	–	22	–	2
Henry	440	72	–	20	–	30	–	18	–	4
Triumph	380	72	–	20	–	26	–	24	–	2
Old James	380	70	–	22	–	26	–	18	–	4
Swiftsure	380	66	–	22	–	28	–	16	–	–
St Andrew	360	66	–	20	–	20	–	26	–	–
St George	360	66	–	20	–	20	–	26	–	–
Unicorn	320	60	–	22	–	14	–	20	–	4
Vanguard	320	60	–	22	–	2	24	8	–	4
Rainbow	310	56	–	20	–	2	22	12	–	–
Third Rates										
House of Sweeds	280	70	–	26	–	–	26	–	–	20
Cambridge	320	64	–	22	–	28	–	14	–	–

Name	Men	Guns	Cannon-of-7	Demi-cannon	24pdrs	Culverins	12pdrs	Demi-culverins	8pdrs	Sakers or Saker-cutts
Defiance	320	64	–	22	–	28	–	14	–	–
Monmouth	320	64	–	22	–	28	–	14	–	–
Rupert	320	64	–	22	–	28	–	14	–	–
Warspite	320	64	–	22	–	28	–	14	–	–
Clove Tree	250	62	–	24	–	–	–	26	–	12
Helverston	260	60	–	24	–	–	–	26	–	10
Golden Phoenix	260	60	–	24	–	2	24	10	–	–
Slothany	280	60	–	22	–	2	24	12	–	–
Fairfax	300	60	–	22	–	4	26	8	–	–
Henrietta	300	58	–	20	–	4	26	8	–	–
Mary	300	58	–	20	–	4	26	8	–	–
Montagu	300	58	–	20	–	4	26	8	–	–
Resolution	280	58	–	20	–	4	26	8	–	–
Revenge	280	58	–	20	–	4	26	8	–	–
Anne	280	58	–	22	–	2	–	32	–	2
Dreadnought	280	58	–	22	–	2	–	32	–	2
Gloucester	280	58	–	22	–	2	–	32	–	2
Plymouth	280	58	–	22	–	2	–	32	–	2
York	280	58	–	22	–	2	–	32	–	2
Dunkirk	260	58	–	22	–	2	–	32	–	2
Lion	260	58	–	22	–	2	–	32	–	2
Monck	260	58	–	22	–	2	–	32	–	2
Essex	260	56	–	12	–	12	–	28	–	4
Fourth Rates										
Greenwich	260	58								
Leopard	250	56	–	22	–	2	–	24	–	6
Seven Oaks	190	54	–	22	–	–	–	24	–	8
Matthias	200	54	–	–	24	–	–	20	–	10
Charles V	200	54	–	–	–	22	–	24	–	8
Princess	220	52	–	10	–	12	–	4	20	6
Yarmouth	200	52	–	–	22	2	–	20	–	8
Bristol	200	52	–	–	–	26	–	22	–	4
Mars	180	52	–	–	–	22	–	24	–	6
Happy Return	190	52	–	–	–	22	–	22	–	8
Antelope	190	52	–	–	–	22	–	20	–	10
Convertine	190	52	–	–	–	24	–	–	20	8
St David	220	50	–	–	–	22	–	–	–	–
St Patrick	220	50	–	–	–	–	–	–	–	–
Newcastle	200	50	–	10	–	12	–	22	–	6
West Friesland	180	50	–	–	22	–	–	22	–	6
Santa Maria	180	50	–	–	–	22	–	22	–	6
Jersey	190	50	–	–	–	22	–	20	–	8
Mary Rose	190	50	–	–	–	22	–	20	–	8
Portland	180	48	–	–	–	22	–	24	–	2
Breda	180	48	–	–	–	22	–	20	–	6
Centurion	180	48	–	–	–	22	–	20	–	6

Name	Men	Guns	Culverins	12pdrs	Demi-culverins	6pdrs	Sakers	Minions
Fourth Rates								
Diamond	180	48	22	–	20	–	6	–
Reserve	180	48	22	–	20	–	6	–
Swallow	180	48	22	–	20	–	6	–
Crown	170	48	22	–	20	–	6	–
Black Spread Eagle	180	48	22	–	18	–	8	–
Gelder de Ruyter	180	48	22	–	18	–	8	–
Advice	180	48	22	–	16	–	10	–
Bonaventure	180	48	22	–	16	–	10	–
Assistance	170	46	22	–	20	–	4	–
Dover	170	46	22	–	20	–	4	–
Foresight	170	46	22	–	20	–	4	–
Kent	170	46	22	–	20	–	4	–
Ruby	170	46	22	–	20	–	4	–
Portsmouth	160	44	22	–	18	–	4	–
Marmaduke	160	42	12	–	22	–	8	–
Elizabeth	160	42	12	–	20	–	10	–
Hampshire	160	42	12	–	16	–	14	–
Golden Lion	170	42	–	20	–	18	4	–
St Paul	160	40	22	–	18	–	–	–
Hope	170	40	22	–	–	–	18	–
Dragon	160	40	12	–	20	–	8	–
Tiger	160	40	12	–	16	–	12	–
Sapphire	160	40	12	–	10	–	14	–
Black Bull	160	40	–	22	–	–	18	–
Delft	160	40	–	22	–	–	18	–

Name	Men	Guns	Culverins	12pdrs	Demi-culverins	6pdrs	Sakers	Minions
Zealand	160	40	–	22	–	–	18	
Amity	150	38	12	–	14	–	14	–
Assurance	150	38	10	–	24	–	4	–
Adventure	150	38	10	–	14	–	14	–
Guinea	150	38	10	–	10	–	18	–
Welcome	150	36	–	–	–	–	–	–
Constant Warwick	150	34	12	–	12	–	10	–
Providence	140	34	6	–	14	–	14	–
Expedition	140	34	–	–	–	–	–	–
Unity	150	–	–	–	–	–	–	–
Fifth Rates								
Falcon	140	36	18	–	–	–	18	–
Sweepstakes	140	36	–	22	–	–	14	–
Fountain	130	36	–	20	2	14	–	–
Great Gift	130	34	8	–	20	–	6	–
Sorlings	130	34	–	–	22	–	12	–
Sophia	130	34	–	–	20	–	12	–
Paul	90	32	–	–	16	–	16	–
Success	120	30	–	–	10	–	10	–
Mermaid	110	28	10	–	20	–	8	–
Pembroke	110	28	–	–	20	–	8	–
Nightingale	110	28	–	–	20	–	2	6
Colchester	110	28	–	–	18	–	10	–
Dartmouth	110	28	–	–	18	–	10	–
Forester	110	28	–	–	18	–	10	–
Guernsey	110	28	–	–	18	–	10	–
Garland	110	28	–	–	18	–	10	–
Milford	110	28	–	–	18	–	10	–
Eagle	100	26	–	–	18	–	8	–
Norwich	100	26	–	–	18	–	8	–
Oxford	110	26	–	–	18	–	8	–
Pearl	100	26	–	–	18	–	8	–
Speedwell	100	26	–	–	16	–	10	–
Little Victory	90	26	–	–	6	–	16	4
Richmond	100	24	–	–	16	–	8	–
Coventry	90	22	–	–	8	–	14	–
Lizard	75	20	–	–	–	–	14	6
Orange	110	–	–	–	–	–	–	–

Name	Men	Guns	Name	Men	Guns
Sixth Rates			Hawk	40	8
Fox	60	14	Hind	35	8
Drake	70	12	Nonsuch	35	8
Little Gift	80	12	Roe	45	8
Little Mary	60	12	Wivenhoe	45	8
Martin	60	12	Swallow	35	6
Paradox	70	12	Giles	20	4
Truelove	60	12	**Fireships**		
Francis	50	10	Young Prince	50	–
Young Lion	50	10	Briar	45	–
Harp	35	6	Hound	45	–
Lily	35	6	Providence	45	–
Cygnet			Land of Promise	40	–
Pinks and Ketches			Spread Eagle	40	–
Blackmoor	50	12	Fortune	35	–
Chestnut	40	10	Greyhound	35	–
Deptford	45	10	Happy Entrance	35	–
Portsmouth	45	10	Little Unicorn	55	–
Colchester	45	8			
Eaglet	40	8			

Appendix IV: Ordnance Establishment of 1677

The ordnance establishment shown below is adapted from a document preserved at the Pepys Library, Magdalene College, Cambridge (Pepys 2867, pp201-210). The document is entitled 'The Numbers, Natures and Weights of the Guns upon each Deck of every of his Majesty's Shipps fitt to bee made & Confirmed according to ye Opinion of the Principal Officers & Commissioners of his Majesty's Navy, humbly presented by them to the Lords Commissioners for executing the Office of Lord high Admirall.' It is actually a copy, certified with Pepys' signature as having been signed and confirmed by the Lords of the Admiralty on 15 December 1677.

The establishment did not include the 30 new ships of the 1677 programme. It also did not include the details of the *Old James*, an old 2nd Rate which at that time was expected to be rebuilt as a 3rd Rate. In addition, the clerk copying the list unaccountably neglected to show the type of guns to be carried on the lower deck of the ships shown on the first page of the document (extending up to the 3rd Rate *Rupert*). Fortunately these details are available from other sources. The Admiralty itself formally issued another version of the establishment – with a few minor changes – to the Ordnance Board on 22 December 1677. This document is also preserved in the Pepys Library. It includes the ships missing from the 15 December list. It does not repeat the weights, but it is accompanied by a separate paper giving the weight breakdown for the armament of the 30 projected ships. The information shown in the 22 December list has here been used to fill in the gaps in the otherwise more detailed 15 December document.

Both lists give two ordnance allowances for each ship. The first is the maximum armament, which was to be carried only during wartime for ships operating in home waters. The second was a reduced armament which was to be carried during peacetime or on overseas stations in wartime. To save space the peacetime establishment has not been shown here. For most ships it was about 10 per cent less than the wartime figure.

The clerk compiling the list made a number of arithmetical mistakes in computing figures for the 'Total Weight' column. By the time he reached the smaller 4th Rates he was evidently either distracted or very tired; in one stretch five out of six entries were miscomputed. Such errors have been corrected in the table below. There were also several of what appear to be transcriptional mistakes from copying the original document. Where these are obvious they have been corrected as well. For example the establishment showed the 4th Rate *Woolwich* as a 54-gun ship, but included 56 in the breakdown. The lower deck armament for 'war at home' was given as 24 guns. For peacetime the number was reduced to 22, *but with no change in weight*. From this it is obvious that the correct lower deck armament was 22 guns for both peace and war, and that is exactly what is shown by the 22 December list. In another case the 46-gun 4th Rates *Dragon, Hampshire,* and *Portsmouth* were shown with a wartime quarterdeck armament of 4 light sakers weighing 3 tons. The peacetime entry showed the same 4

guns weighing only 2 tons. Since the total numbers of guns in both conditions were consistent with the breakdowns, the mistakes here must be in the weights. This seems to have arisen from the clerk's copying method. A large number of preceding entries were listed as carrying in wartime 6 light sakers weighing 3 tons, and in peacetime 4 light sakers weighing 2 tons. The clerk was evidently copying the original table column by column, and failed to note the change in the wartime entry. It is clear from the context that all of the light sakers carried by the 48- and 46-gun 4th Rates actually weighed a half-ton each.

One apparent error could not be corrected. This was the entry for the *Kingfisher*, a 4th Rate shown as a 46-gun ship, but with 48 guns included in the breakdown: 22 on the lower deck, 20 on the upper, and 6 on the quarterdeck. From the 22 December list it is clear that the proper figure for the lower deck was 20 guns. In this case the weights in the earlier list are consistent with the number of guns shown, so the mistake was probably not the copyist's, but the original compiler's. Since the correction would require an arbitrary adjustment in weight, the entry is shown below as it appears in the document, inconsistency and all. The table includes several other possible inconsistencies. The armament of the 6th Rates and ketches is shown simply as 'sakers.' The weights, however, suggest that at least some of these guns were actually light sakers. Other problems of this sort may be noted in the entries for various individual ships throughout the list.

The table distinguishes only two classes of sakers. Such guns actually came in three calibres: a 'light' size, firing a shot weighing about 5lb; an 'ordinary' size, firing a 6 or $6\frac{1}{4}$lb shot; and an 'extraordinary' size, firing a $7\frac{1}{2}$ or 8lb shot. In the 1677 establishment both of the larger sizes are shown simply as 'sakers', without distinction. It is impossible to determine from the list which ships carried which type, but the reader should be aware that such a difference existed.

In the table below, all weights are shown in tons. Fractions are expressed in decimal form and not in the hundredweights shown in the actual document. For the sake of convenience the order of ships in the document has been slightly adjusted. It should be noted that, despite the headings, the establishment did not correspond to the true gunport configurations of the ships. In addition, for most vessels the weights of the guns of each calibre were not homogeneous. For more details about these matters, see Appendix VI.

Name	Guns	Lower Deck		Middle Deck		Upper Deck		Quarterdeck & Forecastle		Poop		Total Weight
		No	Wt	No	Wt	No	Wt	No	Wt	No	Wt	
First Rates		Cannon-of-7		Culverin		Saker		Light Saker		3pdr		
Britannia	100	26	84.5	28	58.8	28	30.8	16	12.8	2	0.5	187.4
				24pdr		Demi-culverin						
Royal Sovereign	100	26	78.0	28	51.0	28	38.0	14	9.2	4	0.8	177.0
				Culverin								
Prince	100	26	77.75	28	50.0	28	36.0	14	8.5	4	0.8	173.0
Royal Charles	100	26	77.75	28	50.0	28	36.0	14	8.5	4	0.8	173.0
Royal James	100	26	77.75	28	50.0	28	36.0	14	8.5	4	0.8	173.0

Name	Guns	Lower Deck		Middle Deck		Upper Deck		Quarterdeck & Forecastle		Poop		Total Weight
		No	Wt	No	Wt	No	Wt	No	Wt	No	Wt	
		Cannon-of-7		Culverin		Demi-culverin		Light Saker		3pdr		
London	96	26	75.25	28	48.25	26	34.25	12	7.2	4	0.8	165.75
St Andrew	96	26	74.5	28	47.5	26	34.0	12	7.2	4	0.8	164.0
Charles	96	26	71.0	28	45.0	26	31.25	12	6.95	4	0.8	155.0
		Demi-cannon										
St Michael	90	26	63.0	26	41.25	26	28.0	10	6.1	2	0.4	138.75
Second Rates						Saker						
9 to be built	90	26	70.2	26	52.0	26	28.6	10	8.0	2	0.5	159.3
Royal Katherine	84	26	58.25	26	41.25	24	26.75	8	5.0	–	–	131.25
Victory	82	24	57.5	26	40.25	24	26.75	8	5.0	–	–	129.0
Henry	82	24	57.0	26	40.0	24	26.0	8	5.0	–	–	128.0
French Ruby	80	24	53.5	24	37.5	24	24.0	8	5.0	–	–	120.0
St George	70	22	50.5	22	35.0	20	24.0	6	3.0	–	–	112.5
Triumph	70	22	50.0	22	35.0	20	24.0	6	3.0	–	–	112.0
				Demi-culverin								
Unicorn	64	22	47.5	22	35.0	14	20.0	6	3.0	–	–	105.5
Rainbow	64	22	46.0	22	34.25	14	18.0	6	3.0	–	–	101.25

Name	Guns	Lower Deck		Upper Deck		Quarterdeck & Forecastle		Poop		Total Weight
		No	Wt	No	Wt	No	Wt	No	Wt	
Third Rates		Demi-cannon		Culverin		Light Saker		3pdr		
Royal Oak	74	28	71.0	28	46.0	16	10.6	2	0.4	128.0
				12pdr						
Edgar	72	26	63.0	26	43.0	16	9.7	4	0.8	116.5
20 to be built	70	26	70.2	26	41.6	14	11.2	4	1.0	124.0
Old James	70	26	?	26	?	14	?	4	?	?
Harwich	70	24	61.5	21	41.5	18	9.2	4	0.8	113.0
Swiftsure	70	24	60.0	24	41.0	18	9.2	4	0.8	111.0
Cambridge	70	26	59.5	26	38.5	16	9.6	2	0.4	108.0
Warspite	70	26	57.5	26	37.25	16	8.35	2	0.4	103.5
Resolution	70	26	56.0	26	36.25	16	8.35	2	0.4	101.0
		24pdr								
Monmouth	66	26	55.75	24	36.0	14	7.85	2	0.4	100.0
Rupert	66	26	53.5	24	32.0	14	7.5	2	0.4	93.4
		Demi-cannon								
Defiance	54	24	57.5	24	37.25	14	8.35	2	0.4	103.5
		24pdr		Demi-culverin						
Mary	64	24	53.0	26	31.5	12	7.1	2	0.4	92.0
Montagu	62	24	53.5	24	31.5	12	7.6	2	0.4	93.0
Henrietta	62	24	50.25	24	29.5	12	6.85	2	0.4	87.0
Revenge	62	24	50.25	24	29.5	12	6.85	2	0.4	87.0
Dreadnought	62	24	49.0	24	29.5	12	5.6	2	0.4	84.5
Gloucester	60	24	50.25	24	29.5	10	6.85	2	0.4	87.0
Plymouth	60	24	50.25	24	29.5	10	5.85	2	0.4	86.0
York	60	24	49.0	24	29.5	10	5.6	2	0.4	84.5
Lion	60	24	48.5	24	29.5	10	5.6	2	0.4	84.0
Dunkirk	60	24	46.5	24	28.5	10	5.6	2	0.4	81.0
Monck	60	24	46.0	24	28.0	10	5.6	2	0.4	80.0

Name	Guns	Lower Deck		Upper Deck		Quarterdeck & Forecastle		Total Weight
		No	Wt	No	Wt	No	Wt	
Fourth Rates		24pdr		Saker		Light Saker		
Woolwich	54	22	47.5	22	28.5	10	6.0	82.0
Oxford	54	24	50.0	22	23.0	8	4.0	77.0
Leopard	54	24	50.0	22	23.0	8	4.0	77.0
Greenwich	54	24	48.0	22	23.0	8	4.0	75.0

Name	Guns	Lower Deck		Upper Deck		Quarterdeck & Forecastle		Total Weight
		No	Wt	No	Wt	No	Wt	
		24pdr		Saker		Light Saker		
St David	54	24	47.0	22	22.0	8	4.0	73.0
Yarmouth	54	24	46.0	22	22.0	8	4.0	72.0
Newcastle	54	24	46.0	22	22.0	8	4.0	72.0
Happy Return	54	24	46.0	22	22.0	8	4.0	72.0
Princess	54	24	46.0	22	22.0	8	4.0	72.0
		Culverin						
Portland	50	22	44.75	22	20.75	6	3.0	68.5
Antelope	48	22	42.25	20	20.25	6	3.0	65.5
Swallow	48	22	41.25	20	19.25	6	3.0	63.5
Jersey	48	22	41.25	20	19.25	6	3.0	63.5
Assistance	48	22	41.25	20	19.25	6	3.0	63.5
Mary Rose	48	22	41.25	20	19.25	6	3.0	63.5
Diamond	48	22	41.25	20	19.25	6	3.0	63.5
Stavoreen	48	22	41.0	20	19.0	6	3.0	63.0
Bristol	48	22	41.0	20	19.0	6	3.0	63.0
Dover	48	22	41.0	20	19.0	6	3.0	63.0
Advice	48	22	41.0	20	19.0	6	3.0	63.0
Reserve	48	22	40.5	20	18.25	6	3.0	61.75
Foresight	48	22	40.5	20	18.25	6	3.0	61.75
Crown	48	22	40.5	20	17.75	6	3.0	61.25
Ruby	48	22	40.5	20	17.5	6	3.0	61.0
Centurion	48	22	40.5	20	17.5	6	3.0	61.0
Bonaventure	48	22	37.5	20	18.0	6	3.0	58.5
Kingfisher	46	22	42.25	20	20.25	6	3.0	65.5
Hampshire	46	22	34.25	20	16.5	4	2.0	52.75
Portsmouth	46	22	34.25	20	16.25	4	2.0	52.5
Dragon	46	22	33.0	20	15.5	4	2.0	50.5
		Demi-culverin						
Adventure	44	22	32.35	18	15.75	4	2.0	50.0
Tiger	44	22	32.5	18	15.5	4	2.0	50.0
Sweepstakes	42	20	27.0	18	13.5	4	1.5	42.0
Constant Warwick	42	20	27.0	18	13.5	4	1.5	42.0
Assurance	42	20	27.0	18	13.5	4	1.5	42.0
Phoenix	42	20	26.75	18	13.25	4	1.5	41.5
Falcon	42	20	26.75	18	13.25	4	1.5	41.5
Nonsuch	42	20	25.75	18	12.25	4	1.5	39.5
		Saker				3pdr		
Charles Galley	32	6	7.5	22	21.0	4	1.5	30.0
James Galley	30	4	5.0	22	18.5	4	1.5	25.0

Name	Guns	Upper Deck		Lower Deck		Quarterdeck		Total Weight
		No	Wt	No	Wt	No	Wt	
Fifth Rates		Demi-culverin		Light Saker		Minion		
Sapphire	32	18	28.0	10	8.5	4	1.5	38.0
Swan	32	18	26.0	10	7.5	4	1.5	35.0
Success	32	18	25.25	10	7.25	4	1.5	34.0
Mermaid	32	18	25.25	10	7.25	4	1.5	34.0
Dartmouth	32	18	22.5	10	5.25	4	1.5	29.25
Hunter	30	18	22.25	8	5.25	4	1.5	29.0
Pearl	30	18	22.25	8	5.25	4	1.5	29.0
Norwich	30	18	22.0	8	5.0	4	1.5	28.5
Garland	30	18	22.0	8	5.0	4	1.5	28.5
Guernsey	30	18	22.0	8	5.0	4	1.5	28.5
Rose	28	16	20.0	8	4.75	4	1.25	26.0
Richmond	28	16	19.75	8	4.5	4	1.25	25.5

Name	Guns	Upper Deck		Quarterdeck		Total Weight
		No	Wt	No	Wt	
Sixth Rates		Saker		Minion		
Lark	18	16	13.25	2	0.75	14.0
Saudadoes	16	16	12.24	–	–	12.25
Greyhound	16	16	12.0	–	–	12.0
Drake	16	16	10.5	–	–	10.5
Francis	16	16	10.5	–	–	10.5
Roebuck	16	16	10.25	–	–	10.25
Young Spragge	10	10	5.25	–	–	5.25
		3pdr				
Fanfan	4	4	0.75	–	–	0.75
Ketches		Saker				
Deptford	10	10	5.25	–	–	5.25
Quaker	10	10	5.25	–	–	5.25
Fireships		Light Saker				
Eagle	14	10	?	4	1.25	?
Holmes	8	–	–	8	3.0	3.0
Castle	8	8	6.0	–	–	6.0
Ann & Christopher	8	8	6.0	–	–	6.0
Wyvenhoe	6	6	3.25	–	–	6.0

Name	Guns	Upper Deck	
		No	Wt
		3pdr	
Yachts			
Charles	8	8	?
Katherine	8	8	?
Anne	8	8	?
Monmouth	8	8	?
Cleveland	8	8	?
Portsmouth	8	8	?
Merlin	8	8	?
Richmond	8	8	?
Navy	8	8	?
Kitchen	8	8	?
Charlotte	8	8	?
Isle of Wight	4	4	?
Deal	4	4	?
Bezan	4	4	?
Sloops			
Bonetta	4	4	?
Spy	4	4	?
Chatham	4	4	?
Chatham Double	4	4	?
Experiment	4	4	?
Emsworth	4	4	?
Dove	4	4	?
Hound	4	4	?
Invention	4	4	?
Prevention	4	4	?
Woolwich	4	4	?
Hunter	4	4	?
Whipster	4	4	?

UNARMED VESSELS

Yachts
Jemmy
Queenborough

Smacks
Bridget
Little London
Royal Escape
Sheerness
Shish

Hoys
Transporter
Unity horseboat
Marigold
Lighter

Hulks
Arms of Horn
Arms of Rotterdam
Slothany
Alphin
Stathouse
Elias

Appendix V: Proposed Ordnance Establishment of 1685

The list below is taken from an ordnance establishment originating from the Ordnance Board on 1 January 1685. This was entitled 'A List of his Majesty's Navy Royall with the Ordnance proposed to each respectively in time of Warr'. Appended to it is an abstract comparing the number of pieces required with the actual inventory of guns. This establishment was probably prepared on instructions from the Admiralty, but there is no evidence that it ever received official confirmation. The document is preserved in the Pepys Library, Magdalene College, Cambridge (Pepys 2879, pp111-122).

The 1685 establishment differed considerably from the 1677 list. In general it conformed better to actual gunport availability than most earlier establishments (see Appendix VI). For most of the larger vessels it proposed a reduction in the number of heavy guns and an increase in the number of medium calibre pieces.

It should be noted that by 1685 the terminology for small-bore guns had reverted to the usage of the 1660s. Thus, the guns which had been called 'sakers' in the 1677 establishment became '6pdrs' and '8pdrs' in the 1685 list, while the 'sakers' of the 1685 establishment correspond to the 5pdr 'light sakers' of 1677.

In the table the short, lightweight, taper-chambered guns known as 'drakes' are distinguished by the letter 'd'. Another class of short guns, known as 'cutts', are indicated by 'c'. These were pieces which had been sawed-off because of defects in the muzzles. All other guns in the table were standard true-bored 'fortified' weapons, noted by 'f' in the abstract only. The format and the order of ships have been slightly modified.

Name	Guns	Cannon of-7	Demi-cannon	24pdr	Culverin	12pdr	Demi-culverin	6pdr	Saker	Minion	3pdr
First Rates											
Britannia	100	22	–	–	32	–	–	–	44	–	2
Royal Sovereign	100	26	–	26	–	28	–	–	20	–	–
Prince	100	24	–	–	32	–	34 10c	–	–	–	–
Royal Charles	100	24	–	–	32	–	30 12c	–	–	–	2
Royal James	100	–	22	–	30	–	–	42	–	–	6
London	96	24	4	–	26	30	–	12	–	–	–
St Andrew	96	26	–	–	26	–	28	–	14 2c	–	–
Charles	96	22	4	–	28	–	30 12c	–	–	–	–
St Michael	96	–	26	–	26	–	26 10c	4	–	–	4
Second Rates											
9 new ships	90	–	22	–	30	–	–	–	36	–	2
Royal Katherine	86	–	26	–	26	–	–	–	34	–	–
Victory	80	24	–	–	24	–	24 8c	–	–	–	–
French Ruby	74	–	22	–	22	–	20 8c	–	–	2	–
St George	68	–	18	–	4	22	–	–	18d 6c	–	–
Triumph	70	–	20	–	24	–	20 4c	–	2c	–	–
Unicorn	60	–	20	–	4	22	–	4c	10	–	–
3rd Rates											
Royal Oak	74	–	24	–	30	–	12 4c	–	–	–	4
Edgar	74	–	24	–	28	–	12 10c	–	–	–	–
20 new ships	70	–	22	–	4	26	–	–	14	–	4
Harwich	64	–	24	–	–	22	14c	–	–	4	–
Swiftsure	66	–	24	–	–	24	–	–	16	–	2

Name	Guns	Cannon-of-7	Demi-cannon	24pdr	Culverin	12pdr	Demi-culverin	6pdr	Saker	Minion	3pdr
Cambridge	70	–	26	–	26	–	2 16c	–	–	–	–
Warspite	68	–	24	–	–	26	14	–	–	–	4
Resolution	68	–	22	–	4	24	–	–	18	–	–
Monmouth	66	–	26	–	–	24	–	14	–	–	2
Rupert	64	–	–	24	2	26	2 10c	–	–	–	–
Defiance	64	–	–	24	–	–	24 14c	–	–	–	2
Mary	60	–	–	24	–	24	–	–	6 4c	–	2
Montagu	58	–	–	20	4	–	24d 10c	–	–	–	–
Henrietta	60	–	–	24	–	–	30 4d 2c	–	–	–	–
Dreadnought	62	–	–	24	–	–	26	–	2 10c	–	–
Plymouth	58	–	22d	–	2	–	26d 8c	–	–	–	–
York	60	–	20d	–	4	–	26d 10c	–	–	–	–
Lion	60	–	–	24	–	24	–	–	10d	–	2
Dunkirk	60	–	–	–	22	–	24 12c	–	2c	–	–
Monck	58	–	24d	–	–	–	26 8c	–	–	–	–

Name	Guns	24pdr	Culverin	12pdr	Demi-culverin	8pdr	6pdr	Saker	Minion	3pdr	Falconet
Fourth Rates											
Woolwich	54	22	–	–	–	22	–	4 6c	–	–	–
Oxford	54	22	–	–	6d	26	–	–	–	–	–
Leopard	54	–	24	–	24d 6c	–	–	–	–	–	–
Greenwich	60	22	2	–	26	–	–	10	–	–	–
St David	54	24	–	–	2d	22	–	2 6c	–	–	–
Newcastle	52	–	24d	–	22d	–	–	6c	–	–	–
Happy Return	48	–	22	–	20 6c	–	–	–	–	–	–
Portland	50	–	22	–	–	22	–	4c	–	2	–
Antelope	46	–	–	22	20d	–	–	4c	–	–	–
Swallow	50	–	22	–	2	20	–	4c	–	–	2
Jersey	48	–	22	–	–	–	22	4c	–	–	–
Assistance	48	–	22d	–	22	–	–	6c	–	–	–
Mary Rose	48	–	22	–	6c	20	–	–	–	–	–
Diamond	48	–	–	22	20	–	–	6c	–	–	–
Bristol	48	–	–	22	–	22	–	–	–	4	–
Dover	54	–	22d	–	24	–	–	8c	–	–	–
Advice	50	–	22	–	–	20	–	8c	–	–	–
Reserve	48	–	22	–	22	–	–	4c	–	–	
Foresight	52	–	22d	–	22d	–	–	4c	4	–	–
Crown	50	–	22d	–	22d	–	–	6c	–	–	–
Ruby	48	–	22d	–	22d	–	–	4c	–	–	–
Centurion	50	–	22d	–	–	22	–	6c	–	–	–
Bonaventure	52	–	–	22	–	22	–	2d	–	6	–
Kingfisher	46	–	–	20	–	–	20	–	–	6	–
Hampshire	46	–	–	20	–	–	20	–	4	2	–

Name	Guns	24pdr	Culverin	12pdr	Demi-culverin	8pdr	6pdr	Saker	Minion	3pdr	Falconet
Portsmouth	48	–	22d	–	–	–	20	6c	–	–	–
Dragon	44	–	5 11d	–	20d	–	–	4d 2c	–	2	–
Adventure	40	–	12d	–	6d	–	16	6c	–	–	–
Sweepstakes	40	–	–	20	–	–	–	2 18d	–	–	–
Constant Warwick	40	–	–	–	18d	–	18	–	–	4	–
Assurance	42	–	10d	–	12d	–	16	–	–	4	–
Phoenix	40	–	–	–	20d	–	–	18	–	2	–
Falcon	40	–	–	20	–	–	16	4	–	–	–
Nonsuch	40	–	–	–	20d	–	–	11 5d	4	–	–
Charles Galley	32	–	–	–	–	–	26	–	–	6	–
James Galley	30	–	–	–	–	–	10	16	–	4	–
Tiger rebuilt	46	–	–	–	20d	–	–	18 8c	–	–	–
Mordaunt	46	–	–	20	–	18	–	8	–	–	–
Tiger Prize	46	–	–	–	20d	–	–	26	–	–	–
Golden Horse	40	–	–	–	20d	–	16	–	4	–	–
Half Moon	40	–	–	–	–	18	18	–	4	–	–
Two Lions	40	–	–	–	–	18	18	–	4	–	–
3 to be built	54	22	–	–	22 10d	–	–	–	–	–	–

Fifth Rates

Name	Guns	24pdr	Culverin	12pdr	Demi-culverin	8pdr	6pdr	Saker	Minion	3pdr	Falconet
Sapphire	28	–	–	–	–	16	–	–	10	2	–
Swan	32	–	–	–	–	16	–	–	16	–	–
Mermaid	30	–	–	–	12	–	–	10 4c	–	–	–
Dartmouth	36	–	–	–	16d	–	–	16d	4	–	–
Pearl	28	–	–	–	12	–	10	4c	–	2	–
Garland	34	–	–	–	16	–	–	12 4c	–	2	–
Guernsey	32	–	–	–	16d	–	14	–	–	2	–
Rose	28	–	–	–	16d	–	–	8	–	4	–
Richmond	28	–	–	–	16d	–	–	4 6c	2	–	–
St Paul	28	–	–	–	16d	–	8	–	4	–	–
Orange Tree	30	–	–	–	–	–	14	–	12	4	–

Name	Guns	Demi-culverin	6pdr	Saker	Minion	3pdr
Sixth Rates						
Lark	18	–	–	16	–	2
Saudadoes	16	4c	6	4c	–	2
Greyhound	18	–	–	16c	–	2
Drake	16	–	–	2 12c	2	–
Francis	16	–	–	–	14	2
Fanfan	4	–	–	–	4	–
Two Lions	16	2 4c	–	10c	–	–
Rose Prize	8	–	–	–	–	8

Name	Guns	Demi-culverin	6pdr	Saker	Minion	3pdr
Fireships						
Eagle	12	4d	–	4d 4c	–	–
Ann & Christopher	8	–	–	–	8	–
John & Alexander	12	4d	–	8	–	–
Peace	6	–	–	–	2	4
Providence	4	–	–	–	–	4

Name	Guns	Demi-culverin	6pdr	Saker	Minion	3pdr
Sampson	8	6d	–	2	–	–
Spanish Merchant	12	4d	–	8d	–	–
Sarah	4	–	–	–	–	4
Thomas & Katherine	10	4d	–	6	–	–
Young Spragge	8	–	–	8d	–	–
Rose	8	–	–	–	8	–

Ketches

Name	Guns	Demi-culverin	6pdr	Saker	Minion	3pdr
Deptford	10	–	–	10c	–	–
Quaker	10	–	–	10c	–	–

Name	Guns	Minion	3pdr	Falcon	Falconet	Rabonet
Yachts						
Katherine	8	–	8	–	–	–
Anne	8	–	8	–	–	–
Monmouth	8	–	8	–	–	–
Cleveland	6	–	6	–	–	–
Portsmouth	6	–	8	–	–	–
Merlin	8	–	8	–	–	–
Richmond	6	–	6	–	–	–
Navy	8	–	4	4	–	–
Kitchen	6	–	6	–	–	–
Charlotte	6	–	6	–	–	–
Isle of Wight	4	–	–	4	–	–
Deal	4	–	4	–	–	–
Bezan	6	–	–	6	–	–
Jemmy	4	–	–	4	–	–
Queenborough	4	2	–	4	–	2
Fubbs	6	–	6	–	–	–
Henrietta	6	–	6	–	–	
Isabella	13	–	10	–	2	1
Mary	8	2	6	–	–	–

Abstract

Size	Type	Proposed	On hand	Excess	Shortage
Cannon-of-7	f	192	267	75	–
	d	–	10	10	–
Demi-cannon	f	994	913	–	81
	d	66	174	108	–
24pdr	f	346	347	1	–
Culverin	f	993	1122	129	–
	d	211	406	195	–
12pdr	f	1004	956	–	48
	d	–	8	8	–
Demi-culverin	f	748	1015	267	–
	d	360	519	159	–
	c	250	286	36	–
8pdr	f	282	424	142	–
6pdr	f	382	540	158	–
	d	–	18	18	–
Saker	f	947	854	–	93
	d	93	155	62	–
	c	218	234	16	–
Minion	f	118	237	119	–
	d	–	8	8	–
3pdr	f	324	422	98	–
	d	–	1	1	–
Falcon	f	46	95	49	–
Falconet	f	4	17	13	–
Rabonet	f	3	8	5	–
TOTALS		7581	9036	1677	222

Name	3pdr	Falcon
Sloops		
Bonetta	–	4
Hound	–	4
Woolwich	–	4
Brigantine		
Whipster	4	–
Smacks		
Royal Escape	–	2
Sheerness	–	2
Shish	–	2
Little London	–	2
Tow Engine	–	–
Hoys		
Transporter	–	2
Unity horseboat	–	2
Marigold	–	2
Lighter	–	2
Hulks		
Alphin	–	–
America	–	–
Arms of Horn	–	–
Arms of Rotterdam	–	–
Slothany	–	–
Stathouse	–	–
Elias	–	–

Appendix VI: Gunport Configurations

The Restoration Navy's official ordnance lists usually make it appear that the ships mounted homogeneous calibres on each deck. Until quite recently these establishments were assumed to be good guides to the actual gunport configurations. It is now known that the gunport arrangements of most vessels did *not* match the ordnance assigned, and distribution of guns was usually more complicated than the establishments make it seem.

The table below gives gunport configurations as shown by the works of the Van de Veldes and other reliable marine artists of the period. It includes only vessels above the 5th Rate for which good portraits can be identified. Even a cursory comparison with Appendix II makes it obvious that some ships had more gunports than necessary, while others do not seem to have had nearly enough to accommodate the assigned armament. In addition, many vessels with identical establishments had considerably different gunport arrangements.

Where extra ports were present, the purpose was presumably to allow guns to be shifted from one side to the other at the tactical situation demanded. Most marine artists – including the Van de Veldes – often showed such ships with a gun in every port. This was probably incorrect in most cases, though many vessels at times carried more guns than they were supposed to.

For ships with apparently insufficient numbers of ports, the evidence from the Van de Veldes can be deceiving. This is partly because the number of ports on the poop, forecastle, and even the quarterdeck were changeable. Some of the portraits were produced in the 1660s and early 1670s, when the assigned ordnance was less numerous than it later became. Other ships were portrayed during peacetime commissions, when the armament was routinely reduced; or in ordinary, when most of the guns were stored ashore. Thus the 70-gun *Lenox* of 1678 is shown with only 30 ports a side. For a wartime commission she would have had perhaps 3 ports a side added on the forecastle and two more on the poop. In addition some ships such as the 2nd Rates *Victory* and *Henry* may have mounted guns where there were no proper ports, pointing over the low gunwales in the waist.

Even when the number of ports agreed with the number of guns, there were often apparent discrepancies in the allotment for each deck. In most cases these anomalies are accounted for by the chase pieces that provided end-on fire through the stern and beakhead bulkhead. For this purpose most ships had at least one pair of guns in each calibre which were heavier than the others, presumably long-barrelled weapons with extra range. They were often not placed on the decks to which they were assigned by the official establishments. Usually such guns also had access to broadside ports, but in a few ships one pair of guns may have been used exclusively as chasers. The actual distribution depended on the preferences of the captain.

In the table an 'R' in the 'Built' column means last rebuilding or great repair. In the body of the table the letter 'r' indicates a gun between the head rails. The letter 'g' indicates a port hidden in the quarter-gallery or its decoration. The letter 'a' indicates a port abaft th quarter-gallery. Notation such as '2 + 6' is used for ships lacking gunports in the waist. The first figure is the number of ports forward of the waist, and the second shows the number of ports abaft the waist. Ship names in italics are those for which the sources could have been misidentified. In the body of the table, italics indicate that the source drawings do not show the gunports clearly enough to make a definite count possible.

Name	Built	Lower Deck	Middle Deck	Upper Deck	Quarterdeck	Forecastle	Poop
1st Rates							
Royal Prince	1641R	13	13g	12	4	2	0
	1663R	13	13g	12	5	2	2
Royal Sovereign	1660R	13	13g	12	7	3	4
Royal Charles	1655	13	12	12	3-6a	0-2	0
Royal James	1658	13	12	12	5	2	0
Charles	1668	15	14	13	5	0	0
St Michael	1669	13	r13	13	6a	0	0
St Andrew	1670	14	13	14	5	0	0
London	1670R	14	14g	13	5	0	2
Prince	1670	15g	r15g	13	7a	0-1	1-2
Royal James	1671	14	r14	13	6	0	2
Royal Charles	1673	14g	r14	13	6	0	2
Royal James	1675	13g	r13	12	7a	2	2
Britannia	1682	14	r14	13	6	0	3
2nd Rates							
Rainbow	1617R	12	10	1 + 6g	4a	–	0
St George	1623	12	11	3 + 5	4	–	0
Triumph	1623	12	11	3 + 6	?	–	0
Unicorn	1634	12	11	2 + 5	4a	–	0
Old James	1634	13	12	3 + 6	2	–	0
Swiftsure	1653R	12	12	3 + 6	0	–	0
Henry	1656	13	12	3 + 7a	5a	–	0
London	1656	13	12	3 + 7	5a	–	0
Royal Katherine	1664	13	14g	3 + 6	5	–	0
Victory	1666R	13	12	3 + 7	3-5	–	0
Windsor Castle	1678	13	12	13	5	0	2
Duchess	1679	13	13	13	6	0	0–2
Albemarle	1680	13	r13	13	6	0	2
Duke	1682	13	r13	13	6	1	1
Neptune	1683	13	r13	13	6	0	2
Coronation	1685	13	r13	13	6	0	0
3rd Rates							
Mary	1650	13	–	12	5	2	0
Dunkirk	1651	12	–	11	6	0	1
Essex	1653	13	–	12	3	0	0
Plymouth	1653	13	–	12	4	0	1
Revenge	1654	13	–	13	5	0	0
Montagu	1654	13	–	13	5	0	0
Gloucester	1654	13	–	12	5	0	0
Anne	1654	13	–	12	4	0	0
York	1654	13	–	12	4	0	1
Monck	1659	13	–	12	4	0	0
Cambridge	1666	13	–	12	6	3	1
Warspite	1666	13	–	12	6	3	2
Rupert	1666	13	–	12	6	0	1
Resolution	1667	13	–	12	6	0	1
Swiftsure	1673	13	–	r12	5	0	0
Royal Oak	1674	14	–	13	5	0-3	2
Lenox	1678	13	–	12	5	0	0
Hampton Court	1678	13	–	12	5	0	0-2
Captain	1678	13	–	12	5	0	0
Anne	1678	13	–	13	5	0	3
Restoration	1678	13	–	13	6	2	3
Hope	1678	13	–	13	6	2	1
Elizabeth	1678	13	–	13	6	2	1-2
Burford	1679	13	–	13	5	3	1
Grafton	1679	13	–	13	6	3	2
Stirling Castle	1679	13	–	13	5	2	2
Essex or Suffolk	1679 1680	13	–	13	5	0-2	2
4th Rates							
Expedition	1637	10	–	2+ 4	1	0	0
Providence	1637	10	–	2 + 4	1	0	0
Constant Warwick	1666R	11	–	3 + 5	2	0	0
Adventure	1646	11	–	11	2	0	0
Tiger	1647	11	–	11	2	0	0
	1681R	11	–	11	5	0	0
Portsmouth	1650	11	–	11	2	0	0
Assistance	1650	11	–	12	5	0	0
Diamond	1651	12	–	11	3	0	0
Portland	1653	12	–	11	3-4	0	0
Bristol	1653	12	–	11	4	0	0
Newcastle	1653	13	–	12	3	0	0
Yarmouth	1653	13	–	12	3	0	0
Happy Return	1654	12	–	12	3	0	0
Mary Rose	1654	12	–	12	4	0	0
Dover	1654	12	–	12	3	0	0
Princess	1660	12	–	11	4	0	0
Greenwich	1666	13	–	13	5	0	0
St David	1667	11	–	10	3-5g	0	0
Phoenix	1671	11	–	10	3	0	0
Woolwich	1675	11	–	10	5g	0	0
Charles Galley	1676	1 + 2	–	11	0-3	0	0
James Galley	1676	1 + 1	–	11	0	0	0
Mordaunt	1681	11	–	12	5	0	0

Appendix VII: Establishment of Cabin Allowances, 1673

In October 1673 the Admiralty promulgated an establishment of shipboard cabin allowances to correct a number of abuses arising from the cluttered condition of the ships. The document is preserved at the Pepys Library, Magdalene College, Cambridge (Pepys 2867, pp526-8). It provides a useful and interesting description of the internal arrangements of the warships of the period.

For Ships of the First and Second Rate

Upon the poop for trumpeters 4
Roundhouse – the eldest captain 1
Afore the roundhouse, on the starboard side – the second captain .. 1
Afore the second captain on the starboard side – the eldest lieutenant . 1
Afore the roundhouse on the larboard side, for the secretary, if an admiral 1
Afore the secretary on the larboard side, for the master 1
In the two bulkhead cabins upon the quarterdeck – the chief mate and judge advocate 2
Bulkhead of the coach on the starboard side, for the second lieutenant 1
On the larboard side – the commander of the land officers 1
Upper great cabin for the commander 1
In the lobby on the starboard side –the minister 1
On the larboard side (if no staircase) – a land officer 1
On the bulkhead of the forecastle on the starboard side, for the carpenter 1
On the bulkhead of the forecastle on the larboard side, for the boatswain 1
Within the forecastle on that side, for his mate 1
The lower great cabin for the reformadoes*
On the second deck, canvas cabins for mates, pilots, pursers, midshipmen, and other officers, as the captain pleases to dispose of them 18
Pantries of wood for the commander's use 2
In the gunroom bulkhead – gunner and chirurgeon 2
In the gunroom, standing cabins for mates 2
Hanging cabins 6
Cockpit for the purser, steward, and chirurgeon's mates 5
Steward room 1

For Third Rate Ships

Upon the poop for trumpeters 4
Roundhouse divided – the starboard side, the master 1
On the larboard side, the lieutenant 1
Afore the roundhouse, on the starboard side, for a chief mate, if no second lieutenant 1
On the larboard side, for the minister 1
In the coach – half-cabins for servants 2
Bulkhead of the coach on the starboard side – a second mate 1
Larboard side – a land officer 1
Bulkhead of the quarterdeck, on the starboard side – the carpenter . 1
On the larboard side – the boatswain 1
In the steerage, cabins for a second mate and pilot 2
Pantries for the captain 2
Forecastle bulkhead, on the starboard side – the cook 1
Larboard side – the boatswain's mate 1
Under the gangway – the coxswain and midshipmen 2
In the forecastle – a midshipman and carpenter's mate 2
In the gunroom bulkhead – gunner and chirurgeon 2
In the gunroom, standing cabins 2

Between Decks, before the Gunroom Bulkhead

Cockpit – the purser 1
The steward's room and cabin 1
The Chirurgeon's mate 1
The captain's storeroom 1

For Fourth Rates

On the poop – trumpeter's cabins 2
The roundhouse (if divided) – the master and lieutenant 2
In the cuddy – two mates 2
Bulkhead of the steerage on the starboard side – the carpenter 1
On the larboard side – the boatswain 1
In the steerage, for a land officer and midshipman 2
Pantry for the captain 1
Forecastle bulkhead on the starboard side – the cook 1
Lardboard side – the boatswain's mate 1
In the gunroom bulkhead – gunner and chirurgeon 2

Between Decks

Cockpit – the purser, steward and chirurgeon's mate 3
Captain's storeroom 1
In the forecastle – carpenter's mate and midshipman 2

For a Fifth Rate

Roundhouse – the master 1
Bulkhead of the steerage on the starboard side – the carpenter 1
Larboard side – a lieutenant 1
In the steerage – two mates and midshipmen 2
Bulkhead of the gunroom – gunner and chirurgeon 2
Cockpit – purser 1
Steward room 1
chirurgeon's mate 1
Bulkhead of the forecastle – the boatswain and cook 2

For Sixth Rates

The steerage bulkhead – the master 1
Cockpit built in hold – the boatswain, carpenter, gunner, and other officers 6

No standing cabins on the middle deck of the 1st and 2nd Rate ships to be more than 6ft long fore and aft, and 5ft wide upon the deck.

No cabin in the steerage and forecastle of a 3rd and 4th Rate ship to be more than 5ft 9in long and 4in (sic) wide upon the upper deck.

In the steerage of a 5th Rate ship no cabin to be more than 5ft 6in long, and 4ft wide upon the upper deck.

*Gentlemen volunteers, serving with commissions from the King, but without command

These drawings are intended to illustrate the rigging and internal arrangements of a 'typical' 100-gun 1st Rate of the1670s. The longitudinal section and deck plans include several early eighteenth century features which may or may not have been present as early as the 1670s. Such conjectural features are indicated by asterisks. The cabin assignments are based on the Establishment of 1673 (see Appendix VII). The rigging plans show a typical configuration of about 1675, but it should be realised that there were many variations.

A. Longitudinal Profile

1. Figurehead
2. Range bitts
3. Head grating
4. Knightheads
5. Beakhead
6. Fore sheet bitts
7. Fore jeer bitts
8. Belfry
9. Fore hatch (all decks)
10. Main hatch (all decks)
11. Gallows and Main sheet bitts
12. Main jeer bitts
13. After hatch (all decks)
14. Coach
15. Lobby
16. Spiral staircase (port side)
17. Great cabin bedplace (starboard side)
18. Great cabin
19. Stern-gallery
20. Cuddy
21. Roundhouse
22. Upper roundhouse
23. Stern lanterns
24. Fireplace

25. Jeer capstan
26. Warping capstan
27. Spiral staircase
28. Whipstaff
29. Lower great cabin
30. Manger
31 & 32. Riding Bitts
33. Pump cranks
34. Main capstan
35. Gunroom; tiller overhead
36. Storerooms; sail rooms
37. Cable tier
38. Cockpit
39. Steward's room and storerooms
40. Fore peak
41. Light room
42. Filling room*
43. Cartridge scuttle*
44. Forward magazine
45. Storerooms
46. Shot locker
47. Main hold
48. Shot locker*
49. Main well and chain pumps
50. Shot locker

51. After hold
52. Spirit room
53. Fish room
54. Powder room or after magazine
55. Light room
56. Bread room
57. Lady's hole (Gunner's stores)*
58. Cutwater
59. Stem
60. Keel
61. Floors
62. Kelson and ceiling
63. Riders
64. Deadwood
65. Sternpost
66. Rudder
67. Forecastle
68. Orlop
69. Lower deck
70. Middle deck
71. Upper deck
72. Quarterdeck
73. Poop
74. Topgallant poop

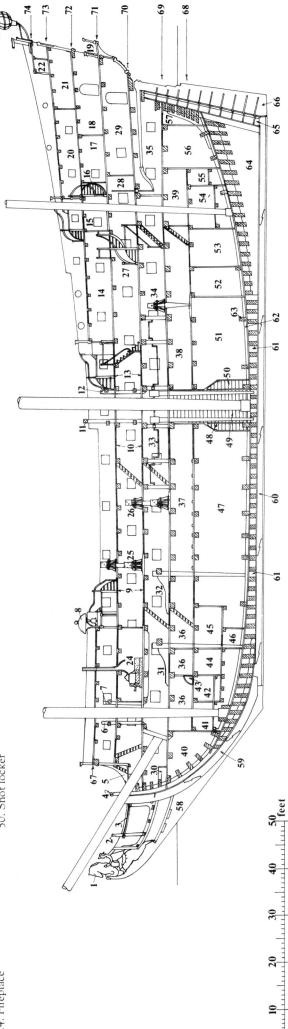

B. Hull and Standing Rigging

Hull

1. Figurehead
2. Headrails and Head Timbers
3. Deadblock for fore tack
4. Cheeks
5. Knightheads
6. Cathead
7. Eking rail or eking supporter
8. Hawseholes
9. Anchor lining
10. Billboard
11. Fish davit
12. Fore channel
13. Chesstree for main tack
14. Skids
15. Lower wale or great wale
16. Channel wale
17. Upper wale
18. Hancing pieces
19. Entry port (port side only)
20. Main channel
21. Mizzen channel
22. Quarter gallery
23. Rudder
24. Stern-gallery
25. Quarter piece
26. Stern lanterns
27. Launch stowed on spare spars

Standing Rigging

28. Lower mast
29. Top
30. Masthead
31. Topmast
32. Topgallant mast
33. Flagpole
34. Bowsprit
35. Spritsail topmast
36. Shrouds and masthead tackles
37–38. Backstays
39–41. Stays
42. Gammoning
43. Toprope (topmast heel rope)
44. Winding tackle

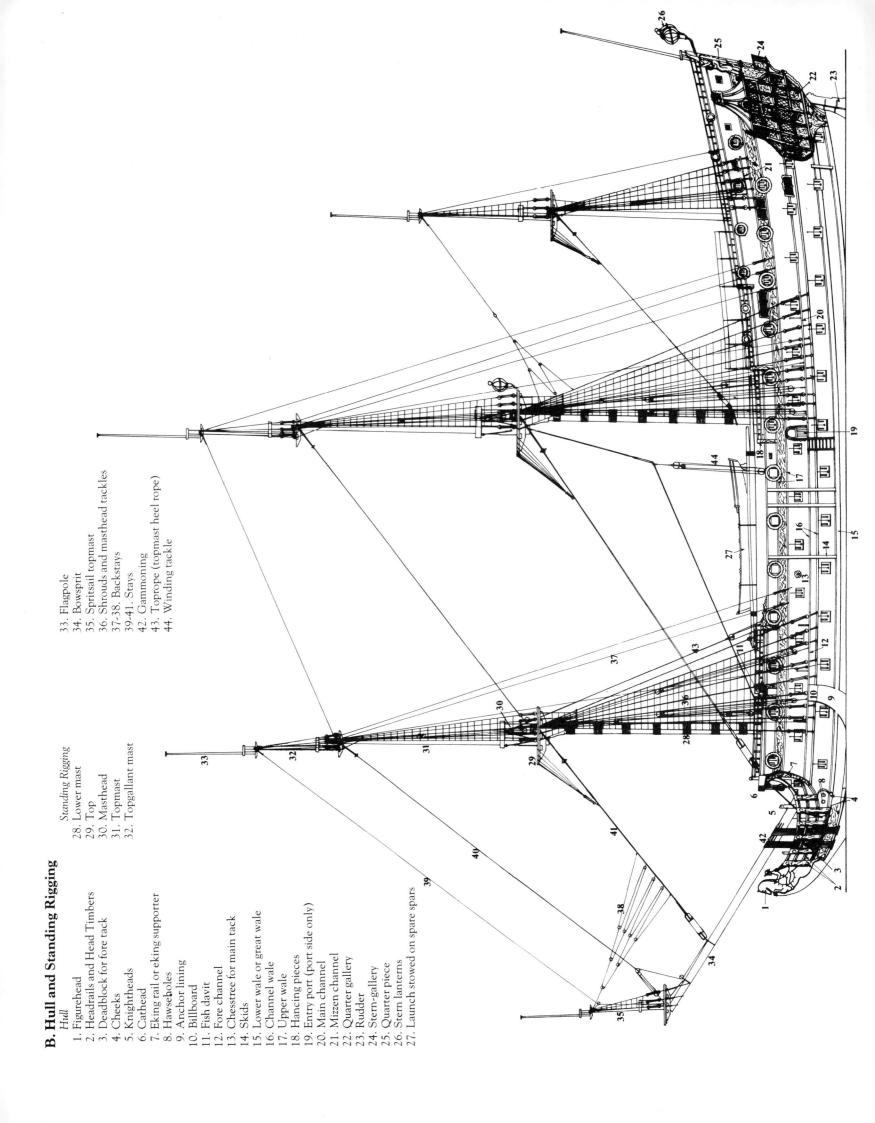

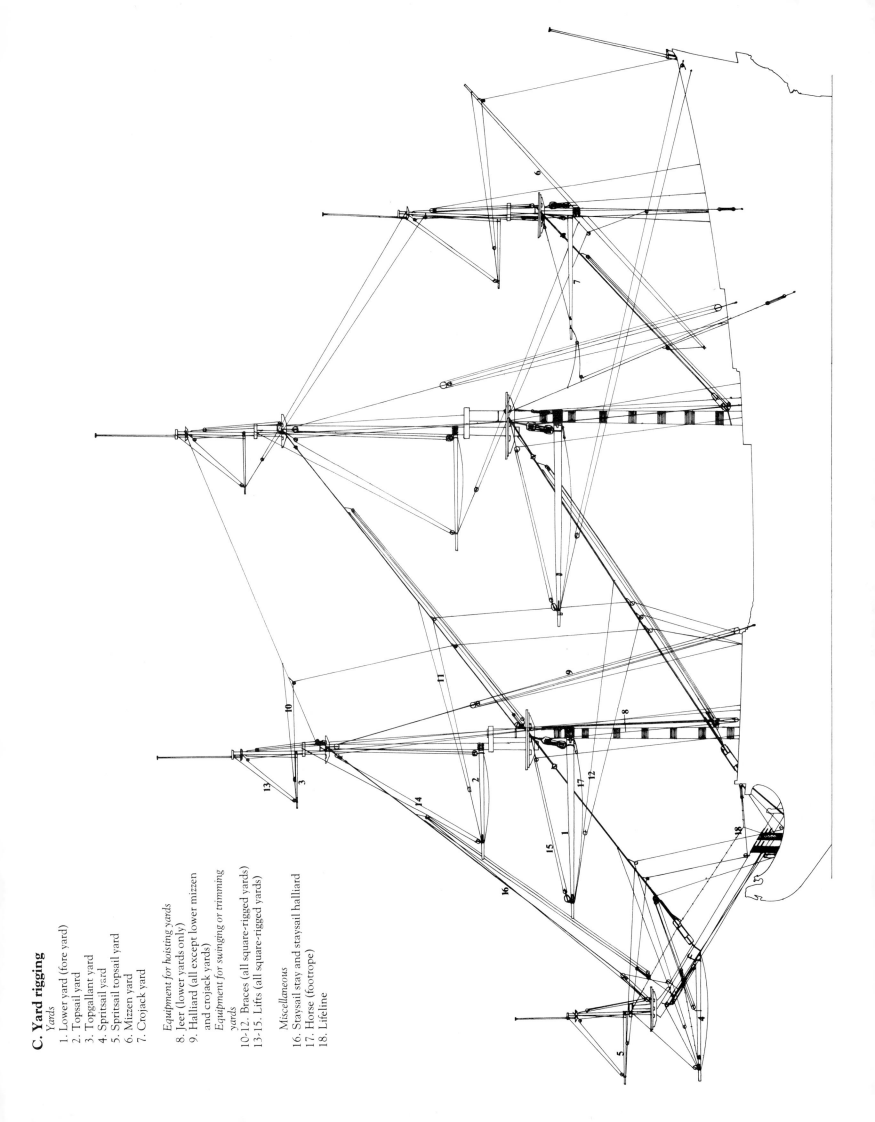

C. Yard rigging

Yards

1. Lower yard (fore yard)
2. Topsail yard
3. Topgallant yard
4. Spritsail yard
5. Spritsail topsail yard
6. Mizzen yard
7. Crojack yard

Equipment for hoisting yards

8. Jeer (lower yards only)
9. Halliard (all except lower mizzen and crojack yards)

Equipment for swinging or trimming yards

10-12. Braces (all square-rigged yards)
13-15. Lifts (all square-rigged yards)

Miscellaneous

16. Staysail stay and staysail halliard
17. Horse (footrope)
18. Lifeline

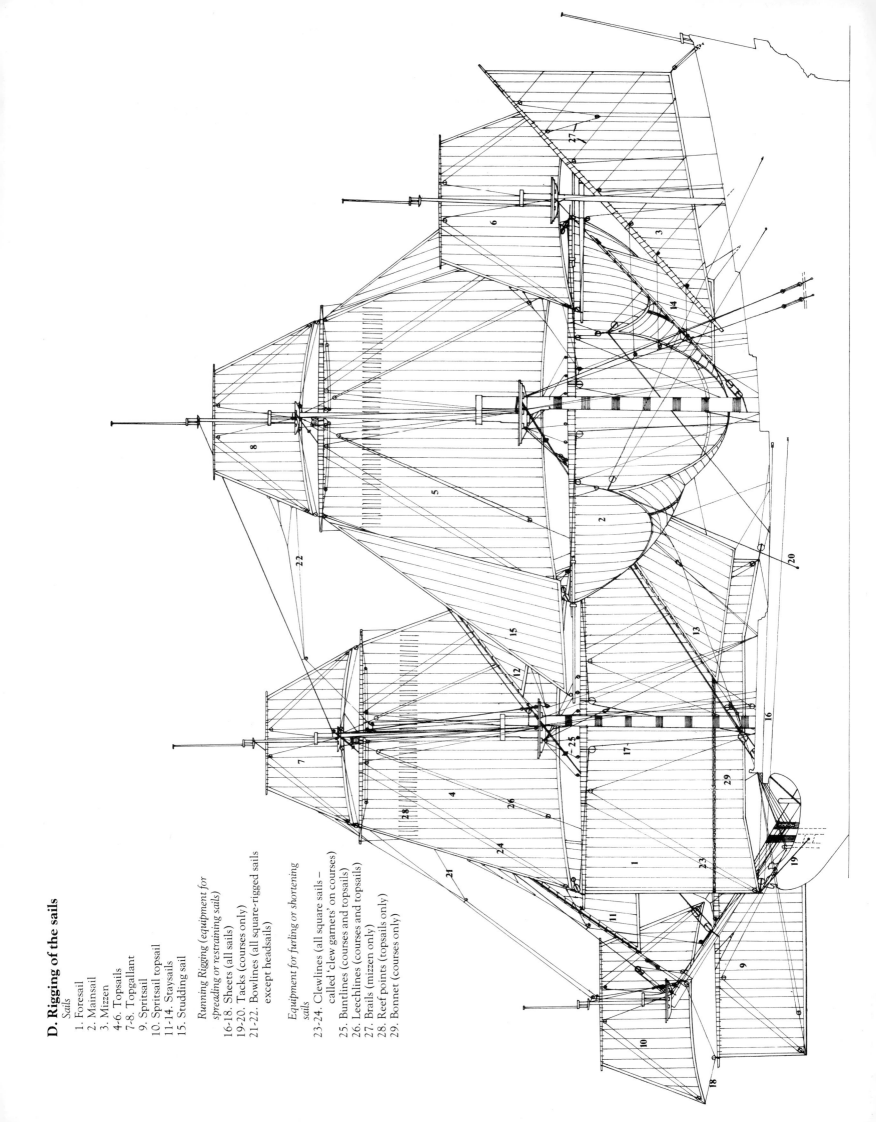

D. Rigging of the sails

Sails
1. Foresail
2. Mainsail
3. Mizzen
4-6. Topsails
7-8. Topgallant
9. Spritsail
10. Spritsail topsail
11-14. Staysails
15. Studding sail

Running Rigging (equipment for spreading or restraining sails)
16-18. Sheets (all sails)
19-20. Tacks (courses only)
21-22. Bowlines (all square-rigged sails except headsails)

Equipment for furling or shortening sails
23-24. Clewlines (all square sails – called 'clew garnets' on courses)
25. Buntlines (courses and topsails)
26. Leechlines (courses and topsails)
27. Brails (mizzen only)
28. Reef points (topsails only)
29. Bonnet (courses only)

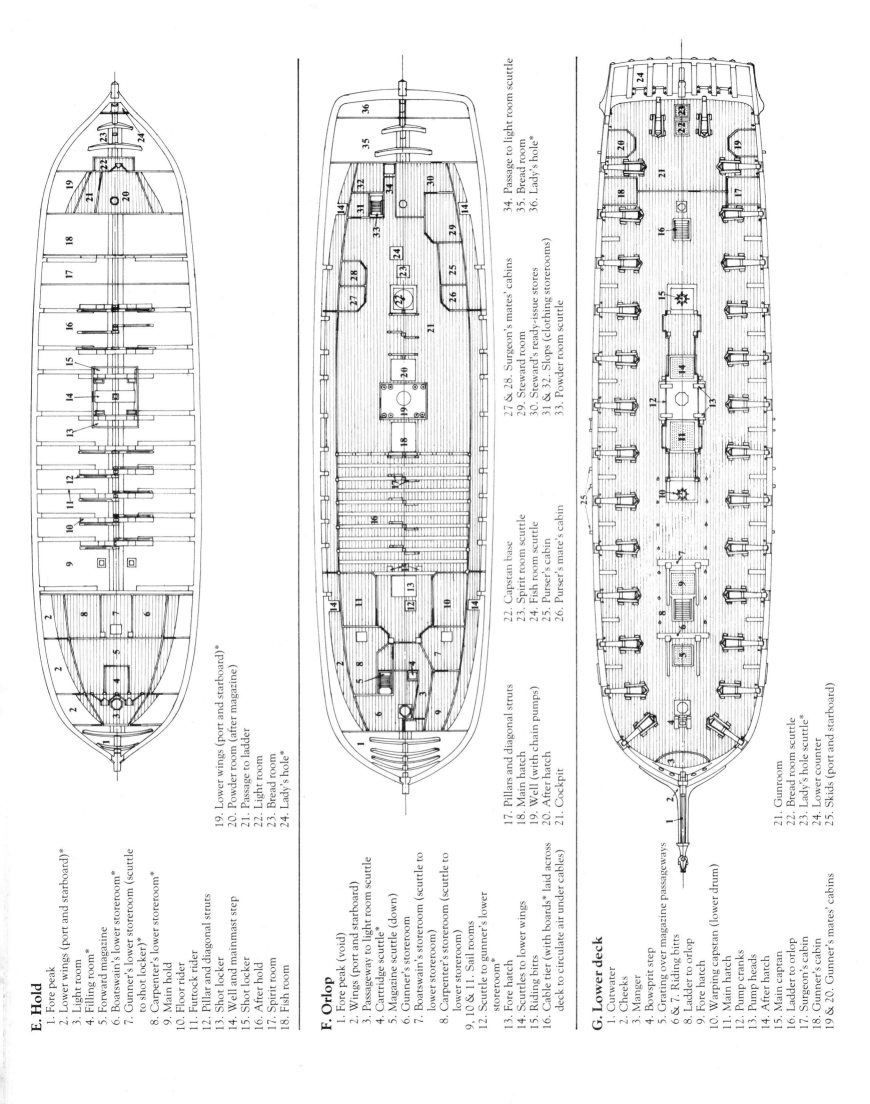

E. Hold

1. Fore peak
2. Lower wings (port and starboard)*
3. Light room
4. Filling room*
5. Forward magazine
6. Boatswain's lower storeroom*
7. Gunner's lower storeroom (scuttle to shot locker)*
8. Carpenter's lower storeroom*
9. Main hold
10. Floor rider
11. Futtock rider
12. Pillar and diagonal struts
13. Shot locker
14. Well and mainmast step
15. Shot locker
16. After hold
17. Spirit room
18. Fish room
19. Lower wings (port and starboard)*
20. Powder room (after magazine)
21. Passage to ladder
22. Light room
23. Bread room
24. Lady's hole*

F. Orlop

1. Fore peak (void)
2. Wings (port and starboard)
3. Passageway to light room scuttle
4. Carrtidge scuttle*
5. Magazine scuttle (down)
6. Gunner's storeroom
7. Boatswain's storeroom (scuttle to lower storeroom)
8. Carpenter's storeroom (scuttle to lower storeroom)
9, 10 & 11. Sail rooms
12. Scuttle to gunner's lower storeroom*
13. Fore hatch
14. Scuttles to lower wings
15. Riding bitts
16. Cable tier (with boards* laid across deck to circulate air under cables)
17. Pillars and diagonal struts
18. Main hatch
19. Well (with chain pumps)
20. After hatch
21. Cockpit
22. Capstan base
23. Spirit room scuttle
24. Fish room scuttle
25. Purser's cabin
26. Purser's mate's cabin
27 & 28. Surgeon's mates' cabins
29. Steward room
30. Steward's ready-issue stores
31 & 32. Slops (clothing storerooms)
33. Powder room scuttle
34. Passage to light room scuttle
35. Bread room
36. Lady's hole*

G. Lower deck

1. Cutwater
2. Cheeks
3. Manger
4. Bowsprit step
5. Grating over magazine passageways
6 & 7. Riding bitts
8. Ladder to orlop
9. Fore hatch
10. Warping capstan (lower drum)
11. Main hatch
12. Pump cranks
13. Pump heads
14. After hatch
15. Main captan
16. Ladder to orlop
17. Surgeon's cabin
18. Gunner's cabin
19 & 20. Gunner's mates' cabins
21. Gunroom
22. Bread room scuttle
23. Lady's hole scuttle*
24. Lower counter
25. Skids (port and starboard)

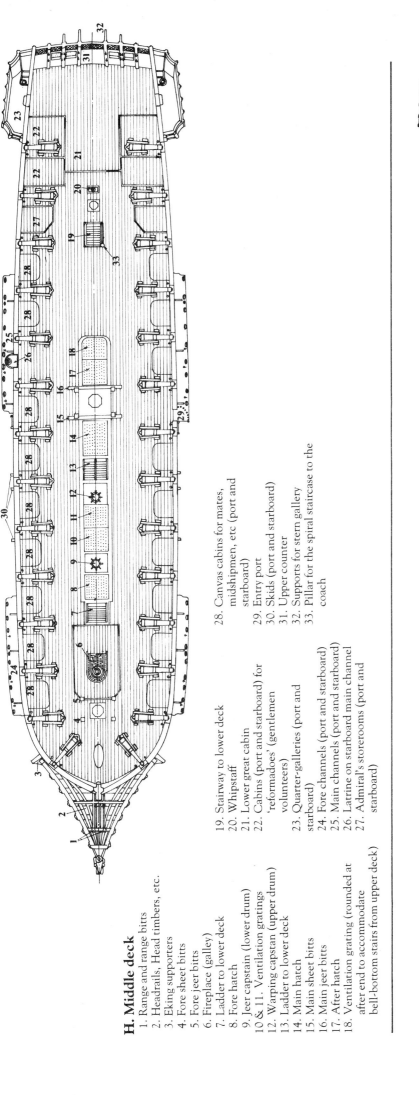

H. Middle deck

1. Range and range bitts
2. Headrails, Head timbers, etc.
3. Eking supporters
4. Fore sheet bitts
5. Fore jeer bitts
6. Fireplace (galley)
7. Ladder to lower deck
8. Fore hatch
9. Jeer capstan (lower drum)
10 & 11. Ventilation gratings
12. Warping capstan (upper drum)
13. Ladder to lower deck
14. Main hatch
15. Main sheet bitts
16. Main jeer bitts
17. After hatch
18. Ventilation grating (rounded at after end to accommodate bell-bottom stairs from upper deck)
19. Stairway to lower deck
20. Whipstaff
21. Lower great cabin
22. Cabins (port and starboard) for 'reformadoes' (gentlemen volunteers)
23. Quarter-galleries (port and starboard)
24. Fore channels (port and starboard)
25. Main channels (port and starboard)
26. Latrine on starboard main channel
27. Admiral's storerooms (port and starboard)
28. Canvas cabins for mates, midshipmen, etc (port and starboard)
29. Entry port
30. Skids (port and starboard)
31. Upper counter
32. Supports for stern gallery
33. Pillar for the spiral staircase to the coach

I. Upper deck

1. Head gratings
2. 'Seats of easement'
3. Beakhead
4. Ladder to middle deck
5. Fore sheet bitts
6. Fore jeer bitts
7. Steam gratings
8. Galley chimney
9. Belfry
10. Fore hatch
11. Jeer capstan (upper drum)
12. Ventilation gratings
13. Ladder to middle deck
14. Main hatch
15. Gallows and main sheet bitts
16. Main jeer bitts
17. After hatch
18. Bell-bottom stairs to middle deck
19. Ringbolts for toprope tackle (port and starboard)
20. Ringbolts for winding tackle (port and starboard)
21. Ringbolts for toprope tackle (port and starboard)
22. Coach
23. Spiral staircase to middle deck
24. Lobby
25. Grating over helmsman
26. Great cabin (Admiral)
27. Admiral's bedplace
28. Quarter-galleries
29. Stern-gallery
30. Carpenter
31. Boatswain
32. Boatswain's mate
33. Marine officer
34. Staff officer (Judge Advocate or Muster Master)
35 & 36. Servants' half cabins
37. Marine commander
38. Second lieutenant
38. 'Minister'

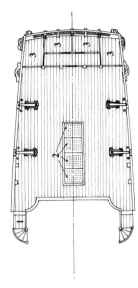

J. Forecastle and Quarterdeck

1. Catheads
2. Ventilation grating
3. Scuttles for foretopsail sheets (port and starboard)
4. Scuttles for fore jeers (port and starboard)
5. Ringbolt for main topmast stay
6. Fish davit
7. Steam gratings
8. Galley chimney
9. Belfry
10. Gangways (port and starboard)
11. Launch stowed on spare spars over the waist
12. Ventilation gratings
13. Grating for passing helm orders
14. Admiral's staircase (spiral) to the lobby
15. Roundhouse (Captain)
16. 2nd Captain
17. Admiral's secretary
18. 1st Lieutenant
19. Master
20. Chief mate
21. Mizzen channels (port and starboard)
22. Quarter-gallery cupola (port and starboard)

K. Poop

1. Gangways (port and starboard)
2. Ventilation gratings
3. Trumpeters' cabins

L. Topgallant Poop

1. Ensign staff step
2. Stern lanterns
3. Ringbolt for mizzen sheet

```
0    5  10      20      30      40      50
|————|——|———————|———————|———————|———————| feet
```

Glossary of Naval Terms

Note: All terms are defined as understood in the seventeenth century. The references in brackets after some definitions relate to the accompanying drawings and keys.

Abaft. Towards the stern relative to some point or object on a vessel, eg, *abaft* the mainmast.

Advice boat. A small, speedy vessel of varying type used to deliver orders and information to and from units of a fleet at sea.

Anchor wale or *anchor lining.* An arc of protective sheathing on each side of a ship's bow. The anchor wale permitted a catted anchor to be swung to or from its stowage position without damaging the hull (B-9). See also *billboard.*

Athwart, athwartships. Across a vessel or from one side to the other.

Backstays. Ropes reaching towards the stern from a masthead or topmasthead, secured at a ship's sides. Backstays helped to prevent a mast from falling forward (B-37).

Badge. An ornamented window on a ship's side near the stern. Badges commonly took the place of quarter-galleries in small vessels.

Beakhead. A short uncovered deck in the space between a ship's stem and the bulkhead at the forward end of the forecastle. It functioned as the crew's latrine (A-5).

Beakhead bulkhead. The athwartships bulkhead at the forward end of a ship's forecastle.

Beat The operation of sailing a vessel on a series of alternating tacks in order to make progress against the wind.

Belfry. A canopy sheltering a ship's bell, usually located at the break of the forecastle (J-9).

Bilge. The parts of a vessel's inner bottom where the frames are more horizontal than vertical.

Billboard. A broad plank angling outward from the upper edge of a ship's anchor wale to the outer edge of the fore channel. It formed an extension of the anchor wale, permitting the flukes of a catted anchor to be hoisted above the channel for stowage (B-10).

Bitts. Short columns of wood to which ropes or cables can be secured (A-6, 7, 12, 31, 32).

Bobstay. A rope running from a point on the forward edge of a ship's cutwater to a point on the underside of the bowsprit. It countered the upward pull on the bowsprit caused by the foretopmast stay. The bobstay was not introduced until the 1690s.

Bonnet. A strip of sail attached to the bottom of a course to provide a temporary increase in sail area (D-29).

Bower anchors. The largest anchors carried by a ship.

Bowline. A rope attached to the side of a square sail to keep it taut when the vessel sailed close to the wind (D-21, 22).

Bowsprit. The heavy spar projecting forward from a ship's bow (B-34).

Braces. The ropes by which a square-rigged yard could be swung around a mast (C-10, 12).

Break. The abrupt drop to the level below at the termination of a deck which was not flush, eg the *break* of the forecastle.

Breasthooks. V-shaped internal ribs at the forward end of a ship's hull.

Brigantine. A two-masted vessel of various builds with two square sails. Not the same as an eighteenth or nineteenth century brigantine.

Broadside. (i) Viewed from the side; (ii) all the guns bearing on one side of a ship, or the shot which could be discharged from one side.

Bulkhead. (i) A vertical partition dividing the space within a ship into compartments or cabins; (ii) short for *beakhead bulkhead.*

Bulwark. The side above the uppermost deck at any point along a ship's length.

Camber. The athwartships curve of a ship's deck, usually bowed slightly upwards towards the centreline.

Cap. A perforated wooden slab at the upper end of a mast, which aligned the mast above.

Capstan. A thick stem fitted into the deck of a ship and used for heavy lifting work, such as weighing anchor or swaying up yards. It was turned by crewmen pushing against long bars which radiated from the central drum (A-25, 26, 34).

Careen. To heave a ship on to one side to expose the bottom of the other side for cleaning or repair. This was usually accomplished on a sloping beach with the ship parallel to the shoreline.

Cat. (i) To hoist an anchor to a cathead; (ii) a merchant vessel (commonly a whaling ship) with a rounded bulbous stern. The taffrail was wide and flat, with one row of windows.

Cathead. A heavy timber projecting over the water from each side of a ship's bow, from which an anchor could be suspended clear of the vessel's side (B-6).

Ceiling. The internal planking laid across the frames surrounding a ship's hold (A-62).

Chains. Iron plates to which the lower ends of the shrouds were fastened.

Channels or *chainwales.* (both pronounced 'channels') Wide planks projecting from a vessel's sides and to which the chains and shrouds were fastened. (B-12, 20, 21; M-24, 25; J-21).

Channel wale. The wale from which a ship's fore- and main-channels projected; the wale next above the lower, or great wale (B-16).

Chase or *chaser.* A gun placed to provide a ship with direct end-on fire.

Cheeks. Large, long-armed, horizontal knees placed on both sides of a ship's stem to ensure the proper alignment of the cutwater (B-4).

Chesstree. A perforated piece of wood, often highly ornamented, fitted on a ship's side abaft the fore-channel and through which a main tack was drawn (B-13).

Close-hauled. The situation of a vessel sailing as near to the wind as possible.

Coach. The compartment sheltered by the forward end of a ship's quarterdeck (A-14; I-22).

Coaming. A raised lip around a hatch, which prevented water from draining to the deck beneath.

Cockpit. A compartment on a ship's orlop abaft the mainmast, which in battle served as a surgery ward (A-38; F-21).

Cornette. A swallow-tailed flag or pendant.

Counter. The arched overhanging area of a ship's stern above the wing transom (G-24).

Course. A sail borne by the lower yard of each mast of a square-rigged ship; a mainsail, foresail, or mizzen (D-1, 2, 3).

Crank. The condition of a ship with an abnormal tendency to heel deeply or capsize.

Crossjack yard or *cro'jack yard* (both pronounced 'cro'jack'). The lower square-rigged yard on a ship's mizzenmast. It served to spread the clews (lower corners) of the mizzen topsail and seldom carried a sail itself (C-7).

Crosstrees. The short athwartships spreaders near the top of a lower mast or topmast. Crosstrees spread the shrouds of the upper masts and helped support the tops.

Crutches. V-shaped internal ribs in the after part of a ship's hull.

Cuddy. A compartment sheltered by the forward end of a ship's poop, serving as an ante-room to the roundhouse (A-20).

Cutwater. A large knee fitted to the forward edge of a ship's stem. Its upper arm protruded forward to form the beak (A-58).

Davit. A long straight timber projecting over the side of a ship's forecastle for hoisting or lowering an anchor to or from its stowage position (B-11).

Deadwood. Areas of solid timbering packed against the foot of a ship's stem and the after part of the keel. Deadwood aided steering and helped support the bow and stern of a ship in drydock (A-64).

Dogger. A seventeenth century craft with a flute stern, having a mainmast with a single square sail and a mizzen with either a square or lateen sail. Called a *buss* if a foremast was present. Doggers and busses were usually fishing vessels.

Drift rail. A thin wale running along the side of a ship's forecastle, quarterdeck, and poop.

Dry rot. Common name for two species of fungus, *Xylostroma giganteum* and *Boletus hybridus*, both of which infect moist, poorly ventilated timbers.

Eking rail or *eking supporter.* An ornamented knee supporting a cathead. Its lower arm usually merged with the second or third headrail (B-7).

Ensign. The flag worn on a staff at a ship's stern.

Entry. (i) The forward edge of the bow of a ship at and below the waterline; (ii) the shape of the underwater part of a ship's hull near the bow.

Entry port or *entering port.* A doorway in the side of a three-decker just forward of the main-channels, providing access to the middle deck. Usually found only on the port side (B-19).

Fall. An abrupt drop, or step, in the level of a deck.

Fights. Strips of canvas rigged for safety above the low gunwales in the upperworks of a ship.

Flagship. A ship carrying a flag officer.

Floor. A ground timber forming the lowest member of a frame of a ship. Floors were locked into the keel and had arms extending outward on either side (A-61).

Flush. In reference to decks, extending in an unbroken line from bow to stern.

Flute. A merchant ship, usually Dutch, having a bulbous, rounded stern with a narrow, flat taffrail.

Flyboat. An English flute.

Fore and aft. Longitudinal or longitudinally.

Fore (i) Pertaining to the forward part of a vessel; (ii) denoting rigging or equipment of the mast forward of the mainmast, eg foremast, fore-channels, etc; (iii) short for foretop masthead, eg a flag worn at the fore.

Forecastle. (pronounced 'fo'c's'le') A deck sheltering the forward end of the upper deck. When no such deck was present, the forward end of the upper deck itself was sometimes described at the forecastle (A-67).

Foresail or *fore course.* The sail borne by the lowest yard on the foremast of a square-rigged ship (D-1).

Forestay. A rope stretched from the foretop masthead to the bowsprit, to prevent the foremast from falling sternwards (B-41).

Frame. A rib of a ship, made up of the assembly of a floor, futtocks, and top-timbers.

Frieze. A band of decoration along the side of a ship.

Frigate. A word of many seventeenth century meanings, some of which were contradictory. The most common uses were: (i) a long, low warship built primarily for speed; (ii) a ship with a raised forecastle; (iii) a warship too small to take a place in the line of battle, specifically a 5th or 6th Rate; (iv) a vessel acting as a scout for a fleet; (v) occasionally after about 1650, a rated warship of any size.

Furring. A process for improving a ship's stability by adding vertical strips of timber to the outside of the frames near the waterline. The result was a lowered centre of gravity and an increased beam.

Futtocks. The timbers of which the underwater frames of a ship are built up from the floors.

Gaff. A spar, attached to a mast at one end, from which is suspended a four-cornered fore and aft sail.

Galjoot. A type of two-masted Dutch craft characterised by a gaff-rigged mainmast and a short lateen mizzen.

Galleon. A type of warship, introduced in the sixteenth century, characterised by a low protruding beak and a forecastle separated from the stem by a beakhead. Technically all large seventeenth century warships were galleons, but by about 1640 the term was seldom used except to describe Spanish ships, especially treasure ships.

Galley-frigate. (i) A relatively narrow, two-decked, ship-rigged warship mounting most of its armament on the upper deck and with the lower deck mainly used for the operation of sweeps. Galley frigates were developed in England and France in the 1670s for use in the Mediterranean; (ii) any 4th or 5th Rate warship fitted with sweep ports.

Galliot. A type of English craft having a tall gaff-rigged main-mast with a square topsail, in addition to a short lateen mizzen.

Gallows. An upright column with athwartships crossarms erected on a ship's upper deck just forward of the mainmast. It supported one end of the extra spars which were stowed over the waist (A-11).

Gammoning. Several turns of a rope passed alternately over a vessel's bowsprit and through a slit in the cutwater, to counteract the upward pull of the forestay on the bowsprit (B-42).

Gangway. (i) A narrow platform placed over the waist of a ship to serve as a bridge between the forecastle and quarterdeck (not common in English ships before the 1690s); (ii) a short, narrow catwalk extending along the inside of a ship's bulwarks, and connecting the break of the forecastle, quarterdeck, or poop with the ladder or staircase on each side giving access from the deck below (J-10).

Girdling. A process for improving a ship's stability by packing an extra thickness of planking to the outside of the hull near the waterline.

Great ship. Originally a specific type of fifteenth and sixteenth century vessel, but in the seventeenth century a common description of a large warship, especially a three-decker.

Ground tackle. All equipment relating to anchoring or mooring a vessel.

Ground timbers. The structural members of a ship's bottom: the keel, floors, and futtocks.

Gundeck. The lowest deck of a warship on which guns were mounted; the lower deck.

Gunroom. The compartment at the after end of the lower deck of a warship (A-34; G-21).

Gunwale (pronounced 'gunnel'). The strip of wood forming the rail along the top of a ship's bulwark.

Halfdeck. A word of several seventeenth century meanings, some of which are not well understood today. It was most commonly used to describe a long quarterdeck.

Hance. The point at which the gunwale of a ship abruptly dropped to a lower level, usually occurring in one or more stages near the beak of a deck (B-18).

Hancing piece. The carved ornament of a hance (B-18).

Harping. The lower or great wale of a ship (B-15).

Hawsehole or *hawse.* A circular hole near the bow of a ship through which a cable passed (B-8).

Head. (i) The structure comprising a ship's cutwater, headrails and headpieces; (ii) a latrine on a ship's beakhead; normally used in the plural, eg *lee heads* or *weather heads*; (iii) of a mast, the part above a top.

Headrails. Slender curved timbers extending from the forward corners of a ship's forecastle and the sides of the beakhead to the figurehead (B-2).

Headpieces or *head timbers.* Ornamented timbers placed perpendicularly across a ship's headrails and fastened to the upper edge of the cutwater (B-2; H-2).

Heel. (i) In relation to a vessel, to lean to one side under the influence of the wind (not a continuous motion such as rolling, nor a permanent cant such as a list); (ii) the lower end of a mast or bowsprit.

Hold. The internal space beneath the orlop of a ship (A-47, 51).

Hoy. A craft without a mizzen, but otherwise identical to a galliot.

Jack. A flag worn on a staff (*jackstaff*) at the bow of a ship or at the bowsprit end.

Jib. A forestaysail or foretopmast staysail.

Keel. The principal longitudinal member in the bottom of a ship's hull; the backbone (A-60).

Kelson or *keelson.* A longitudinal timber bolted onto the upper surface of a ship's floors (A-62) serving as an internal keel.

Ketch. A type of two-masted English craft, usually with a cat or flute stern; usually square-rigged, but sometimes with a gaff mainsail.

Knees. Bent or sharply curved timbers, used to support a ship's deck beams or to buttress some part of the hull.

Knightheads. Two heavy timbers rising vertically at the forward end of a ship's beakhead, and on which the bowsprit rested (A-4; B-5).

Larboard. The left-hand side of a vessel, facing forward; alternative for *port*.

Lateen. A long triangular sail set on a diagonal yard.

Lee. That which is on the side away from which the wind blows.

Leeward (pronounced 'loo'-ard'). The direction away from which the wind blows.

Lifts or *topping lifts* Ropes leading from the end of a yard to the masthead, by which the trim of the yard is adjusted (C-13, 14, 15).

Luff. (i) To sail closer to the wind; (ii) the area of a ship's bow that curves towards the stem; (iii) a gun or gunport sited at the curve of the bow, also *luff port*.

Main. (i) Denoting the rigging and equipment of a vessel's principal mast, eg mainmast, maintopmast, main-channels, etc; (ii) short for maintop masthead, eg a flag worn at the main.

Mainsail or *main course.* The sail on the lowest yard of the mainmast of a square-rigged vessel (D-2).

Mainstay. A rope extending forward from the mainmasthead to prevent the mainmast from falling sternwards.

Manger. An area on the forward part of a ship's lower deck just abaft the hawseholes. It was bounded on its after side by a coaming (the *manger board*) which prevented water entering through the hawseholes from running down the deck (A-30; G-3).

Mizzen or *mizen* (i) Pertaining to the mast and associated rigging abaft the mainmast; (ii) a lateen sail set on the mizzenmast; (iii) short for mizzenmast; (iv) short for mizzentop masthead, eg a flag worn at the mizzen.

Moulded beam. The maximum width of a vessel measured to the outside of the frames, but not including the planking.

Orlop. The deck beneath a ship's lower deck (A-68).

Pay. To cover the sides or bottom of a ship's hull with tar or varnish.

Pay off. In tacking, for a vessel's bow to turn to leeward after having crossed the wind.

Peak. The aftermost upper corner of a lateen or gaff-rigged sail, or the upper end of a gaff or lateen yard.

Pendant. (pronounced 'pennant') A very long and narrow banner worn at the main by private ships of the Royal Navy to distinguish them from merchant vessels. In large fleets pendants were sometimes used to distinguish squadronal subdivisions.

Pink. A small flyboat.

Pitch. In reference to a ship, to plunge longitudinally.

Planking. The longitudinally laid pieces of wood forming a ship's outer skin.

Private ship. A warship which is not a flagship.

Poop or *poop deck.* The deck covering the after end of a vessel's quarterdeck (A-73).

Port (i) The left hand side of a vessel, facing forward; (ii) an opening cut in a ship's side, eg gunport, entry port.

Prize. A captured enemy vessel. The proceeds from the sale of a prize and its cargo were divided among the officers and crew of the capturing ship according to an established ratio of shares.

Quarter. The side of a vessel near the stern, or the corner formed by a ship's side and its stern.

Quarterdeck. The deck covering the after part of a ship's upper deck, extending to the stern from a point abaft the mainmast (A-72).

Quarter-gallery. An ornamented gallery projecting from a ship's side at the stern and used as a privy by the officers (B-22).

Quarter-pieces. Wooden statuary, usually large human forms, placed on each side of a ship beside the upper parts of the stern (B-25).

Rake. (i) The angle at which a mast or part of the hull of a vessel departs from the vertical in a longitudinal direction; (ii) the distance between the forward end of a ship's keel and a perpendicular dropped from the foremost point of the stem (*fore rake*), or the distance from the after end of the keel to a perpendicular dropped from the upper end of the sternpost (*after rake*).

Reef. A part of a sail that can be rolled up to reduce the area presented to the wind (D-28).

Reef-points. Short lengths of rope set in horizontal rows across a sail, by which reefs can be tied down (D-28).

Ribbands. Bands of timber placed along the outside of a hull under construction, to maintain the proper alignment of the frames prior to fitting deck beams.

Riders. Internal ribs laid over the ceiling in the hull of a ship (A-63; E-10, 11).

Riding bitts. Heavy oaken columns on the forward part of a ship's lower deck, to which the cables were secured when the ship rode at anchor (A-13, 32; G-6, 7).

Roll. In relation to a ship, to lean from one side to the other in a periodic motion under the influence of the sea.

Roundhouse. A cabin sheltered by the after end of a ship's poop or topgallant poop (A-21, 26).

Royal. A mast or sail rigged above a topgallant sail.

Run. The shape of the underwater part of a vessel's hull near the stern.

Sally port. A doorway in the lower tier of a fireship near the stern, through which the crew could escape to a boat towed astern after igniting the vessel.

Sheer. The upward curvature of the longitudinal parts of a ship's hull, especially the decks.

Sheer strake or *sheer wale.* A thin wale extending for the length of a ship's hull immediately beneath drift rail.

Sheet. A rope attached to a clew (lower corner) of a sail to extend or restrain it.

Shrouds. Multiple ropes leading from a masthead to a ship's sides or from a topmasthead to a top. Shrouds provided lateral support for a mast or topmast (B-36).

Sill. The upper and lower frames of a square gunport, especially the lower frame.

Skids. Vertical strips of timber placed on the outside of a ship's hull to prevent boats being hoisted in or out from chafing against the sides (B-14).

Sloop. (i) A type of gaff-rigged single-masted craft with a single jib; (ii) a class of two-masted warships built by the Royal Navy between 1666 and 1677, characterised by a square-rigged foremast and a gaff-rigged mainmast, and equipped with sweep ports.

Smack. A type of English single-masted, gaff-rigged vessel.

Snow. A type of two-masted vessel, usually rigged with a single square sail on each mast.

Spar deck. A platform or grating erected over a ship's waist and used either as a gangway or to provide stowage for boats and spars.

Spritsail. A square sail rigged beneath a bowsprit (D-9).

Spritsail topmast. A short mast stepped from the sprit-top at the end of a ship's bowsprit (B-36).

Spritsail topsail. A small square sail set on a spritsail topmast (D-10).

Sprit-top. A circular platform at the upper end of a ship's bowsprit.

Stay. A rope stretched forward or sternward from a masthead or topmasthead to provide longitudinal support for a mast.

Staysail. A triangular fore and aft sail set on a stay (D-11, 12, 13, 14).

Stem. A large timber curving upward from the forward end of a ship's keel and to which the sides of a ship were joined to form the bow (A-59).

Step. (i) A block of wood fixed to a vessel's kelson, into which the heel of a mast was fitted; (ii) the operation of erecting a mast.

Sternpiece. The ornamentation of a ship's taffrail.

Sternpost. A large straight timber rising upward from the after end of a ship's keel, to which the lower sides of a ship were joined at the stern, and to which the rudder was hinged (A-65).

Stiff. The condition of a vessel with a strong tendency to remain upright and resist heeling.

Strakes. The longitudinal lines of planks running along the outside of a ship's hull.

Studding-sail or *stunsail.* An extra sail set on a boom extended from a yardarm (D-15).

Sweep. A long oar.

Tack. (i) To change the course of a vessel so that the wind bears on the other side, when accomplished by turning the vessel's bow into the wind; (ii) a course or distance travelled by a vessel with the wind bearing continuously on one side (when the wind blows from the port side such a course is the *port tack* or *larboard tack*, and if the wind blows from the starboard side it is the *starboard tack*); (iii) a rope leading from the clew (lower corner) of a course or staysail to restrain it when sailing close-hauled (D-19, 20).

Taffrail or *Tafferel.* The flat parts of a vessel's stern above the counter, particularly the upper edge.

Tender or *tender-sided.* The condition of a vessel which tends to heel disproportionately deeply under the action of the wind.

Tier. A row of guns or gunports on one side of one deck of a ship.

Tiller. A bar extending inboard from a vessel's rudderhead, by which the rudder is turned (A-35).

Top. A platform surrounding a lower mast just beneath the masthead (B-29).

Topgallant (pronounced 't'gallant'). The mast and sail rigged next above a topsail (B-32, D-7, 8).

Topgallant poop. A short deck sheltering the after end of ship's poop. Also called *poop royal* (A-74).

Topmast. The mast next above a lower mast (B-31).

Topsail. The sail set on a topmast (D-4, 5, 6).

Top-timbers. Those segments of a ship's frames which extend the futtocks above the waterline.

Touch. The point at which a vessel's keel joins the stem.

Transoms. Athwartships timbers linking a ship's sternpost to the aftermost frame on each side.

Tread. That part of a vessel's bottom which would touch the ground if the vessel rested upright on a flat surface.

Treenails or *trunnels* (pronounced 'trunnels'). Wooden pegs used to fasten the planks and timbers of a vessel's hull.

Trestletrees. Two short horizontal fore and aft timbers placed beneath the crosstrees near the head of a lower mast or topmast. Trestletrees helped support the top and align the mast next above.

Tuck. The shape of a ship's hull beneath the counter.

Tumblehome. The inward curve of a ship's hull from the breadth to the gunwales.

Union or *Union flag.* The British national flag, used as a flag of command by a fleet commander other than the sovereign or Lord High Admiral. The Union was also sometimes authorised as a flag of command for an officer commanding a detached squadron.

Union jack. The Union flag when worn at a bowsprit end.

Upper deck. The highest deck extending for the entire length of a vessel (A-71).

Waist. The area of a ship's upper deck between the break of the forecastle and the break of the quarterdeck. If no forecastle was present, the waist was considered to begin at a point roughly coincidental with the after end of the fore channels.

Wales. Thickened strakes of planking along the outside of a ship's hull, usually extending unbroken from end to end (B-15, 16, 17).

Wear. To change the course of a vessel so that the wind will bear on the other side, when accomplished by turning the bow away from the wind.

Weather. (i) That which is in the direction from which the wind blows (opposite of *lee*); to sail to windward of another vessel, object, or point.

Windward. The directions from which the wind blows (opposite of leeward).

Yacht. A small vessel of varying rig intended primarily for pleasure.

Yard. A spar attached in the centre to a mast, and which bore or extended a sail.

Sources

Most of the original information in this book came from the marine art, ship models, and draughts preserved in museums, art galleries, and private collections around the world. The following is a list of the educational, commercial, and public institutions whose collections proved useful for archaeological research:

Birmingham (England) City Art Gallery
Bristol City Art Gallery
British Library, London
British Museum, London
Danish Maritime Museum, Kronborg
Goethe Museum, Wiemar
Leger Galleries Ltd, London
Los Angeles County Museum of Art
Malcolm Henderson Gallery, London
Mariner's Museum, Newport News, Virginia
Maritiem Museum Prins Hendrik, Rotterdam
Merseyside County Museums, Liverpool
Musée de la Marine, Paris
Musée des Beaux Arts, Besançon
Musée des Beaux Arts, Marseilles
Museo Maritimo, Barcelona
Museum Boymans-van Beuningen, Rotterdam
National Maritime Museum, London
National Trust for Places of Historic Interest, London
Nederlandsch Historisch Scheepvaart Museum, Amsterdam
Orlogsmuseet, Copenhagen
Parker Gallery, London
Pepys Library, Magdalene College, Cambridge
Rijksmuseum, Amsterdam
Royal Canterbury Museum
Rupert Preston Ltd, London
Science Museum, London
Statens Sjöhistoriska Museum, Stockholm
Stichting Atlas van Stolk, Rotterdam
Trinity House, London
United States Naval Academy Museum, Annapolis, Maryland
Vasa Museum, Stockholm
Victoria and Albert Museum, London
Wellesley College Art Museum, Wellesley, Mass
Worcester (Mass) Art Museum

Other institutions provided assistance in the form of collections of photographs of drawings, paintings, and ship models which were otherwise impossible to examine. These organisations were:

Christie, Manson & Woods Ltd, London
Country Life Magazine, London
Sotheby-Parke Bernet & Co, London
Witte Library, Courtauld Institute of Art, London

Bibliography

Albion, R G: *Foresis and Sea Power: the Timber Problem of the Royal Navy, 1652-1862*, Cambridge, Mass, 1926

Anderson, R C: *Journals and Narratives of the Third Dutch War*, Navy Records Society, 1946
　Naval Wars in the Baltic, 1522-1850, London, 1910
　Seventeenth Century Rigging, London, 1955
　and Anderson, Romola: *The Sailing Ship: Six Thousand Years of History*, 2nd Edition, New York, 1963

Archibald, E H H: *The Wooden Fighting Ship in the Royal Navy, AD867-1860*, New York, 1968.

Barfod, H H P: *Orlogsfladen pa Niels Juels tid, 1648-1699*, Copenhagen, 1963

Slaget I Koge Bugt, den 1 Juli 1677, Copenhagen, 1952

Barlow, Edward: *Journal of His Life at Sea in King's Ships, East & West Indiamen & Other Merchantmen from 1659 to 1703*, 2 vols, B Lubbock ed, London, 1934

Bryant, Arthur: *Samuel Pepys: The Man in the Making; The Years of Peril; The Saviour of the Navy*, 3 vols, London, 1933-38

Boxer, C R: *The Anglo-Dutch Wars of the 17th Century*, London, 1974

Charnock, John: *A History of Marine Architecture*, 3 vols, London, 1800-1802

Colledge, J J: *Ships of the Royal Navy: An Historical Index*, 2 vols, New York, 1969

Clowes, G S Laird: *Sailing Ships: Their History and Development*, London, 1932

Clowes, W Laird: *The Royal Navy: A History from the Earliest Times to the Present Day*, 7 vols, London, 1897-1903

Derrick, Charles: *Memoirs of the Rise and Progress of the Royal Navy*, London, 1806

Ehrman, J H: *The Navy in the War of William III, 1689-97*, Cambridge, 1953

Evelyn, John: *Diary*, E S de Beer ed, London, 1959

Fraser, Edward: *The Londons of the British Fleet*, London, 1908

Henry Huddleston Rogers Collection of Ship Models, US Naval Academy Museum, Annapolis, Md, 1971

Jenkins, E H: *A History of the French Navy*, London 1973

Kemp, Peter, ed: *The Oxford Companion to Ships & the Sea*, London, 1976

Landstrom, Bjorn: *The Ship*, Stockholm, 1961

Laughton, L G Carr: *Old Ship Figureheads and Sterns*, London, 1925
Lists of Men-of-War, 1650-1700, 5 vols, Society for Nautical Research, Occasional Publication No 5, 1935-39

The Mariner's Mirror, Quarterly Journal of the Society for Nautical Research, 1911 to date

Ollard, Richard: *Man of War: Sir Robert Holmes and the Restoration Navy*, London, 1969

Oppenheim, M: *A History of the Administration of the Royal Navy and of Merchant Shipping in Relation to the Navy, from 1509-1660*, London, 1896

Padfield, Peter: *Guns at Sea*, London, 1973

Penn, Christopher: *The Navy Under the Early Stuarts*, London, 1920

Pepys, Samuel: *Diary*, 3 vols, J B Wheatley ed, London, 1923
　Memoires of the Royal Navy, 1679-1688, J R Tanner ed, Cambridge, 1906
　Naval Minutes J R Tanner ed, Navy Records Society, 1926

Pett, Phineas: *Autobiography* W G Perrin Ed, Navy Records Society, 1918

Pool, Bernard: *Navy Board Contracts, 1660-1832*, Hamden, Conn, 1966

Powell, J R and Timings, E K eds: *The Rupert and Monck Letter Book, 1666*, Navy Records Society, 1969

Preston, Lionel: *Sea and River Painters of the Netherlands in the Seventeenth Century*, London 1937

Robertson, F L: *The Evolution of Naval Armament*, London 1921

Robinson, M S: *Van de Velde Drawings: A Catalogue of Drawings in the National Maritime Museum Made by the Elder and the Younger Willem Van de Velde*, 2 vols, Cambridge, 1973-1974

Rogers, P G: *The Dutch in the Medway*, London, 1970

Stevens, J R: *An Account of the Construction and Embellishment of Old Time Ships*, Toronto, 1949

Tanner, J R ed: *Descriptive Catalogue of the Naval Manuscripts in the Pepysian Library*, 4 vols, Navy Record Society, 1903-1923

Tedder, A W: *The Navy of the Restoration*, Cambridge, 1916

Vere, Francis: *Salt in Their Blood: The Lives of the Famous Dutch Admirals*, London, 1955

Index

Note: Text references are in roman type, those for captions in *italics*.

Admiraal Generaal 119
Adventure 54, 55, *52*
Advice 61
Albemarle 164, *4*, *114*, *169*
Albemarle, Adm George Monck, Duke of 23, 75, 89-90, *89, 90, 169*
Alexander 119
Allin, Adm Sir Thomas 23, *84*, *93*
Allington, Capt Argentine 61
Amsterdam, Admiralty of 115, 116, *118*
Anne (1678) 158, *161*
Anne, ex-Bridgewater 57, *138*
Antelope (1618) 38
Antelope (1651) 58
Antelope, ex-Preston 57
Ardens, Adm H Des *124, 138*
Armorer, Sir Nicholas 143
Association 169
Assurance 54
Ayscue, Adm Sir George 90, *70, 90, 91*

Balchen, Adm Sir John 114
Banckert, Adm Adriaan *138, 136*
Bantry Bay, Battle of 59, 158
Barfleur, Battle of 37, 100, 103, 104, 114, 158, 164, 170, 172
Basing, see Guernsey
Batten, Adm Sir William 69
Bayley, Francis 12, 80, 139, 143, 157
Beachy Head, Battle of 37, 103, 119, 158, 164
Beecq, Jan van 8
Bergen, Battle of 115
Berkeley, Adm Sir William 23, 89, *84, 90, 91*
Berwick 158
Betts, Isaac 164
Bien-Aimée 149
Blackwall, dockyard at 12, 55, 80, 93, 149, 157, *82*
Bonaventure, ex-President 57
Bradford, see Success
Brakel, Capt Jan van *144*
Brandenburg, Elector of 143
Breda (1679) 158, *4*
Breda ex-Nantwich, 57
Breda, Treaty of 94
Brest, arsenal at 121, 124, *122*
Bridgewater, see Anne
Bristol 60
Bristol, dockyard at 12, 80, 139, 143, 157
Britannia 169-170, *4, 34, 164, 170, 171*
Buckingham, George Villiers, Duke of 154
Bugia Bay, Battle of 59
Burford 159
Byland, Edward 102

Cadiz, Battle of 59
Cadiz, engagement near 55
Callis, Manley 69
Cambridge 80, 82, 151, *81, 100*
Captain 158, *153, 154, 164*
Cartegena, Battle of 158

Castle, Capt William 12, 80-81, 82, 143, 157, 158, *155*
Charles (1668) 9, 95-96, 100, 164, 170, *77, 95, 96, 98, 137, 144*
Charles I 33, 35, 36, 39, 51, 95, *44*
Charles II 7, 8, 11, 17, 20, 21, 24, 29, 31, 37, 57, 69, 70, 73, 75, 82, 89, 92, 94, 95, 100, 113, 135, 137, 140, 141, 149, 151, 153, 154, 156, 157, 171, *11, 44, 71, 104, 122, 156, 164*
Charles V 93
Charles Galley 149, *144, 150*
Charles yacht 22
Chatham, royal dockyard at 11, 37, 69, 73, 78, 80, 92-93, 94, 100, 104, 141, 158, 164, 169, *4, 12*
Cherbourg, Battle of 170
Cheriton, see Speedwell
Chicheley, Adm Sir John 75, *137, 144*
Chopwell Forest 34
Christiana, dockyard at 129
Christianus Quintus 129, *130*
Christmas, Gerard 36
Cleveland yacht 44, 104
Clifford, Sir Thomas 33
Gloucester 53
Colbert, Jean-Baptiste 121, 123, 129, 153
Comeetster 144
Confederacy 149
Conpill, dockyard at 80
Conquerant 119
Constant Reformation 40
Constant Warwick 54, 55, *51, 138*
Convertine 38
Coronation 164, *164, 169*
Couronne 123
Courtisan 119
Cromwell, Lord Protector Oliver 61, 69, 72
Crown, ex-Taunton 57

Dannebrog 132
Dartmouth, Adm George Legge, Earl of *158*
Dauphin-Royal 122, 123
Dawes, Capt Henry 73
Dean, Forest of 14, 73, 139
Deane, Sir Anthony (I) 12, 80, 81, 82, 83, 110-114, 139-141, 149, 151, 153-154, 157, 172, *79, 80, 84, 110, 114*
Deane, Anthony (II) 149
Defiance (1666) 80, 81, 82
Defiance (1675) 141, *17, 141*
Delft 64, 89
Deptford, private dockyard at 12, 80, 143, 157, *24*
Deptford, royal dockyard at 11, 69, 75, 80, 95, 100, 141, 158, 164, *77*
Désirade, Battle of 59
Diest, Jieronymus van 8
Digby, Capt Francis *144*
Dover, Battle of 59
Dragon 54
Dreadnought, ex-Torrington 57, *57*
Duchess, 164, *4, 162*
Duke 164
Dunbar, see Henry
Dungeness, Battle of 59, *38*
Dunkirk, ex-Worcester 57, *54*
Duquesne, Adm Abraham, Marquis *120*
Dyck, Sir Anthony van 36

Eagle, ex-Selby 57
Edgar 139, 140, 157
Eendracht (1653) 84, *84, 115*
Eendracht (1666) 89, *104*

Elizabeth 1647) 54
Elizabeth (1679) 157, 158, *155, 156*
Essex (1653) 90, *91*
Essex (1679) 157, *155, 159*
Estrées, Adm Comte Victor Marie d' 135, 137, *122, 138*
Evelyn, John 12, 36, 69
Evertsen, Adm Cornelis 70, 119
Exeter 157, 158
Expedition 158

Fagons, see Milford
Falcon 151, *152*
Four Days' Battle 33, 40, 70, 75, 89-90, 172, *42, 44, 64, 78, 84, 89, 90, 91, 94*
Fredericus Tertius 130, *131*
French Ruby 141, *44, 138*
Friesland, Admiralty of 115
Furieux 129
Furzer, Daniel 80, 81, 164

Gainsborough, see Swallow
Garland (1620) *38, 151*
Garland, ex-Grantham 57
Gloucester 53
Gloucester, Henry, Duke of 70
Golden Horse 55
Golden Phoenix 93
Goteborg, dockyard at 132
Gouda 4, 44
Gouden Dolfijn 116, *118*
Gouden Leeuw 116, 121, *4, 118, 124, 144*
Grafton 158, *159*
Grancey, Adm the Marquis de *124*
Grantham, see Garland
Graves, Adm Thomas *41*
Great Fire of London 100
Great Storm of 1703 60, 164-169
Greenwich 80, *83*
Greyhound 34
Groot Hollandia 144
Guernsey, ex-Basing 57, 61

Haen, Adm Jan de *144*
Hampton Court 158, *153, 154, 164*
Hannibal 130
Happy Return, ex-Winsby 9, 57, 60, *18*
Harderwijk 116
Harman, Adm Sir John 23, 70, 89, 138, *71, 138, 144*
Harwich 111, 139-141, *141*
Harwich, royal dockyard at 11, 80, 110, 111, 139, 164
Heemskirk, Capt Louis van 151
Helverston 93
Henrietta, ex-Langport 57, *57*
Henrietta yacht 4
Henry, ex-Dunbar 57, 69-70, 72, 74, 78, 79, 89, 136, *70, 136, 144*
Henry, Prince of Wales 32
Heywood, Thomas 36
Hollandia 44, 64, 90, 117, 144
Holles, Capt Sir Frescheville 100
Holmes, Adm Sir Robert 23, 90, 99, *100, 101, 144*
Hope 157, 158, *155, 156*
House of Sweeds 93
Huis te Swieten 116
Hull, dockyard at 139

Intrépide 119
Invincible 119

James, see Old James
James I 32, 38, 95

James II, formerly Duke of York 11, 77, 80, 82, 84, 104, 114, 135-136, 138, 171, 172, *44, 84, 135, 136, 144, 164*
James Galley 149, *104, 150*
Johnson, Sir Henry 12, 80, 82, 157, *159*
Jordan, Adm Sir Joseph 35, 90, *136, 144*
Juel, Adm Niels 129, *130*

Katherine, see Royal Katherine
Katherine yacht 149, *104*
Kempthorne, Adm Sir John 60-61, 103, 138, 150, *138, 144*
Kempthorne, Capt Morgan 150
Kent 157
Kentish Knock, Battle of 33, 37, 59
Kingfisher 149-150, *64*
Kitchen yacht 22
Køge Bugt, Battle of 129, *133*

La Hogue, Battle of 170, 172, *172*
La Rochelle, Siege of 38
Langport, see Henrietta
Lawson, Adm Sir John 23, 71, *71, 84*
Lead sheathing 151
Lee, Robert 37
Leghorn Roads, Battle of 40
Leicester 93
Lenox 158, *4, 153, 154, 164*
Leopard 1635) 33, 40
Leopard (1659) 60, *57*
Liefde, Adm Jan de *136*
Limehouse, dockyard at 55
Line of battle, organisation of 29
Lion 59, 172, *38*
London (1657) 69, 71, 72, 74, 75, *71, 133*
London (1670) 100-101, 102, 103, 114, 172, *4, 102, 104, 136, 138, 144*
Louis XIV 89, 94, 121, 135, 137, 140, 171
Lowestoft, Battle of 30, 33, 59, 84, 89, 91, 115, 172, *84, 115*
Loyal George 64, *94*
Loyal London 75-76, 77, 90, 93, 95, 96, 100, 141, *75, 77, 84*
Lyme, see Montagu

Maagd van Dordrecht 136
Maas, Admiralty of the 69, 115
Maidstone, see Mary Rose
Malaga, Battle of 158
Maria Sancta 93
Marines 30
Marlborough 100
Marmaduke 93
Marston Moor, see York
Martel, Adm Marquis de *122*
Mary I 171
Mary II *24*
Mary, ex-Speaker 57, 59-60, 82, 164, *24, 59, 60*
Mary Rose, ex-Maidstone 57, 60-61, 103, 150, *62, 64*
Matthias 93
Medway raid 69, 72, 75, 92-94, 96, 100, 135, *84*
Milford, ex-Fagons 57
Minnes, Sir John 69
Monarque 123, *120*
Monck 59, 172, *54*
Monck, see Albemarle
Monmouth 80, 82
Montagu, ex-Lyme 57, *54, 58*
Mordaunt 143, *144*

Mordaunt, Lord, see Peterborough
Morelyn, John de 151
Mulgrave, Capt John Sheffield, Earl of *74, 84*
Myngs, Adm Sir Christopher 23, *78*

Nantwich, see Breda
Narbrough, Sir John 104, *104*
Naseby, see Royal Charles
Navy Board 7-8, 11, 12, 21, *77*, 80, 100, 156, 157
Neptune (English) 160, 164, 169, *4, 34*
Neptune (French) 119
Nes, Adm Jan van 64, 89, *144*
Nes, Adm Aert van 89, *104*
Newbury, see Revenge
Newcastle 60, 164, *61*
Nicodemus 53
Nonsuch (1646) 54
Nonsuch (1668) 151, *152*
Noord Quartier, Admiralty of 115
Normand 119
North Foreland, Battle of the 33, 59
Northumberland 157, *154*
Nottingham, Lord High Admiral Charles Howard, Earl of 32

Obdam, Adm Jacob van Wassenaer, Early of 84, *115*
Öland, Battle of 129, 132
Old James, ex-*James* 39, 40, 78, *49*
Olifant, see Witte Olifant
Oranje 84
Ordnance Board 20, 114
Orford, Adm Edward Russell, Earl of 170
Orgueilleux 124
Ossory 164
Ossory, Adm Thomas Butler, Earl of 138, *138, 144*
Oudshoorn 40
Oxford 143

Paris 122
Pendennis 158
Penn, Adm Sir William 23, 60, *60*
Pepys, Samuel 7-8, 12, 37, 54, 57, 60, 69, 72, 75, 77, 80-81, 82-83, 96, 110, 139-141, 153-156, 157, 171, 172, *8, 78*
Peterborough, Adm Charles Mordaunt, Earl of 143
Pett, Christopher 59, 72, 73, 80, 102
Pett, Peter (I) 53, 80, *44*
Pett, Commissioner Peter (II) 12, 69
Pett, Phineas (I) 32, 33, 34, 37, 54, 69, 80, 104, *44*
Pett, Sir Phineas (II) 54, 80, 104, 139, 141, 143, 158, 169-170
Pett, Phineas (III) 80, 143, 149
Phoenix (1647) 54
Phoenix (1671) 151, *152*
Pill of Foudre, dockyard at 139
Plymouth 53
Popish Plot 157
Portland 60
Portland, Battle of 59
Portsmouth, royal dockyard at 11, 73, 78, 96, 110, 114, 164
President, see Bonaventure
Preston, see Antelope
Prince (1670) 104, 114, 133, 136, 137, 138, 169, 170, 172, *4, 24, 34, 104, 109, 124, 136, 138, 140, 144*

Prince Royal (1610) 31-33, 34, 36, 37, 57, 73, 90, *31, 32, 44, 84, 90, 91*
Princess 73, 82, 156, *73*
Prinses Maria 119
Puget, Pierre 129, *120, 122*

Queen, ex-*Royal Charles* 113

Rainbow 38, 40, *41*
Ratcliffe, dockyard at 54, 55
Reigersbergen 64, *84*
Reine, ex-*Royal Duc* 123, *120, 138*
Reserve 164
Resolution (1667) 83, 164, 172, *79, 80, 84, 138*
Resolution, ex-*Prince Royal* 32
Resolution, ex-*Tredagh* 57, 90
Restoration 164, *161*
Revenge, ex-*Newbury* 57, 156, *58*
Richard, see Royal James
Richelieu Armand Jean du Plessis, Cardinal de 121
Richmond, ex-*Wakefield* 57
Riks-Äpplet 132, *133*
Riks-Kronan 132-133
Robbins, James 129
Rochefort, arsenal at 121, 123
Roebuck 34
Royal Anne 103
Royal Charles (1673) 96, 110-113, 114, 133, *111, 112, 138, 140*
Royal Charles, ex-*Naseby* 57, 61, 69, 72, 75, 84, 90, 93, 132, *63, 64, 84, 90*
Royal-Duc, see Reine
Royal George (1715) 113
Royal George, ex-*Victory* 114
Royal James (1671) 110, 136, 138, *104, 111, 136, 144*
Royal James (1675) 113-114, 160, *113, 114*
Royal James, ex-*Richard* 57, 72, 93, 100, 110, *64, 72, 84, 93*
Royal Katherine 73-75, 78, 90, 93, 96, 116, 129, 136, 172, *74, 84, 136, 144*
Royal-Louis 122, 123, *120*
Royal Oak (1664) 73-75, 78, 93, 100, *4, 84, 90*
Royal Oak (1674) 141, *141, 142*
Royal Prince, see Prince and *Prince Royal*
Royal Society 73-74
Royal Sovereign (1637) 33-37, 90, 95, 104, 112, 129, 130, 170, 172, *4, 33, 34, 35, 36, 44, 131, 136, 144*
Royal-Thérèse 122, 124
Royal William, ex-*Prince* 104, 172
Rozenkrans, ex-*Garland* 38
Rubis 141
Ruby 60, 172
Rupert 80, 81, 82, 83, 172, *79*
Rupert, Prince 11, 23, 37, 89-90, 92, 112, 136-138, *40, 44, 64, 138, 144*
Russell, see Orford
Ruyter, Adm Michiel Adriaanszoon De 89, 90, 92-94, 95, 119, 121, 135-138, *84, 89, 117, 139, 144*

Sailmaker, Isaac 8
St Andrew (1622) 39, 40, *41, 44*
St Andrew (1670) 102-103, 114, 139, 160, 172, *103, 104, 138, 144*
St David 80, 81, 82, 83
St George (1622) 39, 40, 93, *38, 42, 44, 138, 140*

St George, ex-*Charles* 96, 98
St James Day Fight 37, 59, 75, 90, 92, 94, *75, 92, 93*
St Michael 96-100, 160, 164, 172, *2, 98, 100, 101, 136, 137, 138, 144*
St Patrick 80, 82
Sandwich 164
Sandwich, Adm Edward Montagu, Earl of 23, 72, 110, 136, 138, 70, 136, *144*
Saudadoes 24
Schakerloo 55
Scheveningen, Battle of 33, 57, 59, *41*
Schooneveld, 1st Battle of 59, 112, 123, 136, *23, 122, 124, 138*
Schooneveld, 2nd Battle of 59, 123, 136-137, *122, 124*
Selby, see Eagle
Seymour, Adm Lord Henry 38
Shaftesbury, Anthony Ashley, Earl of 154
Sheerness, royal dockyard at 11, 40
Sheldon, Francis (I) 132, *133*
Sheldon, Francis (II) 133
Sheldon, Thomas 133
Ship Money Tax 36
Shish, John 158, 164
Shish, Jonas 12, 80, 81, 95, 96, 100, 141, 158, 172, *77*
Shish, Thomas 158, 164, *159*
Shovell, Adm Sir Clowdisley 169
Skane War 129
Slot Honingen 116
Smith, Adm Sir Jeremy 75, *75, 77*
Smyrna Convoy action 135, *100*
Solebay, Battle of 59, 75, 110, 135-136, 138, 151, *35, 100, 136, 144*
Soleil-Royal 122, 123, 170
Sophia Amalia 129-130, *131*
Sovereign or *Sovereign of the Seas, see Royal Sovereign*
Speaker, see Mary
Speedwell, ex-*Cheriton* 57
Spragge, Adm Sir Edward 23, 137, 138, 143, *138, 140, 144*
Stad Utrecht 89
States General 69, *92*
Steenbergen 119
Stirling Castle 164, *160, 161*
Strickland, Sir Thomas 139
Success, ex-*Bradford* 57
Suffolk 157, *4, 155, 159*
Superbe 140-141
Sussex 142
Svan 130
Svardet 133
Swallow, ex-*Gainsborough* 57
Swan of Flushing 53
Sweepstakes 151, *152*
Sweers, Adm Isaac *44, 104*
Swiftsure (1621) 39, 40, 89, *42, 64, 84, 90, 91*
Swiftsure (1693) 110-111, 139-141, *141, 172, 140, 141*

Taunton, see Crown
Taylor, Capt John 37, 69, 75, 100
Taylor, Silas 111
Tenerife, Battle of 59
Terrible 124
Test Act 136
Texel, Battle of the 59, 104, 123, 137, 138, 143, *122, 140, 144*
Thames Watermen's Company 149
Thomas & Elizabeth fireship 29

Tiger 54, 55, *52, 150*
Tippetts, Sir John 73, 74, 96, 157

Torbay, ex-*Neptune* 169
Torpley, Capt John 55
Torrington, see Dreadnought
Toulon, arsenal at 121, 129, 149, *120, 122*
Tourville, Adm Anne-Hilarion de Cotentin, Comte de 170
Tredagh, see Resolution
Tre Løver (1656) *130*
Tre Løver (1689) *132*
Trinity House 33, 80, *77*
Triumph (1622) 39, 40, *42*
Tromp, Adm Sir Cornelis 119, 129, 138, *44, 64, 90, 140, 144*

Unicorn 39, 40, *38, 42*
Unity 93

Van de Velde, Willem the Elder 8-9, 19, 32, 37, 69, 102, 110, 121, 130, 132, 158, 164, *9, 122, 136, 138*
Van de Velde, Willem the Younger 8-9, 19, 32, 102, 110, 121, 132, 158, 164, *10, 144*
Vanguard (1615) 38, 40, 93, 164, *44*
Vanguard (1678) 164
Victoria 133
Victorieux 123
Victory (1620) 39, 40, 78, *42*
Victory (1666) 76, 78, 93, 114, *4, 78, 137*
Victory, ex-*Royal James* 114
Vigo Bay, Battle of 59, 158
Vlie, raid on the 90
Vrijheid 116
Wager, Adm Sir Charles 158
Wakefield, see Richmond
Wapping, dockyard at 55
Warspite 80, 82, 140, *82*
Warwick, Robert Rich, Earl of 54
Waterford, dockyard at 143
Welcome 93
Westfriesland 119
William III 75, 141, 158, 171, 172, *24*
Windsor Castle 164, *4, 162*
Winsby, see Happy Return
Witte Olifant 116, 121, *104, 118, 144*
Woerden 144
Woolwich 9, 143, *24, 143, 144*
Woolwich, royal dockyard at 11, 32, 33, 34, 59, 69, 72, 73, 78, 80, 93, 94, 100, 102, 143, 149, 158, 164, *24, 159*
Worcester, see Dunkirk
Wynter, Capt Sir William 38

Yarmouth 60, 154
York, see James II
York, ex-*Marston Moor* 57, 164, *54*
Young, Capt Benjamin 61

Zeeland, Admiralty of 115
Zeelandia 119
Zeven Provincien 116, *44, 84, 89, 117, 138*
Zon 90

208

de Breda.

The Neptune

...ing on board

Royal Sovereign, 1685. Ships laid up in ordinary.